THE STUFF OF FAMILY LIFE

THE STUFF OF FAMILY LIFE

How Our Homes Reflect Our Lives

Michelle Janning

ROWMAN & LITTLEFIELD
Lanham • Boulder • New York • London

Published by Rowman & Littlefield
A wholly owned subsidiary of
The Rowman & Littlefield Publishing Group, Inc.
4501 Forbes Boulevard, Suite 200, Lanham, Maryland 20706
https://rowman.com

Unit A, Whitacre Mews, 26-34 Stannary Street, London SE11 4AB,
United Kingdom

British Library Cataloguing in Publication Information Available

Library of Congress Cataloging-in-Publication Data
Names: Janning, Michelle Yvonne, author.
Title: The stuff of family life : how our homes reflect our lives / Michelle
    Janning.
Description: Lanham, Maryland : Rowman & Littlefield, 2017. | Includes bib-
    liographical references and index.
Identifiers: LCCN 2016058386 (print) | LCCN 2016058974 (ebook) | ISBN
    9781442254794 (cloth : alk. paper) | ISBN 9781442254800 (electronic)
Subjects: LCSH: Families. | Domestic space. | House furnishings—Psychologi-
    cal aspects. | Personal belongings—Psychological aspects.
Classification: LCC HQ734 .J347 2017 (print) | LCC HQ734 (ebook) | DDC
    306.85—dc23
https://lccn.loc.gov/2016058386

Printed in the United States of America

For Neal and Aaron

CONTENTS

ACKNOWLEDGMENTS

Thanks to Sarah Stanton at Rowman & Littlefield, who assured me all along that it's my voice that needs to be heard, even if it's an impatient voice trying to reach an audience whose members may not always find themselves in pleasant mixed company. Thanks also to reviewers and editors who helped along the way.

Thanks to my Whitman sociology colleagues Keith Farrington, Helen Kim, Gilbert Mireles, Bill Bogard, Alissa Cordner, Alvaro Santana-Acuña, and all past and present colleagues, who amaze me with their kindness, smarts, and support. I'm grateful to Whitman College for providing support for collaboration with stellar students—and thanks to all of my former students, for inspiration in the classroom. I would also like to give a special thanks to all students with whom I have collaborated in research and writing over the years, many of whom are mentioned in this book as my co-authors. Thanks to the College for supporting faculty members who write, and for being a place with amazing past and present students who teach me daily how to ask good questions in order to get good answers and, sometimes, how to be okay with not knowing the answer. I am a better teacher because I write, and I am a better writer because I teach these amazing students. The fact that they keep in touch even after they graduate and continue to ask me good questions is a testament to the amazing liberal arts education they have as a foundation.

Thanks to my Council on Contemporary Families friends, whose tireless work in the name of showing *families as they really are* has been an inspiration for my own work.

Thanks to all of the people who filled out a survey, sat through an interview, or otherwise contributed a voice to my research. You are not data points, you are the stories that make up this book.

Thanks to friends and family members who read bits of the book with an eye toward helping me offer my words with compassion and inclusivity without being superficial.

A special thanks to Louisa Albermann and Anna Jakobsen for letting me be your American mom for a year or so as I watched in awe at your bravery and growth in the States, and as you shared ideas with me about your own homes and families.

Thanks to Amy Davis Bruner, who helped me see myself. Trying is not the same as doing. I see that now.

Thanks to Jennifer Steffens for all of the silly poems and calendars and for trips to cold places that we love—and everything else, including your parents' wise words. And thanks to all my good friends, near and far, for your courage at climbing ice walls, photographing wildlife, teaching little ones, supporting and building up each other's foundations, sharing ideas about books and kids and life, writing, and protesting what isn't right.

Thanks to Auntie Diane Houtkooper, who reminds me at every turn how important it is to "look at the lives we lead every day and how much that can teach us about our small role in the world today and for generations to come." You are loved, and you are lovely.

Thanks to other academics who write about the things I love, many of whom are cited in this book. Necessarily when we write, we take the pieces we know, or that fit into the story we're weaving, or that we stumble upon, and say, "Hey, cool, this is too good not to include." But, inevitably, I have missed pieces of research and writing from others much smarter than I am that would also fit or detail my very general claims. So, thanks to those whom I've cited, and thanks for your forgiveness to those whom I've inevitably and inadvertently left out.

Thanks to Maggie, the aging dog, who is a daily reminder of what it means to care for another being who gives you love no matter what, and who plops herself behind my chair so I can't get up from my writing desk.

Thanks to Mom for your love, penchant for fun, perfect penmanship, and ability to just listen no matter what weird stories your daughter is telling, even and especially if they're about you. Yours is the gift of unquestionable love, and I thank you for loving me for who I am.

Thanks to Mark for giving me that Eiffel Tower "sculpture" made out of an old sock and a coat hanger, and for sometimes dressing like Elvis because that's just what you do. Thanks to Marty for throwing me across the room to Mark (while I was little and wrapped in a blanket like a burrito) and for embodying all that there is to working hard and being devoted to healing people. Thanks to both of you, my big brothers, for your own family stories, and for your love and admiration and good sense of humor, all of which remind me of Dad. You have taught me, in quiet and not-so-quiet ways, how to spin a decent story.

Thanks to Richard and Christina for your endless knowledge about our social world, our kids, and our communities, and for your ability to show the best kinds of love. You model a life that I see embodied in a loving husband every day. Thanks to all of the Jannings and Christophersons and those who are connected to me in a family genogram, for inspiring me with stories, and for letting me tell some of them.

Thanks to Angela Lansbury, whose characterization of J. B. Fletcher inspired me nightly in my binge-watching of *Murder, She Wrote* to write about things I see in my everyday life and not to be fazed when bad things happen. Luckily, I don't write about murder. But still. I'm grateful for the character. And her ability to appreciate how small-town relations may matter as much as solving a big ol' crime.

Thanks to you, the reader. My hope is that wherever I go, people can share stories with me about how their home spaces and objects help to tell the stories of their families. Maybe someday I'll get to hear your stories. Please tell them to me.

Thanks to Neal, whose song lyrics say it best: "Here I am inside this room with no one else but you. It's the first time that I've understood. *I chased you forever until something turned out right.* And coming home has never been so good." You are my husband, my hope, and my home. Keep writing songs and making me listen to them.

And finally, thanks to Aaron, whose wisdom was visible in his eyes the day he was born thirteen years ago, a wisdom that preceded him in another life and exceeds his years. I will always wait patiently for your answers to questions, because you offer them with simultaneous logic and compassion, you are usually right, and sometimes your answers are communicated with a subtly raised eyebrow and a tiny grin. You are made of good stuff, my son.

FAMILIES, HOME SPACES, AND OBJECTS

Welcome Mats and Windows

I have to admit this book is really about me.

I have remodeled two homes, much on my own. I have lived in a dozen different home spaces, from a midcentury rambler in a small Minnesota town to an urban walk-up in Copenhagen; from a college dorm room to a run-down Midwestern rental house where the decades of grease on the kitchen cabinets could never be completely wiped off. And now, I spend my days in a 1930s stucco house in the Pacific Northwest, each room donned with curtains I've sewn and walls I've painted and trim I've secured with a hammer and nails and a bruised thumb. Since childhood, in each of the home spaces I have occupied, I have taken seriously (and have found fun in) the task of arranging the space to make it a place—to make a space seem like it's mine, recognizable perhaps as an extension of what I value and love. Conscientious object arrangement and wall placement have been a part of my identity since I could set my collection of stuffed animals on a low shelf. My subscription to *Elle Décor* as a fourteen-year-old rural Midwestern kid from the middle class always seemed strange to those around me, but it made me happy. I am obsessed with how aesthetics have affected me personally. Now, I am in the privileged position to be able to shape the spaces I occupy, with changes that cost much more than my childhood wall shelf that held my stuffed animals. As I age, I wonder how much my body can take in the form of remodeling injuries, but I'm always thirsty for aesthetic transformation. All of this is to say that I define who I am in part by how I arrange home spaces and objects. *The stuff and spaces of family life are part of my self.*

My affinity for aesthetics has expanded beyond the personal. I have organized a fund-raiser featuring a tour of child-centric home spaces in my community. I have redesigned a nursery in a church seeking to attract more families with young children. I have served as a color and furniture consultant for the remodel of a college classroom building. I have served as a participant in a collaborative project between a college and an architecture firm in the research, design, and building of a new residence hall and dining facility. I have submitted an application and portfolio for a national design television show (which did not, in fact, result in me being on HGTV, but they don't know what they're missing). I have given seminars on the use of color in workspaces. I have had my home featured on home tours for creative kid spaces (thanks, neighbors, for letting me paint a mural on your garage that borders our yard), for innovative design of small kitchens (thanks, 2008 windstorm, for tipping over the beautiful walnut tree that is now my countertop), and for environmentally friendly gardens (thanks, solar panels, for allowing us to show off our love of the environment using metal and glass). I have performed building, sewing, fixing, and design help for friends in exchange for wine or child care. *The stuff and spaces of family life are part of my social interactions with others, including in a wide variety of institutional realms that extend beyond my own family and friends.*

My affinity for learning about home spaces has led me to understand their importance not just at personal and interactional levels, but also as a way to understand my place in larger social groups. My research as a sociologist has centered squarely on the intersection between social relationships and material objects and spaces. By social relationships, I mean the everyday interactions with those we hold near and dear, but I also mean the really large groups in society of which we are a part—groups organized by age, geography, social class, gender, bodily ability, sexual orientation, and race, among others. The groups to which we belong can shape our values, aesthetic choices, and access to time and money and energy that matter in any consideration of what homes we have and what we have in our homes. And these groups sometimes have unequal access to things we find valuable in our society. Our homes and domestic objects tell as much of the story about our group identities as they tell about our own individual preferences. And homes also tell us about how family lives are impacted by changing societal roles, cultural views, economics, science and technological innovation, and political trends. *The stuff and spaces of family life are not just part of my understanding of self or interactions with people I know; they are part of my understanding of the structural, political, economic, and technological arrangements of a society filled with inequalities.*

Now you know my passions and my qualifications. Really, though, this book is not about me, even though every author will tell you that a piece of her is in everything she writes. It is about *us*. It is about the realization that understanding others helps us understand ourselves. Understanding the story of family lives requires understanding the spaces that families occupy and the objects they use.

And so, I bid you welcome into my project about home spaces and objects. I hope you can imagine yourself within these walls and within the ideas in this book, preferably without a bruised thumb from fervent page turning.

DEFINING HOME

What is home? Is it about a physical space, or about the people and feelings associated with that space? Is home where the heart is, or where the hearth is, or both?[1] These questions do not belong in the domain of any single academic discipline, nor are they new questions. The most common thread among the definitions of *home* is that it is a space that has socially defined meaning attached to it. While a house is the physical dwelling, a home is what it all means to the people who are there. Homes are connected to families, especially if we define *family* as a close social group, often (but not always) connecting people in kinship terms, that provides ongoing support and resources to its members. Often, but not always, if people are included in a definition of a home, the people occupying the space are some form of family.

Home is often a physical space that offers or provides something to people in the form of security, nurturing relationships, warmth, connection to others, or refuge from the public world or their public selves. Importantly, it can also be a place that brings sadness, fear, and loneliness, evident in stories about intimate violence, child neglect, or alienation within our aging populations in the news and in our own neighbor-hoods. In any of these cases, a home is imbued with meaning that its inhabitants may or may not consciously recognize. And the meaning can be nurturing, harmful, and everything in between. But the meaning is still about the relationships between the people who are there, and those relationships are often defined as familial—having to do with the family.

How home is defined depends on the social circumstances sur-rounding it, and on the kinds of interactions that take place there. Home is a space with possibilities for its inhabitants to inscribe personal meaning, as in "Home is where my family is," which means home doesn't always have to be an actual physical space. Home is also a subject of academic inquiry, as in "This is a book about the American home." We can study how the meaning of home may change from person to person, and how it may change over time, between big groups of people, and across geographic space. Home is thus an important subject of study using both a microsociological (small group, interac-tional, or individual level) lens and a macrosociological (large societal, historical, and group level) lens.

Home, then, is where this book will go. It is physically visible and touchable, an objective place. It is also a subjective place that is filled with meaning, often attached to family relationships, that often contains or at least references rooms and objects that, when visited, show us important patterns about both possibilities and constraints that matter for contemporary American families.

LOOKING THROUGH THE SOCIOLOGY WINDOW

If homes can be defined as meaningful by people who live there, it's important to include people's experiences in any discoveries or inter-pretations about homes. But how people's experiences are included in a book about homes can vary depending on what disciplinary window you look through.

I really like data about people. Numbers, quotes, emerging themes, typologies, tables, charts, statistics, drawings that can be analyzed, word clouds. All of it. I'm a social scientist, which means I have spent more time than the average person crafting good (and probably not-so-good) survey questions, learning how to interview people without losing eye contact after they've been talking for forty-five minutes straight, attending conferences about data visualization, categorizing lengthy interview stories into thematic tables, and trying to systematically observe public social life without seeming creepy.

I appreciate approaches to the study of homes, families, and objects from many disciplines that are less inclined to, and perhaps even averse to, describe what they're observing as "data." But when I look at these, I'm always thirsty for a more social scientific approach to organizing the observations, an approach that favors being systematic and noticing patterns rather than exceptions. And if exceptions are included, they help us understand larger patterns. For example, you may read this book and wonder whether your unique experience of living in a tiny house can fit into whatever research findings are presented about other kinds of houses. Or you may wonder if your experience as someone in a wheelchair means this book is somehow not as applicable to your life. While I can't do all things with one book, I do believe that what is presented here, especially in terms of patterns that emerge from good research, is applicable in many places to many people with varied experiences. This is because, no matter what the individual story or circumstances are, there are always larger patterns that contextualize that story. So, one person's decision to live in a tiny house can be understood as part of a larger trend where people are increasingly interested in building projects that save space, cost, and energy (and that are even featured on HGTV shows about living in small spaces). And another person's task of remodeling a newly purchased home to alter the counter height for wheelchair access can be understood alongside changing technological advances in both home design and bodily mobility, and in light of building code revisions that are meant to comply with the Americans with Disabilities Act. An exceptional story, for a sociologist, can always point to, and connect with, larger social patterns.

As a sociology professor with a background in anthropology and art history, I try to understand how and why our everyday interactions and aesthetics are connected to larger social issues within our economy, media, religion, politics, schools, and technology. Sociologists are quite good at figuring out patterns relating to large social issues. There's also a rich history in this discipline of thinking about the role of objects in social relations, from early writing about the importance of sacred objects in religion to the role that urban housing plays in building ties among neighbors and, at the same time, in reinforcing inequalities between neighbors of different groups. But it has only been recently that people in my field have started to intentionally include things and spaces as central pieces in our research. We now see books and articles that explicitly mention the sociology of things, or the importance of spaces and places for sociology. I hope to add to this growing body of knowledge with this book.

No single piece of research tells the whole story in one place that I'd like to tell here. As you read, you'll notice that I reference lots of ideas from my own research and observations, and from those of other scholars, trying to combine ideas that may not have been in conversation before. Some research I cite takes place outside the United States, or it covers only individualized stories without reference to larger social patterns, or it relates to spaces and objects that are more about public life rather than private homes, or it covers private lives well but without reference to the importance of home spaces and objects. To put it another way, there is wonderful research on home spaces and objects in other countries, but it may not apply to U.S. family lives. In U.S. research, the focus of home spaces and objects in family lives sometimes glosses over group differences and inequalities because it focuses so much on individual psychology. I love reading old and new sociology works that stress the importance of the built environment as it relates to important issues such as immigration patterns, neighborhood racial segregation, or urban planning, but I wish there was more focus on what happens *inside* the buildings that are in the neighborhoods. I also wish that there was more written about how both qualitative and quantitative research findings can help to collectively tell the story of how family lives, spaces, and objects intersect. And finally, I love U.S. sociology that looks at family relations, but spaces and objects in homes are largely absent from that work.

To address some of these wishes, I've had to look "under the couch cushion" of existing research—into qualitative realms, into non-U.S. realms, into nonsociological realms—in order to be able to tell this story. By doing this, I have to be careful not to overgeneralize, or to assume that what happens in one place happens everywhere, or to lose focus with so many methodological and disciplinary voices in the mix.

Hopefully I am able to uncover some treasures that add up to a new take on families and home spaces and objects.

* * *

I always say that I am confident in my home remodeling ability, as long as what I am working on is not inside any walls. For mysterious home maladies that reside behind walls and under the floors, like electrical wiring, plumbing, or rodents, I hire a professional. But as a sociologist, my job is *precisely* to uncover what's underneath the surface. To use a sociological perspective means to uncover just how bizarre our everyday lives can be. This means that as the chapters in this book unfold, seemingly familiar household objects and spaces will be dissected and unveiled to reveal what is strange and mysterious about them as they relate to research findings about contemporary family relationships. If nothing else, my aim is to have you take away a handful of "aha" moments that may make you take a different look at family spaces and objects. Hopefully you'll never look at a toilet or a dining room the same way again. Hopefully you can find concrete ways to incorporate this new understanding into your own experiences and values. Maybe you'll start to look at families, home spaces, and objects through a new sociological window. This book, then, has as its goal to talk about U.S. families' home spaces and objects as largely hidden-from-research, but immensely important, dimensions of family lives. And the spaces and objects are not merely symbols or metaphors for other research on family life. They are the subjects of the research presented.

I seek to explain why things happen the way they do, using home spaces and objects as the location for explanation. Sociologists like to explain why things happen using empirical (can be seen, heard, smelled, touched, tasted) data from our social world, but we also like to be able to try to predict how and why these things may happen (or perhaps why they should not happen) in the future. If we are to think about what home spaces and objects (and accompanying family roles and relationships) will look like in the future, we need to understand how they are operating now. We need to look at how the pipes are plumbed to see how long the water pressure will stay strong.

FOUNDATIONS: REFLECTING ON OUR STUFF

There are a handful of central foundational themes that organize my writing. This is the set of ideas that support the book; they are my assumptions about families, home spaces, and objects. I use these themes to ground the questions I'm asking and the research findings I unveil that answer the questions. If this book were a home, these ideas provide the foundation. Without a foundation that threads everything together, the walls and rooms and furniture may sink into the mud or seem superficially propped up. I incorporate three supportive foundations about home spaces and objects that uncover what is happening in contemporary family life, which I return to at the end of each chapter:

> *Foundation 1: Homes show how the boundaries between public and private matter for families.*
> *Foundation 2: Homes tell us about individual families, but also about broader social issues.*
> *Foundation 3: Homes are not only symbolic, but also shape our lives.*

I'll begin with the first foundation: *Homes show how the boundaries between public and private matter for families.* The private realm, when it is labeled as separate from the public realm, tends to be hidden, or only seen as occupied by people and activities that are often deemed as insignificant, unimportant, or not very valuable in economic or political terms. This can even happen in academic research, when studies about homes and families become labeled as somehow less important, less political, or less impactful than more public topics. The problem with this is that what happens in a home becomes nobody's business but the ones who live there, thus reinforcing the boundary between public and private and rendering private life as hidden and devalued. This can be especially dangerous when people's homes are filled with anger and violence. And it can be politically problematic if policy is based on a lack of understanding of the hidden world inside homes. I find it valuable to bring to light those aspects of life that are deemed more mundane. If we don't do this, then family relationships will remain in the background of louder political and rhetorical (and social media) conversations about our world, and voices and subjects that are labeled as more appropriate to be heard in private will remain silenced.

Studying home spaces and objects is important today because the difference between public and private life is increasingly blurry and messy, at least relative to the last century or two. Certainly the home, especially in the West, and especially in the last two hundred years, has been depicted as a retreat, a haven, a secluded space separated from the harsh public (and valued, and male) world of work, politics, economic marketplaces, and strangers. But the notion of public and private as separate realms is itself a social and historical construction. The only reason homes are seen as separate spaces from the public world (and that there are rooms within our homes that are more public or more private) is that we say they are, and because there are numerous ways that social, economic, and political structures at play in today's American society reinforce this. But it's important to note that this is not the case everywhere, nor has it been the case throughout history. From farmsteads in the 1800s to communities across the globe where public spaces and family spaces are intermingled (such as a cohousing community in Denmark or an Israeli kibbutz), seeing a strict border between private and public life provides a limited picture of real family lives. Further, seeing the home as entirely private can even reinforce damaging ideas that closed doors are somehow better than open ones when it comes to caring for others in our communities.

In contemporary U.S. society, to see homes and families as entirely removed from the public world is inaccurate. Because of shifting gender roles that have brought about increasing numbers of women into the paid work force, as well as communication technologies that allow for things such as telecommuting or talking with faraway family members on a webcam, it is clear that where the walls of a home are placed is increasingly flexible. Of course, the boundaries of home spaces have always been permeable (there are doors and windows, we allow visitors in our homes, and we have long combined paid work and home tasks), but we have different ways that we control how permeable or porous or blurry the boundaries are. As sociologist Christena Nippert-Eng says in her 2010 book *Islands of Privacy*, homes are territories of families that have the capacity both to allow people in as well as to shun people.[2] We let certain people into our homes, and not others. Once invited inside, we let certain people into our living room, but not into our bedroom. Homes are both public and private, and looking at sociological research about the spaces and objects within them can show us how and where the boundary between public and private becomes interesting. As you read the next chapters, you'll see ways that changing family relations, changing technologies, and changing norms about spaces and objects in homes matter in people's ability and desire to integrate or separate their public and private lives.

* * *

The second foundation supporting this book states that *homes tell us about individual families, but also about broader social issues.* Home is where we can see social and personal values play out. It is where building policies, norms about architectural design aesthetics, and structural inequalities that make some homes more affordable than others intersect with private family life. Thus, singling out the importance of home spaces and objects as areas to study and write about calls attention to how homes show important patterns about relationships within their walls as well as to how these patterns may relate to broader social life. As I said in the first few paragraphs of this chapter, I have always loved designing rooms, remodeling, and talking with friends about home décor. This stuff tells the story of who I am. But only talking about individual self-expression, habits, or design preferences is not enough. If we are to acknowledge that homes are where both personal *and* social values are enacted, then we must go beyond the level of the individual. As social researchers Tony Chapman and Jenny Hockey articulated in their edited collection of sociological research on social change, home design, and inequalities, "We can think of the home as a site of habitual practice where a culture's ways of doing things are set up between persons, practices and domestic objects/environments."[3]

Put another way, beyond individual family dynamics, it is important to acknowledge that large social groupings and status inequalities are represented by home objects and spaces. Things can be viewed as a depository of social and cultural meaning,[4] where they are used to classify their owner into such categories as lifestyle, interests, occupation, race, class, or gender, among others. Objects can also show power differentials and inequalities, most visibly represented in what social theorist Thorstein Veblen[5] called conspicuous consumption (we buy expensive things if we can, and we show them off in our homes so others know that we have achieved a certain social and economic status). Our homes show our consumption of products, from new couches to paint colors. The stuff that we choose to buy and display (and where we display it) shows not just what may be the latest trend in home design; it also shows that we are participating in a social process. When we paint a wall or buy a couch, we are not just consumers picking out something based on personal preferences. We are often actively trying to show our status, roles, and tastes, and these play out within a larger cultural context that defines what counts as high status, appropriate, and tasteful at the time.[6] Home objects and spaces actually play a big role in people's accomplishment of social identities that are much larger than any individual preference. Objects (and the spaces those objects occupy), thus, tell us about broader social issues in the form of groups, status, and cultural context.

To go further, I find that turning everything into an individual-level analysis can actually cause problems. I believe I have a responsibility to consider home spaces and objects as existing within a larger social system because our private worlds are always part of the larger public world. Living in a particular time period, place, economic system, and culture makes us think about homes in a certain way. We live in a Western capitalist system that emphasizes individualization and privatization and, as some may argue, that reinforces inequalities, economic and otherwise. An emphasis on how homes matter only at the individual level can miss important points about structural problems that create privilege for some and disadvantage for others. My personality and individual effort alone do not make it possible for me to afford a nice house. My identity in particular groups, in a particular historical era, in a particular geographic location, and within a particular network of people, all play a huge role in my life chances. The stuff in our lives can seem trivial or only connected to personal preferences, but there are lots of deeper social issues at play when we buy, use, and get rid of stuff—issues such as environmental degradation (what to do with all our old TVs), labor issues (who makes our smartphones), and even market issues (who can afford what homes and with what interest rate).[7] And studies about homes that include primarily individual-level stories about personalities, mood, cognitive processes, or self-expression, while important and interesting, miss that larger stuff. I seek to point out how home spaces and objects represent larger cultural ideals about family and can serve to reproduce inequalities and what geographer Allison Blunt calls "inclusions and exclusions" from contemporary social and family lives based on inequalities.[8] These "inclusions and exclusions" are part of the broader social issues that go beyond individual family circumstances. Plus, by recognizing that there are group inequalities, we can better understand any individual family.

❄ ❄ ❄

If we drew pictures of our families, how many of us would include a couch in the picture as a member of the family? Probably very few of us. This strange question brings us to the third foundation: *Homes are not only symbolic, but also shape our lives.* I know that it is not the case that my closet arranged itself or my desk made me sit down and work on this chapter. Or that my couch has a conscience or set of emotions that would guide it into believing it was a part of my family. Or that my smartphone made me remember to go to the dentist.

Or is it?

My best friend's mom once said, "You make your space and then your space makes you." Home spaces and objects are certainly part of the dynamic processes that make up our family lives, but do they really act upon us as if they had intention and consciousness of their own? Let's say for a moment that this is possible. Objects and spaces are, as archaeological scholar Carl Knappett termed it in 2002, "socially alive."[9] But how "socially alive" spaces and objects are depends on how much you think they are equals with humans in any given social interaction. Author Winifred Gallagher's work references this idea in her book *House Thinking: A Room-by-Room Look at How We Live.* She highlights research by psychologist Roger Barker, who called the intersection of our behaviors and the places where they are enacted "behavior settings." Familiar environments like our homes are not just passive pieces of our daily lives. Rather, our behaviors and habits mingle with our physical setting and the objects therein to create a "person-environment dynamic."[10] For example, if we think of LEGO bricks as household objects, we can ask both "How do we build the bricks to matter in our lives?" as well as "How might the bricks built in a certain way make our lives matter in a certain way, especially if they're visible on a low shelf?" Or, we can think of our kitchens not just as the place where we create a meal, but as a place where the location of pots, pans, and spoons shapes our meal-making movements and behaviors, and as a place where our kitchen work triangle serves to choreograph the dance that is our cooking pattern. The definition of spaces also matters in how we think about our family roles. Anthropologist Antonius Robben found that spaces within homes are divided into areas that have distinct social functions (e.g., cooking or entertaining friends) and are characterized by specific roles (e.g., some people are supposed to cook and others are not).[11] Spatial arrangements, thus, help to define what people do in those spaces.

To break down the role of home spaces and objects as actors in our social lives, let's start with the idea of *spaces*. The importance of physical space is one that is sometimes overlooked by sociologists, but it is increasingly recognized in the field as a significant aspect of our social world, especially in terms of subjects like racial residential segregation or social impacts of land use or environmental toxins. Back in 2000, in an article that I return to often when trying to articulate why it's important for sociologists to study places and spaces, sociologist Thomas Gieryn noted that "nothing of interest to sociologists is nowhere. . . . Everything that we study is emplaced; it happens somewhere and involves material stuff, which means that every published piece of sociology legitimately belongs [in a discussion of place]."[12] Space is not merely a setting or backdrop, but a player with *agency* (another word for individual freedom to shape one's circumstances) and with detectable and significant impacts on our families.

Everyone has space that is meaningful, determined through their acts of defining, naming, and attaching meaning to spaces.[13] And the meaning of a space can be good or bad, freeing or limiting, vast or hardly even there. I felt this most strongly in 1979 when my older brothers made a habit of walking through *my* bedroom without knocking to take a shortcut to the kitchen. So I decided to start charging them a toll. Gieryn not only acknowledges the notion that we attach meaning to spaces; he also says that these same spaces have significant effects on people by shaping the possibilities of their behaviors. My attempt at charging a toll for my brothers to walk through my room was an attempt at control over a space that was valuable. It worked until they ran out of nickels, at which point my parents intervened and told my brothers to stop trespassing.

The same has been said more recently by cultural sociologists such as Wendy Griswold and her colleagues, who researched how art museums end up steering patrons into certain paths and rooms.[14] They suggested that the space we occupy may influence us as much as, if not more than, the way we attach meaning to the space (and art pieces). Add to this the fact that some spaces are easy to access for some and hard to access for others, and we can also see that space shapes inequalities. To illustrate, I may attach meaning to my dining room by recovering the chairs with new red fabric, but the room's shape, structure, fit within a larger set of norms about what *counts* as a dining room (e.g., it should have a table and chairs), and even who can afford a house with enough space to have a dining room, are situated in a larger set of social patterns that can constrain how much freedom I actually have to attach meaning to it. That dining room is thus constructed both by its actual physical existence and also by my understanding of it as a dining room (or not) and my ability to access a space like a dining room in the first place. A dining room, like any other home space, is part objective and part subjective. It allows some creative freedom in the form of my decision to recover chairs, but it constrains my creativity because it is still defined as a dining room as opposed to, say, a bathroom. To extend this beyond the home, just think about how an attractive public town square may be easier or harder for teenagers to access depending on anti-loitering laws in place. Forbidding certain groups from certain places can highlight whether we think people deserve to be in those spaces or not. And, as with my above story about my bedroom toll, I needed the help of my parents to have enough power to enforce my brothers' access to the space.

People become attached to their homes, and home "space" becomes "place" when it is filled up with people, activities, and objects that are meaningful. It is as if the home becomes a site for the accumulation of biographical experiences. That's what makes moving so hard for people who love the places they're leaving behind, and easy for people who hate them because they're filled with bad memories. A space turns into a place. A house turns into a home. To leave the space means to leave behind the accumulated meanings attached to it. The place we live acts upon us by containing memories and meanings. And sometimes we don't even know this is happening. People are rarely aware of the significance or impact of the spaces around them, unless they are transitioning into or out of a space. For sociologists, uncovering what is unseen can be as important as understanding what is seen. If our home spaces act upon us in ways we may not even think about, that means the spaces are quite powerful social actors in their own right.

And what about *objects*—the things we sit on, move, place on walls, toss underneath something, trip over, wear, use to store other objects, look at, throw away, and give to others? Just like spaces, objects are made meaningful by us, but they may act upon us and our family relationships in powerful ways. How people use household objects can help in their identity and relationship formation, whether it's through passing along an heirloom to the next generation, trying not to grimace when you receive a gift you don't like, or displaying a certain item in your home to show off to others that you have good taste. Anthropologist Daniel Miller's approach to how objects act upon us, even and perhaps especially when we are unaware of their impact, is articulated in his aptly titled book *Stuff*, where he says,

> Objects are important, not because they are evident and physically constrain or enable, but quite the opposite. It is often precisely because we do not see them. The less we are aware of them, the more powerfully they can determine our expectations, by setting the scene and ensuring appropriate behaviour. . . . They determine what takes place to the extent that we are unconscious of their capacity to do so.[15]

What purpose do our home objects serve? According to research on cherished possessions of aging adults in Florida by Heather Whitmore, objects are "concrete and enduring representations of achievements and social relationships." They are also "external embodiments of personal goals and feelings."[16] Objects represent past memories, and, because we can show them to others, and because others' views help us shape how we think about ourselves, the objects also help us maintain our values and our sense of self. Our identities are not just held in our minds or bodies. They are shown in the travel souvenirs, family photos, or inherited tables that are displayed in our homes.

Objects tell us something about their possessor. Objects, much like spaces, become significant when people assign personal or collective meaning or value to them. Things are imbued with meaning when they are used as physical representations of who we are. Not only can objects provide information about their owners to others, they can also help the owner develop their sense of self by telling and retelling the story associated with the objects. For example, I am reminded of my husband's Greek heritage every time I look at the Socrates trivet in our kitchen cabinet. Souvenirs and other mementos can symbolize places or identities that social actors have in different spaces, which is what the little fabric Danish flag in our hallway does when it reminds me of my time teaching in Copenhagen and being a host mom to our wonderful Danish exchange student, Anna.

Our behaviors and our cultural identities are woven into home objects. Sociologists would argue that objects are given meaning intentionally by people. But they can even be meaningful, and often powerful, when people are unaware of their meaning. This is why it's important to look at things that people would not usually consider to be meaningful. For example, it may be easy to see how a childhood stuffed animal represents a past identity and set of memories, and it may be harder to see how a power tool might do the same. Part of the job of any good sociologist is to not only look at how people craft meaning out of objects that are easy to see as memory or identity markers but also to look at objects that are not automatically understood as personally or socially meaningful. In fact, both are sociologically interesting.

As you continue to read, keep in mind the foundational ideas that hold this book together: first, we should value the study of home spaces and objects in order to learn things about how our public and private lives are defined today; second, this investigation must move beyond individual-level explanation to uncover larger social processes, including those that show how unequal our society is; and third, we must consider that the objects and spaces themselves may influence us as much as we design, arrange, use, and influence them, sometimes when we don't even know they're doing this.

THIS BOOK

The chapter that you're reading now has served as a sort of welcome mat to an understanding of our family lives. Each of the next chapters covers a broad swath of past research, but sticks close to those studies that present research findings that cover family life as told through stories of home spaces and objects, and that align with the book's foundations. I introduce rooms in homes that connect closely to each chapter's focus and tell how those rooms showcase important patterns of contemporary U.S. family lives. I incorporate my own and others' research findings about the family experiences highlighted in each chapter, and about the spaces and objects featured. At the end of each chapter I connect the topics back to the three foundations of this book: homes show how the boundaries between public and private matter for families; homes tell us about individual families, but also about broader social issues; and homes are not only symbolic, but also shape our lives.

Chapter 2 brings us to a space that symbolizes transition. We visit *basement bedrooms* and *college dorm rooms* as home spaces that represent a transition from childhood to adulthood, often in contrast to a childhood bedroom. These spaces show us that the movement from childhood to adulthood takes place in particular spaces that are transitional, just like the life stage of their occupants. The objects of focus are, first, *blankets and stuffed animals,* and, second, a *wall poster.* These things and the studies that include them in their findings demonstrate that moving from childhood to adulthood includes the use of objects and spaces that mark transitional identities.

Chapter 3 focuses on couplehood, with (usually) two people who have joined in living space, sexual relations, and some kind of merging of financial and material resources. We visit *owner's (or master) suites,* the space that symbolizes the movement into adulthood, private sexual relations, and the shared intimate space for sleeping. The two objects we uncover are *love letters* and *beds,* which help us see how objects signify the importance of memories and communication in couples, as well as how sleeping surfaces shed light on the movement into couplehood, sexual relationships, conflict resolution, and thoughts about privacy within families.

Chapter 4 allows us to enter a space that is often seen as an adult space, but is just as likely to be used as a place for objects that facilitate parent-child interactions: *living rooms.* We delve into the importance of the social construction of childhood and parent-child relations in our understanding of contemporary family lives. To get at how parenthood is understood in light of changing family relations, we flip through a couple *family photo albums.* Our second object that helps us understand childhood and parenthood is a big box of *LEGO* bricks, which we'll need to be careful not to step on as we find a spot to sit in the multipurpose living room.

Whether there are children in a home or not, deciding who does what tasks to keep the household running—what sociologists call the household division of labor—is the important area we examine in chapter 5. For this topic, we enter two spaces: *toolsheds* and *kitchens*. We examine closely a *toolbox* filled with hammers and nails used for household fix-it and construction projects, and kitchen *spices*. By looking at these, we uncover the importance of gender roles and how they may intersect with racial-ethnic identity and social class. We also gain an understanding of the current do-it-yourself home décor and remodeling culture in terms of changing gender roles.

Earlier I argued that the walls of homes are increasingly made blurry, in part because of people and tasks who enter our homes. Chapter 6 investigates the pathways that connect homes to other realms, in particular the paid workplace. We enter *home offices* (or spaces where someone plops down their work tasks), where paid work is quite literally found at home. The objects featured in this chapter are a *work bag* and a *calendar*—both of which provide tangible and visible ways we can see family and work lives intersect or be kept separate, sometimes in the face of societal changes that allow for work to creep increasingly into our family lives.

Often in books about families, there is a chapter devoted to divorce, focusing in particular on how problems may emerge for children if there is a high level of conflict in a home. I do something a little different in chapter 7, though I do have divorce as a primary focus. I also include mention of geographic separation of family members for work, including transnational work, living-apart-together relationships (LATs), and commuter marriages.[17] Because this is a book about home spaces and objects, it becomes interesting to see how they may seem different to people who need to spend time in multiple home spaces, and who may use objects to help stay connected to conceptions of home between the spaces. In this chapter, I look at *two bedrooms of a child in two homes* whose parents have divorced. One object I examine is a *sofa bed*—one that serves as a temporary sleeping space for a child who spends time in more than one home. I then focus on *laptop computers* and *cell phones*, which can symbolize and facilitate a child's ability to transport tasks between two different homes or to communicate with family members who don't live under the same roof.

Just as there are myriad home designs, there are multiple ways that families can be constituted. While a variety of family forms are connected to all of the chapters in this book, chapter 8 includes the explicit and focused consideration of how spaces and objects matter in families that are *not* nuclear families. While it may seem as if retirement homes, granny pods, and cohousing communities are very different from each other, this chapter ties them together by arguing that they all challenge the notion that the private nuclear family in a single-family home is the only model of family life in contemporary society. We visit *dining rooms*, some private and some communal, where shared meals between whoever is defined as a member of the home occur. The objects of focus are a *dining table* and *inherited dishes*, which get at the significance of ritual, shared space, how people decide what counts as a family (and what doesn't), and the role of inheritance practices surrounding family heirlooms in defining what constitutes a family and how its members relate within and across generations.

Chapter 9 explores ideas about the future of American families. I do this by visiting, of all places, *bathrooms*, in order to show how families deal with bodies and cleanliness and waste. Bathrooms help us think about how ideas of privacy have changed over time, and how home spaces and objects have connections to bodies in our consideration of family roles and relationships. The objects of focus in this chapter deal with how water is constructed to be either dirty or clean, first with the *toilet* and then with a *shower*. These objects help to show how technological change, globalization, and environmental sustainability matter in family roles and relationships, especially in terms of how we think about privacy. We venture into bathrooms with an eye toward thinking about what future home spaces and objects will look like if we want to understand families several generations from now.

I end the book with a step outside of the home, by examining the ways that literal and figurative fences and pathways hinder or allow our ability to move forward with an understanding of future family lives, and of ourselves.

The topics of the chapters in this book, as well as the order in which they are presented, may look familiar to those who have encountered textbooks on marriage and family life. Often, these books are arranged

in a loose temporal order of life stages, starting with partnership creation and ending with old age and a discussion of future families. The
problem with this is that the experience of family lives over time is often
blurrier and messier than this order may allow. Lots of people are
single. Marriage is not a given for young people. Parent-child relations
don't matter for some, and may matter differently when children are at
different ages, such as when they leave the nest (or come back in their
twenties because they cannot find a job). The cost of arranging a book
into chapters that mimic life stages is that actual home and family life is
(thankfully) not as tidily arranged. The benefit of organizing the book
like this, though, is that what is presented here can be aligned with
other sources on the same topic, so that readers interested in a particular life stage may know where to look. And, throughout, I try hard to
present the kind of blurriness and messiness that shows just how varied
experiences can be even with a topic that seems fixed.

Within each chapter, I figured that overwhelming you with data and
all the research that's fit to print may not be the best route. Instead, I
give you an overview of how scholars have looked at this part of family
life in terms of home spaces and objects, and then share stories of
research projects that exemplify the importance of a room in a home
and a couple domestic objects. I include my own research in each
chapter because I am most familiar with it, and because I want to
thread my research findings together in one book. I'm excited that
these chapters will allow me to highlight research findings that I've
collected over the last two decades on college student conceptions of
home, the nostalgic importance of love letters, the management of family photos, the use of power tools in home remodeling and redecoration,
the use of objects and spaces in work-family boundaries, post-divorce
children's attachment to bedrooms and belongings, and cohousing communities' impact on social relations.

My research is centered in the United States and may not include
findings that represent all types of families or people. Because of this, I
include others' findings that give a more complete integrated picture of
how inequalities may be operating in home spaces and objects—inequalities and social groups that extend beyond the focus of my research projects. But, of course, I leave out a lot, and cannot focus on
every kind of group or inequality or home type.

Some advice for your reading: please remember that the spaces and objects in each chapter not only represent the literal spaces and objects and homes (and research on them), but they also get at the symbolic dimensions of family life that can be seen in other spaces and objects. So, if you live in a home without a dining room, if you don't have any love letters, if you're afraid of power tools, or if you don't sleep in a bed, read these parts anyway. They may relate to what you do have, or what you want, or what you need to know about the importance of home spaces and objects in understanding contemporary family lives.

Welcome home. Now that we know we have a good foundation, let's look at some stuff together.

2

FROM CHILDHOOD TO ADULTHOOD
Stuffed Animals, Blankets, and Wall Posters

Hypothetical parent to eighteen-year-old just after high school graduation: "Okay, it's time to take out that twin bed with the rainbow unicorn bedspread on it, so we can make room for the new elliptical machine I just bought at a yard sale."

Hypothetical eighteen-year-old to parent: "But wait, Mom, I'm still living here for two more months! Don't take away my unicorn!"

BASEMENT BEDROOMS AND COLLEGE DORM ROOMS

I remember coming home from college for the first time to discover that my mom had placed folded towels carefully on my bed for me to use during my fall weekend stay. This generous gesture, though, felt uncomfortable to me. I was not prepared, at that point, to be seen as a guest in my own room. My. Own. Room. Not a guest room, not a future put-all-the-extra-crap-in-here room, not anything but the room with pink walls that surrounded me throughout my childhood. My mom, gracious soul that she is, understood my consternation, and immediately put the towels back in the hallway linen closet so I could retrieve them myself, just as I had done for the years preceding college. Just as I had done as a child living in my pink childhood room.

What to do with the stuff of childhood is a lifelong project for many families, and the stuff itself can signify different life stages, just as the items I refused to label "guest towels" did for me on that defining fall weekend in my eighteenth year. Depending on your circumstances, you may recall a conversation with a parent or guardian (or sibling) about whether they may repurpose your childhood bedroom into something else once you leave. Or you may recall deciding whether you want to take that favorite unicorn bedspread with you when you move into an apartment or college dormitory. Or you may recall moving from a childhood bedroom into a different room in the same house, perhaps in a basement or above a garage, in order to signify that you were moving out of childhood and into adulthood (even if the move was only fifteen feet away). Or you may have moved out of that bedroom for a few years and now find yourself back there, but feeling as if you really hate unicorns now that you're a grown-up. Or you may have stayed in that room this whole time, looking forward to leaving, or seeking a job, or filling out college applications, or helping with household duties as the other members of your household age. Or you may have just left to go get married and never thought this much about how a childhood bedroom could signify so many things! In all of these cases, and even if your circumstances do not fit what you think most people your age are doing, the room where you spend your time can signify what life stage you (and your parents) think you're in.

Millennials—those eighteen to thirty-four years old—have surpassed other generations as the largest generation in the United States today, comprising over seventy-five million people.[1] Around eighteen million people, most who fit into the millennial category, currently attend nearly five thousand colleges and universities in the United States.[2] While that is a lot of people, and while more people are going to college than in past decades, it is not a life path that is possible for everyone, nor is it a path that even those who can afford it may choose. Nonetheless, spaces like college dorm rooms (often referred to now as residence halls, so they sound less institutional) are important locations for understanding roles and relationships. And college residence halls are increasingly likely to intentionally contain elements that people associate with home spaces: warmth, opportunities for socializing, personalization, and emotional connection.[3] The movement of a person from a family home into a college residence hall can symbolize the transition to adulthood and, for many, the path to forming the next generation of families. The transition into this new space is part of the process of increasing independence, separation from parents or guardians, voting rights, more control over time and space, and often intimate or sexual relationships. These things would also be present if we thought about a basement, studio apartment, new home with a partner or spouse, or even a childhood bedroom transformed into an adult space. In all of these cases, one life stage is visibly transformed to represent another, or at least the person is transformed into a different identity (which can sometimes be at odds with the space, as when an adult returns to a childhood bedroom and feels out of place amidst the unicorn bed-spread, the clothes from younger years, the stuffed animals, or the posters of rock stars from one or two decades ago). Studying places where life stage transitions occur can help us understand that these transitions can vary from person to person based on where they live, where they move to, and with whom they live.

In this chapter, while a lot of the discussion of research will relate to college dorm rooms, consider those references to represent any space that someone occupies as he or she is thinking about whether and how to launch into adulthood. It could be a childhood bedroom with an adult body occupying it after returning home. It could be a different room in a home that is redecorated in such a way that the mementos of childhood are rendered less visible. It could be a four-hundred-square-foot micro-apartment in a big city or a house rented with five other people in a small town. It could be any kind of space that signifies the transition between childhood and adulthood—one that, if all the accou-trements of childhood were visible, would somehow feel strange or unrepresentative of the life stage that the room's occupier wishes to feel he or she is in.

TODAY'S CHILDHOOD-TO-ADULTHOOD TRANSITIONS

What ingredients are necessary for someone to be labeled an adult? As with any recipe, the ingredients can change depending on available time, resources, and individual desires. But as sociologists (and chefs) are inclined to say, despite different ingredients in any recipe, we can still notice some intriguing patterns that result from how we mix those

ingredients. In this section, I describe three topics that help us understand what's going on today with the transition between childhood and
adulthood: first, I discuss how the life stage that we know as *adulthood*
is itself a social construction; second, I describe what is going on in
contemporary housing and living arrangements that illustrates the importance of money in the transition between childhood and adulthood;
and third, I uncover the importance of future ideals about finding a
partner and having children as people become adults.

The Transition to Adulthood Is Socially Constructed

Family life is full of transitions. In textbooks these are often labeled
paths to family formation, with the presumption that the end point is to
create a family of some sort. But the thing is, the paths can be winding,
intertwining, forward, backward, and sometimes straight as a line. That
makes talking about transitions into family life and adulthood a little
challenging. But let's try anyway. For the sake of convenience, let's say
that our aim is to figure out how people go from being in one family
(often called a *family of orientation*) into another that they create later
(often called a *family of procreation*, even if children do not end up in
the picture). In contemporary U.S. society, this often means that one
goes from being young to not-so-young, from being dependent on people who are older within your household to becoming those older people upon whom others might rely. This transition can involve greater
independence (economic and otherwise), sexual maturity, and geographic movement away from the family of orientation (at least eventually). It often involves either a change in home space or at least a change
in views about one's childhood space.

Sociologists are likely to be *social constructionists*—people who believe that things in our lives that we think are real are defined that way
because we collectively decide so. That's going to keep coming up in
this book. For example, as I discuss more in chapter 4, even though
children are defined as different from adults, especially when we try to
understand parent-child relations, the boundary between the stages of
childhood and adulthood can change depending on historical era or
geographic location, or even depending on a given person's circumstances. For centuries, the transitional time between childhood and
adulthood has been in flux, and the age that people have thought

marked the end of adolescence has varied. In addition, the popularity of the terms used to refer to that transition has changed. Specifically and perhaps surprisingly, the terms *adolescent* and *teen* have been used for centuries to refer to young people nearing adulthood, though the word *teenager* gained popularity in the 1940s. The concept of *preteen* emerged in the 1920s, and *tween* first appeared in the 1940s but has become popular in the last two decades.[4] Since words are important, and since these words refer to specific life stages, knowing that the words have changed over time means that we also know that the definitions of childhood and adulthood have changed, too. So keep that in mind as you read further; the way this chapter talks about childhood needs to be situated in a particular time and place.

Geographer Gill Valentine, in the inaugural issue of the academic journal *Children's Geographies*, talked about how defining childhood and adulthood, and the boundary between them, is elusive. The liminal, or in-between, period of time when young people are less "circumscribed by parents, teachers, or other adults" happens differently for different people.[5] Sometimes people mature early and take on adult-like tasks like paying bills when they're very young. And sometimes people who are in their thirties or older have never had a credit card. Despite these variations, there are some commonalities among young people today who leave home and move into a place separate from their childhood home, or who leave to attend a residential college or university for a few years. They are all venturing into spaces that allow for identity formation and distance from parental control, and they have been classified as "incompletely launched young adults."[6] Not quite ready for take-off, but nearing the launching pad.

Some scholars have labeled this stage of life as *emerging adulthood*, which often occurs after moving out of a childhood home and before permanently settling down as an adult in a different home, but that increasingly can include people who are still living with parents or guardians (which is now the most common living arrangement for young adults, a recent trend I discuss further below).[7] The circumstances surrounding people who are poised to launch into adulthood vary tremendously, and scholars don't all agree about what constitutes this launching or emerging (or even if these are the right words to use). But in many cases the experiences include the interplay between "independence and dependence, autonomy and reliance on others, distance and closeness, [and] change and stability."[8] And the experiences also often include *rites of passage*—relatively public displays of the transition between life stages that symbolize one's changing identity and status. They are ritual traditions that publicly mark the different stages through someone's life course, signifying a transformation of some kind, as happens with bar mitzvahs, confirmations, *quinceañeras*, graduations, weddings, and funerals. Today in the United States, rites of passage that signify a transition between childhood and adulthood often involve entry into some kind of housing market, whether it's paying parents rent, getting a job to save up money for future independent living, seeking an apartment, or buying a home. Today, there are many ways that young people find their way into the housing market: sometimes they intend to leave their childhood home but can't and start paying rent to a parent, sometimes they have no choice, sometimes they do so with economic constraints, and sometimes they leave because they have been accepted into college and are going to live near or on the campus where they'll take classes.

The transition to adulthood varies across people, but there are enough patterns in place that help us to see how differences between childhood and adulthood have implications for how we live and how we think about people's roles and responsibilities. Movement from one type of home space into another can be part of a transitional process that highlights, and even complicates, these patterns.

Where People Live as They Transition into Adulthood Depends on Money

One of my favorite slogans of all time is from a furniture store in my childhood home town. It was, and still is, plastered across a huge sign above the entrance saying, "Feather your nest with a little down!" Today the slogan is also plastered across the store's website at larsonfurniture.com. Now that I know what it means to make a down payment on something expensive, I find this slogan to be particularly clever. As a child, I didn't yet understand the concept of a down payment for those who wanted to buy furniture by paying for it in installments, because I did not make it a habit of buying couches before junior high (and I don't think the $14 of birthday money I had saved would have gone far to get me a decent couch). But I did understand that a nest represented a home and that down was something that came from birds and was sometimes used inside blankets.

A bird's nest is an oft-cited metaphor for a home, in furniture store slogans and in academic research. Social scientists dabble in studying birds, or at least their metaphorical practices, when they research nest-leaving, the empty nest, and labels like "feathered nests" that refer to affluent homes.[9] Whether it's making a down payment or buying an expensive down comforter, money matters in how people experience life stage transitions in different "nests."

People are taking longer to "leave the nest" and establish themselves as adults.[10] For the first time since the late 1800s, eighteen- to thirty-five-year-olds in the U.S. are most likely to live with their parents, as compared to other living situations such as living alone or living with a married or cohabiting partner.[11] This living situation is far from new, and the proportion of people doing this is not necessarily higher than in the past. But it is now the most common living situation relative to others, due in part to people delaying the age at which they settle down with a long-term partner, to a downward trajectory in men's wages, and to a greater likelihood of people to go to college (and then sometimes return home after graduating, though this group is less likely than their non-college peers to live with parents).[12] This shift in housing patterns is huge news, not just because it has never happened before, but because it makes us consider whether living independently will be included in the ingredient list for someone to be labeled as an adult in the coming years.

Clara Mulder, a population researcher in the Netherlands, notes that leaving a parental home is one of the few family events that always requires relocating to a different residence. She also says that whether people leave the nest depends to a great extent on economics.[13] Kids who go to college, for example, are more likely than those who do not go to college to have parents or guardians who own their homes. If the parental home is rented rather than owned or on the way to being owned via a mortgage, children are not as likely to stay as they enter adulthood. We know that a high-quality and spacious living space looks attractive to children as they enter adulthood. We also know that how much money parents have affects where people live in their transition to adulthood. All of this is to say that there are inequalities in people's ability to attain this kind of adult space.

The student pathway is, in many cases in the United States, a privileged one when it comes to housing, mostly because students can access housing via college or university resources (e.g., a housing office for both on- and off-campus residences).[14] College students, then, even though they may be in debt or feel as if they are not in an economically independent situation, are able to access home spaces that are often unavailable to others, perhaps making their interpretation of home a bit different from someone who has to find an apartment and get a job at the age of eighteen. Rites of passage that launch people into housing markets, then, vary depending on a person's goals and resources, which includes whether they go to college.

Unless they have a large inheritance, young adults who are not attending college, or who have graduated, feel economic constraints when it comes to finding a home. Certainly individual economic circumstances may lead someone toward or away from leaving a parental home. But there are larger societal-level economic conditions that matter, too. If we want to understand why and whether young adults leave home and move into their own places, we should look at any pressing housing crises or economic downturns that may affect these people's housing choices. Case in point: the economic recession from nearly a decade ago, along with changing job market prospects and troublingly high student loan debt, has rendered some housing and rental markets untenable for young adults to enter. In Manhattan, for example, developers are creating apartment buildings with micro-units that resemble dormitories—small private sleeping spaces with shared spaces for other tasks such as cooking and eating—because rent prices in this urban area are too high for most to be able to afford.[15] They are personalizable, but small. They are private, but communal. They are designed for adults, but do not contain all of the elements of a private adult home space. They are more affordable than private rental properties, and yet the mortgage lies upward of a half a million dollars for four hundred square feet.

What about college students? For them, a dorm room is often the first home space where they live after a parental home, yet it can seem impersonal, institutionalized, and less likely to connote adult status than a Manhattan micro-apartment. And yet, we know that college students actively seek ways to gain adult status, often using their living spaces to do so.[16] The ideal of adult status consists of control over space and belongings and the ability to personalize a space, so college students spend time and money trying to make their dorm room into a more adult home-like space, even if it includes spending ten dollars on a used couch with a questionable past. This desire to move into adulthood even among those who live in institutionalized settings such as college residence halls is called forth by companies such as Dormify, a business that sells dorm-room-type furniture and accessories to students and others who want to personalize their space.[17] Of course, the ability to purchase these items depends on a student's financial standing. The transition into adulthood requires money. Financial considerations, whether it's income, job prospects, college costs, securing rental insurance or a mortgage, or expenses associated with furnishing a space, must be part of any discussion of how space matters in this transition.

Aspirations about Couplehood and Kids

While the next chapter delves more deeply into couple relationships, the idea of pairing up to venture into adulthood, at least as an ideal, is relevant in a discussion about the transition away from a childhood home. Not everyone who turns eighteen is involved in a romantic relationship, let alone married. In fact, fewer people are entering long-term relationships at this age than in the past, because partnering is not as necessary as it used to be to find housing, feel economically secure, take part in sexual relationships, or consider yourself to be an adult. There are increasing numbers of single people, greater numbers of college attendees, and a decreasing desire to marry at a young age (or marry at all) than in the past. These patterns affect where and how young adults live. For example, as Clara Mulder found out in her review of research on leaving the parental home and housing choices, increasing numbers of single people want to maintain flexibility so they can move without high costs. This desire among singles may be an economic necessity, but it is also about seeing singlehood as a potentially temporary life stage. This is why they are more likely to rent, often in spaces shared with other single renters. Buying a house, whether single or partnered, is a commitment to a long-term stay in one place. While this may still be a symbol of adulthood for many, it is not the only ingredient, it may be lessening in importance, and it is not always possible.[18]

All of this points to the idea that young people who are not in a long-term partnership are more likely to live in temporary rental housing. That may seem obvious, but what may be less obvious in our everyday thoughts is this: how people play out family relationships is deeply connected to our housing patterns—what's built, what's popular, what's available, what's not. While marriage and cohabitation are looking increasingly similar in U.S. society, and while people are much more likely to live together without marrying than in the past, even when adding children to the mix, both marriage and home ownership are still normally known as part of the transition into responsible adulthood. Even if a couple buys a home without being married, their chances of marrying go up a lot. And it is still the case that people who want to have children are also more likely to desire home ownership over renting. Agreeing to partner with someone for a lifetime and buying a house are both visible symbols of commitment to a larger collaborative (and economic) adult project. On the other hand, with increasing numbers of people remaining single into adulthood, we also see lots of home buying among individuals who are not in a long-term partnership.

Leaving a childhood bedroom with an eye toward a larger space to start a new adult life stage is not just about the relationships that may change or be affirmed. It is also about the spaces and objects that are part of that transition, which include those spaces' availability and the preferences of the space's occupants to define it as temporary or permanent. These spaces and objects signify new roles and relationships that are less about being a child and more about being an adult.

STUFFED ANIMALS AND BLANKETS

Bringing an object from a childhood bedroom into an adult space can symbolize the transition into adulthood. Cherished possessions can be lifelong reminders of our memories and our shifting identities and statuses as we age. Psychologists Jane Kroger and Vivienne Adair remind us of this in their research on valued personal objects in late adulthood.[19] As people move out of their homes and into places such as assisted living facilities or retirement communities, they, like young adults leaving a childhood home, need to decide which items to keep and which ones to toss. This deliberation is not always easy, because, as I discuss in chapter 8, to get rid of a valued possession can feel as if you're getting rid of part of your identity. The objects people wish to retain and leave behind as they transition between life stages tell us a rich story of both the lived experience of moving into a new life stage, as well as the larger ideas we have as a society about what it means to be in a particular life stage. This is as true for aging adults as it is for young people moving into adulthood.

For young adults who are considering whether they can or should leave their childhood home, researchers have uncovered the importance of objects that can symbolize, and sometimes assist with, wrestling with the strange period of time when leaving a childhood identity doesn't feel quite right, but entering a full-fledged adult role doesn't either. Sociologist Ira Silver's work highlights how objects brought from a childhood home into a college dorm room (such as clothing, photographs, and pieces of technology) can anchor a person to childhood identity at the same time as they mark new identities for someone entering college.[20] Pediatricians who have studied young adult transitions say that about a quarter of young women bring things like teddy bears and blankets to college with them (young men do, too, but at lower rates because there's a stigma attached to stuffed animals for men). These *transitional objects*, a term coined by British psychoanalyst Donald Woods Winnicott in 1953, lessen the challenges of separation from a childhood home and family.[21]

Silver's work highlights how objects brought to college can signify attachment to a childhood home (which he calls *anchors*) and those that signify the transition into adulthood (transitional objects). The decision to bring something from home can require a strategic choice on the part of the college student to either retain a childhood identity or connection or to form a new college identity. Sometimes bringing things such as stuffed animals can be risky, since they carry a stigma of being too childlike. As Silver noted, "Regardless of how close incoming students felt toward their parents, they carefully considered how much of their biographies they wanted to leave behind in the settings where they had lived most of their lives."[22] The work of media and youth culture scholar Siân Lincoln echoes this idea, noting that the more public nature of college dorm rooms (as opposed to childhood bedrooms) means college students are in between staying connected to their childhoods (as displaying a stuffed animal may symbolize) and crafting new adult identities among new friends (as hiding that same stuffed animal may symbolize).[23]

Unless it has a unicorn on it, a blanket from a childhood bedroom brought to college is less likely to be stigmatized as too childlike as compared to a stuffed animal. But this doesn't mean that an item as seemingly benign as a blanket or bedspread does not connote identities that matter in our social world. In research on lower-income students' college experience, psychologist Elizabeth Aries and sociologist Maynard Seider found that dorm room objects such as blankets and bedspreads can affect whether students feel as if they belong.[24] Surely the presence of wealth can be seen among students who bring expensive electronic equipment, cars, and designer clothes, but even the display of designer bedding—an object that is both intimate and publicly displayed—can engender feelings of inferiority among college students who do not come from affluent households. Sometimes scholars who study class differences reference something that famed social theorist Pierre Bourdieu named *cultural capital*—the set of information, knowledge, skills, and resources someone from a wealthier background has that can perpetuate his or her class standing and showcase certain tastes (e.g., access to a good education, art museums, books, and technological expertise). I would make the case that even knowledge about thread count in sheets or a desire to buy sheets that are all cotton counts as cultural capital, and can be a location for someone to feel that she or he has a certain status among a new group of peers like college residence hall mates.

Despite bedding and blankets serving as visual symbols of class inequalities, these items can indeed serve as anchors and transitional objects for college students from all backgrounds. In 2016 Maya Volk and I conducted survey research on how college students conceptualize home.[25] We asked students a question about the ways their first-semester residence hall room was the same as, or different from, their precollege room, which yielded fascinating results. Respondents (229 of them, all from a U.S. residential four-year college) were prompted to discuss both the physical and emotional aspects of the rooms. Most mentioned objects or decoration that connected them to their childhood bedroom. Sometimes this included bringing the actual objects from one place to the other, and sometimes it meant decorating the dorm room with similar colors or items that could be found in the precollege room. And guess what? They talked about stuffed animals and blankets.

Aside from pictures and art pieces, one of the most commonly mentioned items brought from home was a blanket (and sometimes respondents mentioned a stuffed animal alongside reference to bedding). Student survey responses included sentiments about comfort (the blanket from home was "so comforting"), or home-like personalized space ("I have the same bedding. It feels homey and like my space."). But some answers were a little more complex, such as, "I had the same quilt on my bed that I had had on my bed at home. I also had my favorite stuff[ed] animal on my bed, a childhood teddy bear that I still sleep with to this day. These two things made the rooms feel similar but for the most part everything else felt different."

Bringing a blanket from home is a necessity for any student whose family cannot afford to shop for a new designer cover from Dormify.com. But sometimes the meaning attached to the bedding is also about the transition between childhood and adulthood. A blanket (and sometimes stuffed animals snuggled into it) serves as an anchor to a childhood identity, but also as an item that is situated in a room where "everything else felt different." The rest of the room is about a new adult identity, and perhaps the activities under the blankets look different from those found in a childhood bedroom. But leaving that childhood blanket (and that stuffed animal hidden in the dorm room drawer) behind may have made the transition too abrupt.

A WALL POSTER

When I was twelve I had a huge poster of Michael Jackson hanging on my wall. To hang it up I used tape that contained an adhesive so weak that the poster was constantly falling down, and yet so strong that when I took it down for good, a large patch of paint came with it. In college, I opted not to bring my cherished Michael Jackson poster, but instead hung a Pink Floyd "The Wall" poster to show that my music taste had become different, given my assumptions about the new peers with whom I was associating. While nobody can deny the talent of Mr. Jackson, Pink Floyd was somehow defined in my eighteen-year-old brain as more sophisticated. Or deep. Or good to listen to while trying to act deep and sophisticated with cheap beer. What was not sophisticated was my use of chewing gum to serve as adhesive on my dorm room wall for a poster about "The Wall."

Wall art and posters were as common as blankets in the responses to Maya's and my survey question asking college students how childhood and dorm rooms were similar. A poster or wall display was often described as bridging childhood and college identities, as this quote illustrates: "One of the walls of my bedroom at home I call the 'wall of stuff,' and it was covered in pictures and posters . . . that either were meaningful to me or just looked cool. . . . I made a new 'wall of stuff' [at college] with a combination of things from home and new things I gathered." For this student, the display of items on a wall became a visual symbol of a transitioning identity from child to adult.

Putting things on the walls of a dorm room or rental space carries with it the ability of its owner to convey their interests and identities to anyone who enters the space. Personalization is something that students in residence halls and residents in rentals prefer.[26] However, unlike in a home that is owned, this personalization usually needs to be done with impermanent changes so as not to damage the walls, as a hammer and nails would do when hanging a picture or wall paint would do (unless you're really good at painting over that exquisite painted headboard that I may or may not have added to my husband's and my first apartment bedroom wall because we couldn't afford a real headboard).[27] Hanging a poster on a dorm room or bedroom wall can also connote territoriality. It's a kind of personalization that connotes control over space, even if the borders of a poster do not extend literally into the room space and the space is divided into territories with imaginary lines.[28] If that weren't the case, my Pink Floyd poster would have hung over my first-year roommate's bed, and her Bob Mould album cover would have been on my desk.

During the transition to adulthood, peers become very important as *reference groups*—people with whom someone feels a connection and finds to be similar and can offer social support. The transition to college carries with it a lot of uncertainty in terms of social roles and acceptance from peers. Objects hung by new students in dorm rooms can serve as ways for the students to introduce themselves to peer groups and networks of people whose opinion may matter. These tell newcomers about the owner's identity, interests, and ability to balance fitting in with an expression of individuality. As college students said in Silver's study about college transition objects, "The Beatles poster . . . well, I've seen lots of posters of the Beatles, but this one is so original. You don't see it in a lot of music stores," and, "I was going to get the James Dean poster, but everyone else has it."[29] Of course, these posters that are used to signify uniqueness among peers still follow genre and style conventions that are common among college student décor choices. I may have thought I was unique in displaying Pink Floyd instead of Michael Jackson, but likely the dozens of other students doing the same thing (and who probably bought a poster at a poster sale on campus like I did) would have had the same thought.

In addition to children transitioning into adulthood, parents undergo a transition when their children leave the family home, evidenced by one of Silver's interviewees describing how his mother cried when he rolled up his childhood bedroom posters to bring them to his college dorm room. He said, "In fact, she went out and bought a new poster for my room. They keep my room exactly as it was. It's like in the movies when a daughter or son dies and the parents retain the room. . . . I think they would mind if I took everything out of my room. I think they still want to keep pieces of me there. These things are reminders that I am still around."[30] What all of this research tells us is that something as mundane as a wall poster carries with it important meaning about the person's identity during the transition into adulthood. Parents may wish to have their children remain young, but if we are lucky we all grow up. While we're doing this, the people with whom we associate and the things we put on our walls illustrate the changes in our identities.

REFLECTING ON OUR STUFF

Homes show how the boundary between public and private matters for families. The definition of *adulthood* has changed over time, and it can vary across geographic space and in different people's experiences. Life stage transitions are a fascinating place to delve into the importance of public and private boundaries, often because they contain rituals and rites of passage relating to private family moments that are made quite public (e.g., hauling a box full of posters and blankets to a new place). Even the display of a blanket in a college dorm room signifies the transition between a private conception of one's childhood experiences and a more public, and socially accessible, version of the self that is meant to be accepted by a new set of peers. Designers of college residence halls, and even the new "dorms" for young adults in expensive urban areas, must take into consideration a balance between privacy and access to public and communal space. And those of us who have people in our lives undergoing a transition into adulthood would be wise to remember that the "stuff of childhood" may actually be one of the most important things to examine when people work on establishing a new adult identity. While this kind of understanding is important to consider for all life stage transitions, it is in the shift between childhood and adulthood—where one goes from being taken care of in private spaces to visibly (and sometimes publicly) enacting adultlike rituals like moving into a new home—that the public-private boundary is particularly salient.

Homes tell us about individual families, but also about broader social issues. What is expected as an adult is not uniform across groups in society. Sociologists know that access to information, resources (including warm blankets), and experiences that help shape one's desire and ability to own a home must be situated in that person's economic standing, along with his or her racial, gender, and sexual identities. What an adult is supposed to do, or can do, depends on others' expectations for that person. And expectations affect how we go from childhood to adulthood in terms of our identities. If that weren't the case, we wouldn't still be impacted by societal expectations about men's and women's roles, racial residential segregation, and the legal and social approval of someone's right to partner, marry, and sign a mortgage. What this tells us is that, as we read news articles about housing availability, or read college marketing materials over the shoulder of a college-bound high school student, we always have to remember that not everyone has equal access to affording certain kinds of spaces, let alone items that can symbolize adulthood. Even though this chapter focused primarily on economic status, it is important to remember that feathered nests and safe spaces, just like down blankets, are not available to everyone, due in part to inequalities that stem from more than just access to money.

Homes are not only symbolic, but also shape our lives. Heaven forbid that a unicorn or a stuffed animal or a "wall of stuff" comes alive. But maybe, if we take a step back, we can see that these items, and the spaces that contain them, act upon their owners in interesting ways. Homes can symbolize and shape the life stages of childhood and adulthood. When a college student walks into her dorm room to see the new wall poster hung above her childhood quilt, she may not even know that she is seeing herself differently. Not quite ready to give up childhood, but not quite ready for a mortgage. A poster is more than just a poster; it is a tool used in the transition into adult identity.

Not only are life stages socially constructed, the concept of home is, too. If homes are now taking shape as multifaceted, not uniform, and varied, then the notion that a transition to adulthood including a particular life path that includes single-family home ownership is outdated. Home is not a fixed place. Perhaps, just as we examine the transformations in identity and status as children move into adulthood, we also need to consider homes as important players in this transition. As architecture scholar Judith Thomsen says, people's increasing geographic mobility, changing family patterns, and altered workplaces (including virtual ones), mean that we can no longer think of homes as fixed or uniform. If homes are "stages on the housing pathway" for young adults, she notes, then "the home is in practice not that stable anymore and . . . the differences between temporary homes and permanent (fixed) homes are less clear than implied by these terms."[31] And yet, despite homes not being as fixed as they used to be, the built environment around us may shape our behaviors and identities. The college dorm room walls that are not supposed to contain nail holes reinforce a transitional identity from childhood to adulthood.

If decorating a home is how we communicate our identity to others, and if identity transformation via housing and home decoration increasingly matters for young people in a world with a diverse set of pathways toward adulthood, and if home spaces and paths to family formation are decreasingly fixed concepts, then it is especially important to wrestle with the ever-changing conceptions of home for people as we label them adults. And to wrestle with the label of "adult" itself. To be sure, scholars note that the paths to family formation are changing. What I'd like to add is that the locations where the paths are paved, the signs along the way, the road debris, and the ultimate destinations are also changing.

How exciting. Seems to me that all of our posters ought to be hung with chewing gum from now on—really strong chewing gum that can either last forever or be easily removed.

3

COUPLEHOOD

Love Letters and Beds

OWNER'S (MASTER) SUITES

When my husband and I signed our names on the mortgage for our home nearly two decades ago, we had just finished graduate school. We had lived for years in rentals that had their fair share of cockroaches and rusty cabinet hinges. It was the first time we were looking at living spaces that had more than one bedroom, and we were excited about the possibility of home ownership and a bedroom that was not also used as an office. On our tour of the house, we noticed that the large bedroom at the back of the house had an interior door frame with a chain lock on it, like you would see at a Motel 6. I vividly remember us noticing it, glancing at each other with a smirk, and hoping the real estate agent didn't see us have a little moment of "I know what that's for. Hee hee."

When we turn on our televisions and stumble upon (or intentionally binge watch) episodes of *House Hunters* or *Property Brothers* on HGTV, two things are clear: first, for episodes with a pair of adults who are in a long-term relationship with each other, a separate and private sleeping space is required for the implied purpose of intimacy and escape; and second, regardless of whether there is a couple involved, the biggest sleeping space is often referred to as the master bedroom or suite (or more recently, as I discuss next, the "owner's suite").[1]

The term *master bedroom* is both recently constructed and interestingly defined.[2] This room, usually larger than other bedrooms and reserved for adults in a household, was made prominent across homes available at a wide variety of income levels during the 1980s, when houses and rooms within them were built bigger (which small-homes guru Sarah Susanka called McMansions), and when modern technology was in place that could more easily heat and cool separated and larger interior spaces than in the past. Because of the twentieth-century introduction of central heating, which replaced central fireplaces that required family members to sleep in one space together, and with an increased focus on homes as retreats from the harsh world of paid work and social ills, people across social classes started sleeping in separate rooms and treating them as smaller retreats within the home. Add to that the focus in the latter half of the twentieth century on leisure time and an increased emphasis on individualism in American society, and voila! There was now an expectation that a home's grown-ups would have their own space to sleep, and the space reserved for the home's grown-ups was made large enough to accommodate more activities than just sleeping. And now, there is an emerging trend to have homes built with *two* master suites, one upstairs for the adult couple when kids are small (to be near them), and one on a main floor for when they want distance from older kids, need a space for a grandparent to stay, or anticipate trouble with stairs. Of course, this emphasis on the prized master suite (or two) presumes that people live in new homes, which most do not, and that they can afford homes with more than one floor, which many cannot.

The term *master suite*, though widely used, has its share of critics, largely due to its connection to wider social inequalities. A *Washington Business Journal* article reported that some realtors and home builders are moving to change the term because it connotes a problematic racist, classist, and sexist past of landowners (and sometimes slaves) and male heads of households. The movement now is to refer to the space as the owner's bedroom or suite, which is what some home building companies are doing in their floor-plan room nomenclature.[3] But if you turn on HGTV or ask most realtors, the term *master* is still widely used. Despite my tendency to use the term *master suite* in my everyday language, in this chapter I will use the term *owner's suite* or *owner's bedroom* (even though many adult couples do not own their homes) to be consistent with what may be an interesting emerging new term that at least acknowledges the strangeness of the term *master* when referring to a bedroom. Plus, I don't think *mistress bedroom* sounds quite right.

No sub-unit of a family is relegated to only one room in a home, but the owner's bedroom is a space where couplehood plays out well, both literally and symbolically. What happens in this bedroom captures that the space is defined as adult space. In addition, the owner's bedroom or suite is often described as a space requiring privacy from other household members or visitors (or their objects). And finally, the space is designed, especially in contemporary homes, for two people. All of these are true whether the owner's suite is just one room or holds one person rather than two, or whether it is an entire suite complete with walk-in closets and a full bathroom. With two sinks.

What happens in an owner's bedroom? Having sex, changing clothes, watching television, working, talking, fighting, exercising, laundry folding, reading, eating, and sometimes even sleeping. Some of the most interesting moments in this bedroom are when the space is infiltrated by people, tasks, or objects that pollute the sacred private adult space with childish or profane public things, and that end up reinforcing the notion that the space is for adults, is a private space, and is designed for two people. Like when my son's field trip permission slip or a stack of papers I need to grade find their way onto my bed and I cease seeing my bed as a retreat from grown-up responsibilities.

Sociologist Margaret Gibson notes that bedrooms are reinforced as private and sacred spaces because the objects located in them "are generally personalized through their use and displacement outside of circulation." In her research on household objects that are discussed and dealt with after a family member dies, she found that these "sacred" objects "were usually set apart in the household, placed in intimate spaces or additionally housed within multiple storage boxes within drawers."[4] What this tells us is that an owner's suite contains private activities, private bodies, and private objects, regardless of whether there's a chain on the door.

Thinking about historical change in homes, anthropologist Marianne Gullestad said that modern homes have "lost several functions in the process of modernization, but they have also taken on new functions. The most important, in my view, is to provide a setting for modern intimacy."[5] The home, then, is no longer where the grain is ground or the clothing sewn. Now, it is almost entirely about where matters of the heart (and libido) play out. And where these matters are at play, we think of couples—two people whose lives are shared in intimate ways. It follows, then, that adult dyads in intimate relationships that take place in private and separated bedrooms form the basis for this chapter on couplehood.

CONTEMPORARY COUPLEHOOD

What's the old saying? First comes love, then comes marriage? And what's the saying now? First comes an online dating connection, a swipe to the right, then sex, then maybe love, a subsequent change in social media status to "in a relationship," and perhaps an eventual decision to stay over at each other's house three nights a week, which may or may not lead to an engagement ring. With all of the reality TV dating shows, marriage self-help books, and social media romance listicles, you'd think we know all we need to know about couples. But alas, I'd like to offer more, to organize how we think about couples in our understanding of home spaces and objects. Plus, there are myths and misconceptions out there about couplehood that gloss over social change and make people feel as if their version of it may somehow be wrong or strange. As a sociologist, I uncover what is strange about familiar things. To that end, I'd like to point out what is strange about something as familiar as the "couple." And so, I turn now to three things we need to know about the state of couplehood in contemporary U.S. families: first, that the default intimate partnership among U.S. adults is two people; second, that couplehood looks different than it used to, which includes an increase in the number of people who remain single for longer periods (or forever), as well as new arrangements that place couples in two different homes; and finally, that the reasons why people pair up have changed over time.

The Dyad as the Default

The tales of modern couplehood are still about two people whose lives are intertwined in intimate and important ways, but the modern tale looks a lot less like the old adage about love and marriage (which may or may not involve a baby carriage, depending on the couple's jobs, economic situation, and access to reproductive technologies). Additionally, it has never been the case that all people have formed themselves into couples, gotten married, and had children, in that order and including all of those ingredients. Marriage is a socially constructed institution, just like the ideal that couples staying in pairs for their entire lifespan is. This social constructionist claim is supported by the fact that marriage has only recently become legal for same-sex couples. If you can't do something legally, it's because it has been decided socially that it is not allowed.

We love marriage, given that most Americans eventually marry (sometimes over and over again!) and given that tremendous attention is given to the wedding ritual as a key transition into adulthood moment. But even without marriage per se, we also love couplehood, which may be starting to more accurately define our ideal than marriage. We love the idea of couples so much that even people who split apart are often found in the arms of another person, perhaps with another wedding (though probably less elaborate than the first one, and more likely to occur among older men than older women, since, at least among heterosexuals, older men tend to marry younger women). Social historian Stephanie Coontz has captured all of these changes well with the subtitle *How Love Conquered Marriage* for her 2005 book *Marriage, A History*.

The couple is indeed a prevailing concept in how we think about homes and families. The dyad is the default, in belief, in practice, in home spaces, and home objects. A dyad is a group of two people. While it seems obvious, it was not until famed social theorist George Simmel, just over a hundred years ago, talked about what happens to group dynamics when you move from a group of two to a group of three that we all realized how important understanding the social processes of couples is.[6] Turns out, the bond between two people is quite strong. Add a third, and the whole system changes. A group of three, while perhaps stronger (since it'd still be a group if one person left), does not contain the same kind of deep bond that a dyad may.

If you open up a book about contemporary American families, like this one, the category of couplehood usually appears as part of the larger picture being painted. To a great extent, this makes sense, given that much of what goes on in our everyday lives and in our research and policies about adult life uses the couple as a focus. The study of human couplehood, in a romantic sense of the word (as opposed to sibling or friendship dyads), spans many areas of inquiry, from communication research about conversational style and conflict to social science research on compatibility; from studies in demography on the number of married and cohabiting couples at the national level to the analysis of romance in literature; and from legal research on rules and benefits associated with partnerships to neurological research on sexual attraction. Further, the investment in couplehood as a life experience is threaded through our shared values about romance and commitment, our laws and norms about marriage and partnerships, and our religious and economic systems. The construction of romantic love between two people (and the idealization of it lasting forever) is so powerful that it shows up in our social media feeds, our everyday conversations, the novels that we read, the movies that we watch that are based on those novels, and commercials for the latest scientifically grounded online dating websites. Even the debates about what is best for children involve whether two parents are optimal. Our nation is governed by a set of laws, a shared set of values and social arrangements, media depictions, and an economic system that, while increasingly dedicated to multiple forms of partnerships in terms of demographic categories, still use the notion of two people (and not more) as the defining characteristic of a clearly defined union in a family. In short, from joint tax returns and legal prevention of multiple spouses to double-occupancy vacation accommodation rates, and from "plus one" event invitations to every single romantic comedy ever made, images of romance between two people are everywhere. This isn't to say this is bad or good, just powerful.

In our home spaces and objects we also see couplehood play out. TV shows about people searching for a home disproportionately feature couples, perhaps looking for a house with an "en suite" bathroom with two sinks and maybe even two showerheads. Doing an online search for mattresses yields more images of queen- and king-size beds than images of twin beds. Holiday cards with photos of people are way more likely to be sent if there are at least two people pictured (sure, sometimes single people send them, but it is not as common to get that retouched studio portrait of just Uncle Nik in his snowflake sweater as it is to get one showing Uncle Nik with a partner and the dog they just adopted). And while there are gift registries for single people moving into a new dwelling, most retailers that offer registries are all about the couples. It seems, then, that our home spaces and objects predominantly feature two as the magic number.

Monogamy is exclusive participation in a committed bond with another person, usually sexually, and often emotionally and financially. But the form that adult relationships have taken in families throughout history and in different geographic locations is not limited to the monogamous dyad. In fact, that form has been less common than other forms that include marriage to multiple people, nonexclusive sexual relationships, and singlehood.[7] Sometimes the version of monogamy that we see is a sort of "one at a time" model—referred to as *serial monogamy*—where people partner up, but then break up and partner up with someone new later. In addition, we know that just because two people form a couple does not mean they are always connected or see themselves as a strong dyad. So, it's important to venture forward with a discussion about couples with a little suspicion about just how common they are, just how successful they are, and just how uniform they look across time and space. Just because the couple is a powerful image does not mean it plays out uniformly across people's actual lives.

To omit a discussion of couples from a larger discussion of families would be like having a wedding without the cake. But, importantly, to include only married couples in a discussion about couplehood would leave out a growing share of our adult population who are forming dyads without a marital bond. And so, for this chapter, couples needn't be married, but they need to see themselves as a couple. Often, but not always, this involves sharing a big private bedroom at the back of a home, which may or may not have a chain lock on its door.

What Couplehood Looks Like Now

Despite the fact that the couple is a defining unit in many parts of our lives, the default notion of two people who have a romantic attachment to each other, and who may also commit to a lengthy or lifelong partnership with attachment in emotional, sexual, financial, and spatial ways, has never looked uniform across groups of people, and the variety of its form is more visible today than ever. What many lives are like looks less and less like a traditional pair of people who are attracted to each other and want to marry and stay together in the same home forever and ever amen. At the same time that marriage is declining as a requirement for long- or short-term partnership, we also see a huge investment in weddings and marriage, and we see marriage still defined as a desired social, legal, and economic privilege among both heterosexual and same-sex couples. After all, around two million couples get married each year in the United States.[8] And while marriage is still valued by virtue of its presence in our culture and its connection to legal rights, we also see couplehood valued in forms that are not marriage.

As the previous section highlights, couplehood as we know it in the study of today's American families is a type of relationship that must be situated in a particular time and place, and it may be that focusing too much on an idealized form of relationship can neglect forms of family life for adults that do not contain this element. Increasing attention on singlehood and valuing multiple partners has to be as much a part of the story as marriages that last sixty years and those that last six months. Couplehood can take many forms. Some say this lessens the value of the dyad. Yet others point to the fact that, even with break-ups, the dyad is still highly prized for adulthood.

Families have changed, which can be seen in contemporary configurations of home spaces and objects. Despite changes, being in a couple is still the preferred goal for adults, finding a partner is still seen by many as the default prerequisite for raising children, and the single-family dwelling—preferably owned and not rented—is still portrayed as the ideal space for committed couples to continue their lives.[9]

But both the people and the spaces are a little different than they used to be. People who live together before, or instead of, marrying are increasing in number, including among older adults, thus making a wedding gift registry for household items more symbolic or about notching up the quality of already-existing home tools for a cohabiting couple.[10] And, as the collection of recent conferences I've attended on family relationships has shown, researchers (both academic and governmental) are increasingly likely to include *cohabiting* (living together) couples in their analyses about contemporary households.

New types of couplehood are also emerging. For example, because people often don't want to figure out how to blend devotion to people who are already situated (e.g., elderly parents, children, and new partners), we see an increase in people who are in *living-apart-together relationships* (LATs) that require maintaining separate households while identifying formally as a couple.[11] LATs are increasingly common and more socially accepted, evidence that there is less pressure to settle in one dwelling for couples than there used to be. And the fact that these situations can occur with couples in different life stages suggests that the notion of couple formation is not reserved for young adults just starting their families.

We also see a more informal and less long-term version of this among people who participate in *stayovers* with romantic partners, sleeping over at one partner's home at least half of each week, which serves as a stopgap tool in the transition between casual dating and more formal commitments like cohabitation and marriage.[12] In terms of home spaces and objects, we can imagine that couplehood in the case of LATs and stayovers takes place in two home spaces, with doubled-up objects like toothbrushes and underpants to use in each space, and a large enough bag to transport things besides toothbrushes and underpants from one home to the other.

For all of these reasons, we can see that while it may be that two people are still the norm for paths into adulthood and family life, what the couple looks like and whether they have formally named themselves as a couple can take many shapes and forms, and can play out different-ly in home spaces and with everyday objects.

Why Become a Couple?

In addition to knowing that couplehood looks different than it used to (and different from any ideal), we know that why people organize them-selves into couples has changed, too. Comedian Aziz Ansari and sociolo-gist Erik Klinenberg wrote a popular book in 2015 entitled *Modern Romance*, in which they uncovered past and present trends in how people look for potential romantic partners.[13] They note that the crite-ria used to discern whether a potential partner will meet one's needs, along with the technological tools to meet potential partners, have changed drastically. Some of this has to do with the fact that we simply have more choices about whom to partner up with. The authors relay stories from couples who've been married for decades about their meeting each other because their families lived in the same apartment building—a finding, I would note, that is primarily relevant for city-dwellers (though you can imagine rural couples finding each other because of geographic proximity, too, likely in terms of being a few acres away rather than in the same building). And then they tell stories from twenty-somethings who use Tinder to find sexual partners on short notice. Even the definition of *romance* now has a more explicit connection to a sexual relationship, with an eventual committed relationship as a distant future "perhaps." The home spaces that potential dating partners occupied in the past, and the technological objects in present hands, are key players in contemporary paths to couplehood, and they help us see how the dyad has become less connected to geographic closeness, marriage, living together, or necessarily any long-term commitment. But it usually involves a sexual relationship.

One of the most fascinating lines of research that shows how much we've changed in our understanding of couplehood is about how people end up living together. We know that living together connotes a more formal commitment than a stayover or maintaining two separate households. It is often paired with marriage, but not necessarily. Recent work by sociologists Sharon Sassler and Amanda Miller shows us that it is increasingly common for people to live together, often forgoing marriage, and historian Stephanie Coontz articulates that, compared to fifty years ago, couples who choose to live together without being married are more likely to be stable than in the past.[14] But the reasons why couples live together vary tremendously. People may live together to save money, especially if they are just entering the job market. These situations are more likely to be defined as temporary, as opposed to cohabitation arrangements by couples who opt to forgo a legal marriage. People who opt for this second arrangement tend to be more educated, have philosophical problems with the requirement that the state recognize their union, or be older and wish to avoid complicating any inheritance arrangements for their grown children. All in all, what we are seeing is an increase in people's desire to live together without marriage, and we are seeing cohabiting couples look increasingly diverse in terms of their reasons why they live together. Most interestingly, we are also seeing that cohabiting couples are more similar than in the past to married couples in terms of relationship stability and general societal acceptance.

LOVE LETTERS

Not too long ago, I was cleaning out a basement cabinet and found a box of old letters. After I spent an afternoon unfolding, rifling, and reading these letters (from friends and past lovers) on the living room floor, and after my husband walked into the room with a bewildered look at the mess of tiny spiral notebook paper scraps I had strewn about me on the carpet, it occurred to me that there were no letters from him in the mix. And then I reminded myself that the letters from my husband were kept in a different place. Not in the dark cold basement to be stumbled upon while cleaning, but snugly situated in an underwear drawer in our bedroom, a special place amidst my private things.

A 2013 *New Yorker* article highlights a South Korean app called "Between," a digital system for romantically involved couples to privately exchange everything from text and voice messages to photos, notes, and stickers, all of which are saved in a virtual pine-colored "memory box" meant to digitally mimic the keepsake under-the-bed boxes and underwear drawers where special romantic messages were once preserved.[15] How people talk to each other in today's romantic relationships is increasingly likely to take place using information and communication technologies such as smartphones and computers. Even the way such communication is preserved is also changing in the digital age. This means that love letters now are digital as well as paper—and stored in places like clouds and computer folders rather than basement boxes and dresser drawers.

How do we assess how much meaning we attach to our love letters, or to our stuff in general? Is it by how much we use it? Where we store it? Whether we are willing to part with it (and if we part with it, how much money we may want for it in our yard sale or on eBay)? Objects are actually parts of our definition of self (they are what communications scholar Russell Belk calls *extended selves*) and they can be placed in certain areas of a home to "cool" off, thus making them perhaps less connected to a person's identity. Often these cooling processes are in locations that are hard to access, such as a garage or basement. In this process, objects may change their meaning in the eyes of their possessor, including in terms of how much they are part of our self.[16] That greeting card in the basement or the garbage? Less a part of my "self" than the greeting card in my dresser drawer, or so this line of thinking goes. Of course, it could also be that some people are just better at storing or throwing away things than others, or that something like a greeting card doesn't really mean as much to them as just being able to think about the person who sent it.

Romantic communication—the words and linguistic cues we use to share ideas with a partner—can be a fruitful place to look if we want to understand how an object tells the story of couplehood. And so, we turn to the different ways that meaning is attached to love letters. Especially the ones we keep in underwear drawers in our bedrooms (or maybe in that box in the basement, depending on if we need to "cool" them off).

In 2013 I conducted a survey research project where I asked 373 men and women across the country between the ages of eighteen and eighty-six to talk about the love letters that they had saved from a past or present romantic relationship. I figured that people's saving practices could tell an interesting story about what was meaningful to them and how they defined the relationship that the letters symbolized. Keepsakes like love letters, whether stored in a bedroom or basement, can trigger an emotional response. This is what *nostalgia* is—the feeling you get when you see something that reminds you of a past memory or person. Love letters symbolize an interaction between people. Saving love letters means preserving a connection with another person, and perhaps thinking of the self as part of that connection.

The survey findings, which have been published in a book chapter that I co-authored with my husband, Neal Christopherson (that collaboration seemed appropriate given the topic; plus he's a really good sociologist), reveal several interesting patterns. First, nearly nine out of ten respondents believe that the practice of handwritten love letter writing is fading away.[17] And yet, when it comes to saving love letters, paper wins—even though most of the relationships referenced by people taking the survey had begun in the last decade. Over two-thirds of the respondents save paper communications (68 percent save letters, 73 percent save cards, and 67 percent save handwritten notes), while digital communications are saved less (47 percent save emails, 32 percent save text conversations, 23 percent save Facebook message conversations, and 6 percent save captured Snapchats).

One way to think about stored love letters is to imagine that they can be "curated," or arranged, visited, and taken care of, as any special set of objects might be. One of the most interesting pieces of the love letters research is in people's curatorial practices—not just whether they saved them, but what their actions surrounding them looked like. Most people revisit saved love letters only occasionally, perhaps a few times a year. People are as likely to revisit a saved letter accidentally (e.g., while organizing things) as they are to revisit it intentionally to stir up nostalgic feelings. The location of where the letter is stored may relate to the frequency of seeing it. For people who save paper communications (letters, cards, handwritten notes), they are more likely to store them in hidden locations like in a drawer or under a bed or in a special box. About one in ten people store them in more visible locations like on a desk or pinned to a bulletin board. For the saved digital communications, about a fifth store them in e-mail folders or on computers, and about a tenth store them on smartphones. And the emotional response can be positive or negative. In fact, many of the respondents in the study talked just as much about looking at old letters in order to reminisce fondly as they did to remember to avoid making the same mistakes in a present relationship that the past relationship had.

Love letters, especially paper ones, are likely to be stored in places that are hidden and not immediately accessible. Being stored in these locations may serve to "cool" the letter or make it less connected to a person's definition of self. But a deeper analysis of the survey responses suggests that keeping something hidden not only means it may be looked at less often, but also that it may be rendered even more meaningful because its hidden location can connote a private sacredness. Plus, the hidden locations referenced were not likely to be basements, but rather boxes or drawers in a bedroom. A love letter may therefore be rendered meaningful (and maybe more a part of the "self") by keeping it private, but perhaps not too far away.

BED(S)

If you are of a certain age, I can ask you if you remember *The Dick Van Dyke Show* and you would likely say yes. I grew up watching reruns of black-and-white television shows like that one, where the adult couples were always depicted as married, but when shown in their bedrooms, were depicted as sleeping in separate twin beds.[18] Flash forward many decades. Now we see TV commercials that advertise beds in scientific terms—foam that conforms to aching bodies, flame retardants that are supposed to make us feel safe but have strange and dangerous-sounding chemical names, numbers that signify how boardlike or cloudlike each half of the bed can be, temperature control, and everything-pedic. Our bodies and our beds are now machines that work with each other. Sleeping has become a science project. (Oh, and speaking of science, don't forget the Ambien.)

Given all of this ergonomic and chemical emphasis, it may seem strange to think about sleep as *sociologically* interesting. What can something that seems very biological, and done when we're unconscious, tell us about social relationships? If most of what we know and hear about sleep uses the individual sleeper as a reference point, then how can we think about beds in our understanding of couples' relationships?

About three-fourths of U.S. adult couples who are married or in long-term partnerships share beds when they sleep.[19] In 2006, Paul Rosenblatt, a family social scientist at the University of Minnesota, published a book that discussed interview findings about people's experiences sharing a bed with another person. He wisely introduced his book by saying, "Almost everything that has been published in the social and behavioral sciences and in medicine about adult sleep has looked at adult sleep as in individual phenomenon. Yet millions of adults sleep with another adult. For them, sleep is a complicated, changing, and often challenging social experience."[20] We live in a society where most couples, when they become couples, are expected to share a bed. Sharing a bed acts to reinforce the cultural belief that couples should show their intimacy and togetherness in material, spatial, and bodily form, even when they're not awake. When couples become couples and share a bed, at least for a majority of people who fill out surveys about whether they sleep alone or with someone else, "my sleep" becomes "our sleep."

Thinking about sleep and beds sociologically allows us to point out how, even when we're unconscious, our social world is at play.[21] In addition to noting how sleepiness has been turned into a public health issue, with media portrayals of problematic sleep and its remedies amplifying anxiety about right and wrong ways to sleep, and right and wrong ways to consider sleepiness, sociologists point out how there are different ways that sleep is experienced across geographic locations and types of people. These types include: *monophasic* (all in one time block), *biphasic* (in two blocks, often including a short afternoon nap and longer nighttime sleep), and *polyphasic* (a long sleep at night and multiple unscheduled naps during the day) cultures. The United States primarily consists of monophasic sleepers, and most Western medical and cultural reference to sleep presumes this. But in populations such as shift workers, adolescents, and even workers whose offices have purchased the latest model of napping desks, napping or sleeping in segments that may or may not be at night is certainly present in the lives of contemporary Americans. Even so, the emphasis on building and buying and using private spaces for sleep (in larger and larger owner's suites), as well as anxiety-inducing health information disseminated about sleepiness, means that American households consist of people whose sleeping spaces and cultural preferences end up lending themselves best to (idealizing) monophasic sleep.

Sociologists examine interactional processes—what happens between people. Since the transition into couplehood is already sociologically interesting because it requires a shift in perspective about space, roles, and sharing, and since one of the main differences in this transition is co-sleeping on a regular basis, it is important to look at sharing a bed as part of what we know about couplehood. Sleeping in the same bed with another person not only increases the chances to be awakened, it also requires negotiation, which by itself raises the level of analysis from the individual to the interactional level. Paul Rosenblatt calls this *couple politics*.[22] When to go to bed, when to wake up, whether to have a screen lit up to watch a show or do work, whether to make the bed daily, how hot to make the room in couples' "thermostat wars," whether to touch or keep separate zones, how much light to allow in the room, and what kind of bedding and pillows to use—all of these are factors that impact sleep patterns, and that are often part of couples' negotiations about how to define their bed rituals.

Beds are also sites for sociological investigation of couple conflict and group inequalities in terms of gender and social class. Women focus more than men on the aesthetics of the bed, and make it more often than men, suggesting that it is a gendered symbol of domestic order and norms about taste. This means that for women, more often than for men, the use of the bed for other tasks during the day (e.g., putting on socks, napping, watching TV) is desired less.[23] There are gender differences in how well people sleep, too. For example, in research on heterosexual partners' coping with co-sleeping annoyances like snoring, cover-stealing, or midnight bathroom visits, more often women are found to be the ones who adapt (and have more sleep trouble) than men. The association of poor sleeping as tied to long work hours has been made more by men than by women, but with the increasing participation of women in the paid labor force, this pattern is changing. Women report more sleep problems than men generally, which may relate to women's greater likelihood to report health problems, due in part to gender normative perceptions that women's bodies are not as healthy as men's, and that women are perceived to be weaker and therefore more prone to experience (and report and seek help for) health problems. It may also be that women's lives are more likely to include responsibilities that disrupt sleep, such as caring for children even when it's dark outside.

In terms of *socioeconomic status* (SES), we know that the more economically stable you are, the higher sleep quality you're likely to have. This is because living with disadvantage may mean a greater likelihood to experience ongoing stress about money or work, and perhaps less access to health information about getting a good night of sleep. What all of these findings about gender and class reveal is that sharing a bed involves not only negotiation at an interactional level, but also couple politics that shine light on the importance of group status in bed.

Beds help to define spatial territories, family rules and roles, and habits for couples. We know this because most couples who share a bed sleep on the same side each night. The reasons for this vary from habit to proximity to the bathroom or the door (for escape, access to kids, or protection, depending on who is asked). We also know this because whether couples allow others onto the bed is a creation of their desires and habits. If the couple has children, and their family has open boundaries in terms of privacy, it is likely that children will be allowed to sleep in (or jump on, or cuddle in, or hang out in) the couple's bed. And sociology teaches us that families' ideas about privacy and boundaries can emerge from their own personal preferences, but they can also stem from values associated with religion, region, or other factors that are much larger than any individual family.

Beds are locations for activities that symbolize transitions and values. The shift from being awake to being asleep can be filled with activities like praying, watching television, reading, working, and sex (which, by the way, is more likely to be defined as the primary activity in bed for couples in early stages of their relationship). And many couples use the bed, especially before sleeping, as the location for important relationship-defining conversations or discussions about larger issues that are defined as necessary to hold away from other members of a household. The transition into couplehood requires defining expectations about sexual intimacy, communication, attentiveness, privacy, and roles, and it is in bed (and on the bed) where many of these dynamics are figured out and enacted. The bed is where the stuff of couplehood often gets played out.

REFLECTING ON OUR STUFF

Homes show how the boundaries between public and private matter for families. We don't hear much on the news about politicians or pundits talking about the importance of a good bed or a thoughtful love letter to make our world a better place (even though the sex lives of politicians are far too often discussed in the news). Beds and stored love letters are some of the most private objects in our homes, and they symbolize relationships that are culturally defined as private, too. But we need to understand that these objects, and the bedroom where they're located, connect the public and private dimensions of couplehood in interesting ways. The owner's bedroom, or any space devoted to sleeping for adult couples in a household, is portrayed on home decorating and real estate television programs as retreats, adult havens where children are sometimes not allowed, or even sacred spaces where very private and mysterious things happen that are only mentioned using code words that signify things that are not usually discussed explicitly on HGTV. What this means is that not only are homes themselves important locations for understanding the boundaries on the spectrum between public and private lives, but spaces within homes themselves are located in different spots on the public-private spectrum. Plus, where we put things in the spaces of our homes can signify their importance, and private spaces may connote meaningfulness and sacredness as much as accessible ones (and maybe even more so), as the research on love letters uncovers. Importantly, though, the creation of private spaces within other private spaces (a bedroom in a home) can hide sadness, violence, or stress that, unless brought into the light, may continue to make some couples' lives really difficult.

Homes tell us about individual families, but also about broader social issues. I recognize that not everyone reading this has been, or is, a member of a couple. I also recognize that many do not want to be, and many cannot. But we still design houses, sell beds, define romance, and talk about adulthood as if couplehood is both a normal and desired part of family life. So powerful is the romantic dyad that we rarely define a happy ending as one where a single adult happily falls asleep in a twin bed in a human-scaled room after reading a love letter she wrote to herself (though, given the current focus on self-care in our media, I can imagine a love letter to one's self could be prescribed as part of the latest recipe for happiness).

Earlier I noted that expectations for couplehood have changed, given men's and women's role shifts, revised expectations about sex, and technological tools that connect people in new ways. Despite an increasing number of single people in society and delayed movement into formal couplehood, we have also seen the perpetuation of couplehood as the ideal state of adult achievement, made complete not just by having a job and securing a permanent home, but also by finding a soul mate who can meet all of the needs of any person—a person who has no trouble expressing emotion in a letter or having fresh morning breath. Of course, this is an unrealistic expectation.

The lived experience of couples, whether through their love letter saving practices or their late-night bedroom chats, is more likely to include some fights and frustrations over morning breath and inadequate emotional expression on stationery than it is to include a fairy-tale ending. We never hear the fairy-tale princess—in an epilogue that resembles the original dark (and probably either Danish or German) fairy-tale ending upon which the Disney-fied movie was based—gleefully sing, "My Prince Charming snores, has bad handwriting, and leaves his toenail clippings in bed. Tra la la." That doesn't fit the picture of high expectations that we have come to normalize in our search for a partner. I suspect that the smart researchers who have uncovered the sociological significance of beds for our understanding of couplehood would have this advice for the princess, or for the young man crafting his online persona for Match.com in order to find the perfect partner:

You can try to find a soul mate and live out your life with that perfect person, or you can find a good enough person and watch the soul mate emerge over time. Or, for goodness' sake, stop assuming one person can be a soul mate or prince, or meet all of your needs. The same holds true for a mattress, by the way.

Homes are not only symbolic, but also shape our lives. What stories about you would your bed tell? A bed could tell a great many stories about what couplehood looks like in contemporary American society. If objects are part of our selves, then we have to acknowledge that they play a role in how we see ourselves as part of a couple. It is easy to understand how the firmness of a mattress can affect our mood, since how we feel physically after a well-rested night can decrease our chances to feel grumpy. Similarly, getting a letter in the mail from a lover acts upon us as a hypnotic force that plunges our emotions into a state of either bliss (for those who love receiving love letters) or bewilderment (for those who are nervous to open the envelope). And hearing a smartphone "ding" with a text from a partner can make us stop what we're doing, check the message, and then go back to work. Some people say we are only a stone's throw away from being controlled by our technology, with the dinging phone as the oft-cited behavioral control example. In any case, the objects and spaces of couplehood act upon the couple not only to symbolize the relationship dynamics, but also sometimes to serve as a third member of the dyad.

You and me and the (choose one: bed, smartphone, love letter, bedroom) make three.

4

PARENTS AND CHILDREN
Family Photo Albums and LEGO Bricks

LIVING ROOMS

Did you know that you can buy special slippers that prevent the sharp pain that comes with stepping on LEGO bricks strewn about your living room floor?[1] I learned about these after years of landing squarely on pointy brick edges that pierced my feet and made me start to swear but then remember that my kid was in earshot. "What the fu—dge brownie is this LEGO doing here next to the shelf holding our photo albums?!"

The scenario above tells an interesting sociological story that helps us go beyond the individual pain I may suffer after stepping on a brick: first, I am part of a social class that can afford LEGO bricks; second, I adhere to a cultural belief that having them (and perhaps not swearing in front of my child) shows that I am a good parent; and third, my living room intermingles items from both kid and adult worlds. How much money parents have, what they define as good parenting, and how much kid and adult worlds are intermingling make for great sociological discussion. So, let's discuss.

Within the United States, not everyone who has children has a home big enough to have a separate space for them. For families that do have room, sometimes children's things end up crossing into nonkid spaces anyway. Like the LEGO bricks noted above, a lot of children's things end up in the living room (or, in some people's homes, a family room).

At times, our living room has been a playroom, a sitting room, a game room, and an event space. It also serves as the first room people enter when they come through our front door and go up one step. When our son was a toddler, the entryway landing proved a perfect spot for his puppet theater curtain to be hanged (it was a fabric square with another fabric square cut out of it, draped using a tension curtain rod—a flash of crafty and thrifty parenting brilliance, if I do say so myself). And so my husband and I would sit with our grown-up beverages on our living room couch, turned not toward each other or toward the TV, but toward the entryway and the tiny face accidentally peeking through the curtain opening next to the little plush puppet animals whose voices sounded strikingly like our son's. We would then watch whatever rendition of Ninjago-meets-Diego-meets-Thomas-meets-Grandma-meets-a-friendly-lion puppet play our son was making up out loud and in his head at the same time. The kid world and adult world existed simultaneously in the entry to our living room.

When you were a child, did you have any favorite toys or cherished objects? Where did you keep them and play with them? Whether you had toys and/or a private and separate space to keep them depends on where and when you grew up, as well as what resources and beliefs about home spaces your family had. Today, the living room is a space that some families use as adult-only space, but that many increasingly use as children's play space, too. It's a space where adults and children interact and sometimes cross kid-adult boundaries and get into each other's things.

What exactly is a living room? British architecture critic Edwin Heathcote asks, "Living room, as opposed, I used to wonder, to what exactly? Not living room? Living dead room? Dying room? Dead room?"[2] Heathcote, with more seriousness, continues by defining the typical living room of Europe and North America as the former parlor—the room my rural Midwest grandma called the *front room*, where special occasions (yes, including funerals) took place, at least until a handful of generations ago. It was, and to a great extent still is, the room that families use to project to the world who they are, and often is situated near the front door where nonfamily members are likely to enter a home. A public space in a private home. Sometimes this means it's where the formal furniture is (situated under a mantelpiece or near a credenza where the inherited urn or ancestral photo is displayed, and sometimes near a window in places where people who don't know what a credenza is reside). Now, though, the living room is more likely to be where the TV is, or where the cabinet is that hides the TV so judgmental visitors aren't able to see the DVR light on during a show starring one or more Kardashian. And sometimes, if there's enough space, families may have two living rooms, with the more informal one sometimes labeled the *family room*. Or perhaps one giant space that is so vast it has earned the title of *great room*. All of these room types are more public home spaces than bathrooms or bedrooms would be. For the rest of the chapter, let's just call these kinds of spaces *living rooms*.

Families are also less likely now to have furniture that is differentiated between formal and informal in their living rooms. When I chatted with Certified Professional Organizer Tammy Schotzko about whether she's seen any changes over time in people's homes, she noted that today's young parents tend to be interested in functional and affordable furniture for their living rooms, rather than expensive antique heirloom pieces that their parents want them to inherit.[3] Ikea is preferred over Great-Uncle Bud's coffee table. The front room in many homes today is thus the same as the back room, whatever that may be, or whatever that may have been. In many homes, there is no other space besides a living room to serve as a sort of common space. What we consider to be a living room today still carries with it the formality and publicness of past parlors, but it is also more likely than in the past to contain elements of family life that are deemed more informal and private.

The living room has also transformed into a children's space, and today's open spaces in home designs (often referred to as *open concept*) make children and their stuff even more visible than in the past because everyone is more likely to gather in one spot than a few decades ago. Importantly, as chapter 2 discussed and as the next sections elaborate, it hasn't always been the case that adulthood and childhood were so distinct so as to define some objects as solely for grown-ups and others as solely for kids. But today, childhood is defined as different from adulthood in the United States in particular. And now we also see more children's activities taking place indoors than in the past, in part due to an increased focus on supervision and structuring of children's time by parents, and in part due to the availability of countless toys and pieces of technology that allow for more and more indoor play.[4] In an interesting way, then, children are now sequestered by virtue of them performing more of their roles inside; but they are more visible inside with the proliferation of multipurpose great rooms and open-plan spaces (or even separated living rooms in old houses where toys are next to the couch or stored in storage cubes in the corner). The playroom, for many families of all walks of life, *is* the living room: the place where everyone sits, plays, looks at family photo albums, and crosses paths with each other and with little plush puppets. And where people have to step over LEGO bricks in order to sit down on a couch and enjoy an adult beverage.

CHILDHOOD AND PARENT-CHILD RELATIONS TODAY

There seem to be as many news features about what children's and parents' lives are supposed to be like as there are children and parents. From stories about parents arrested because their children were alone at a playground to videos of little girls singing "Let It Go" at the top of their lungs in the back of the minivan or subway train, what kids and parents do, and what they're supposed to do, is constantly being defined and redefined in our society. What it means to have a good childhood or be a good parent is defined in moral, legal, social, and economic terms, and its definition gets played out loudly on plenty of social media platforms. Below I discuss three topics that we need to know to understand how childhood and parent-child relations matter not just in our homes, but also in larger conversations about cultural values and our economy: the social construction of childhood; changing norms about privacy for children and their things; and the role of buying things.

Childhood Is Socially Constructed

If you wonder how much of the U.S. population is made up of children, you may find yourself looking up tables and charts on various governmental websites, which would tell you that our country's population is made up of about 22 percent of people who are under eighteen years old (that's about seventy-eight million people labeled under the heading of "child population").[5] But what do we really mean by the word *child*? I'm sure my U.S.-born grandpa, if he were alive, would say that being a child in contemporary U.S. society means something different than being an American kid in 1925. And one child's experiences can drastically differ from another's in a different geographic place, which I'm sure my German-born grandpa would agree with if he were alive. Neither grandfather, by the way, would know what the word *tween* means.

Children's things are interesting to children themselves, to be sure. But they are also featured in some great photographic essay collections targeted at adult book-buyers, such as Gabriele Galimberti's *Toy Stories: Photos of Children from Around the World and Their Favorite Things*, James Mollison's *Where Children Sleep* or *Playground*, or Peter Menzel's *Material World: A Global Family Portrait*. In these collections, children's (and families') things are featured (including some LEGO bricks) not just because they tell the individual kids' stories about what toys or decorations they may like, but because they tell the story of the cultures and time periods in which the children live, the affluence of their families, and the availability of certain goods in the marketplace.

What children do and how and whether they are defined as different from adults depend greatly on a family's circumstances, which are impacted by historical era and geographic location. Parenthood and childhood are acted out in spaces and using objects that are not the same in every time and place. Where kids spend their time at home, what they do in those spaces, and what objects they use are all part of the social construction of childhood. If that weren't the case, my son would have spent the last five years playing with farm tools that were my grandfather's. More likely, he would have been working on the farm.

Childhood today is often presented by parents, teachers, and toy manufacturers as a time of play and growth. It is defined as a stage in life that is separated from, and leads up to, adulthood.[6] But this hasn't always been the case, and the conception of childhood as a pre-adult stage is changing in the minds of many researchers. So, while there have been six-year-olds as long as we have been counting calendar years, there has not been consistency over time and across places about what six-year-olds are expected to do, how they're supposed to look, where they're supposed to be, what they're allowed to see and say, and how they have been defined by researchers.

Psychologists, especially developmental ones, spend a lot of time talking about ages and stages of life that fall under the heading of *childhood.* Sociologists, despite using ages and stages of childhood in their own research, are more likely than psychologists to talk about how ages and stages themselves can vary across time and space, thus challenging more linear models of child development. They are more likely to believe that things in our lives that we think are real are merely defined that way because, over time, we've collectively agreed to define them that way. So, for example, saying that it is a problem if a child sees a movie with violence in it is only a problem if a concerned group proclaims it as such. Because this (and the definition of *violence*) may not be defined the same way across time and geographic region, or by all groups of people, the "problem" is socially constructed. Regardless of where one stands in this discussion, all of this suggests that what is good for children, and what a good definition of childhood is, can change across time and space, and from group to group.

Despite all of this social construction, we do have some operating definitions of childhood that seem to be prevailing, and there are some claims about childhood that few would refute are important. Children are defined as different from adults, to be sure. You would have a hard time finding even the biggest fan of social constructionism saying that a six-year-old is the same as a sixty-year-old. I'll discuss this more in a bit, but it's important to note here that, as childhood expert David Buckingham said in *The Material Child: Growing Up in Consumer Culture*, childhood in contemporary U.S. families is often defined as a time of innocence, meant to be sheltered and set apart from the harsh adult world of violence, sexuality, and greed. And parents are supposed to monitor their children, structure their lives with an eye toward safety and development of useful skills, and consult experts to find out if they're doing it right. In what may seem like a paradox, children are to be protected and perhaps even enclosed in order for them to have the freedom to feel safe and eventually explore and succeed in the world. This is not to say this is correct; it is just to say that this is a prevailing and powerful image of childhood and parenthood. Not meeting this image is a reality for many families, which matters throughout the rest of this chapter. But nonetheless, ideals about how we define what is good for kids are pretty strong.

Even though children are defined as different from adults, the boundary between childhood and adulthood continually changes. If it didn't, we wouldn't see terms such as *tween* that are meant to capture the ever-shifting transitional boundary between childhood and adulthood. We also wouldn't see research and writing on adolescence and something called "emerging adulthood," which I discussed in chapter 2.[7] This is a time when people are old enough to vote and drive and live on their own but may still be doing "childlike" things such as relying on parents for money and housing.

Whom do we ask questions when we want to understand children today? Imagine a reporter at the premiere of the latest Disney movie interviewing a child about her experience. Just as the girl is about to say how much more she likes the funny side characters than princesses in movies, imagine her dad leaning over and whispering to his daughter that she should talk about how her room is decorated with princess curtains from the movie they're about to see, because wouldn't that show just how much she likes these movies. Adults sometimes speak on behalf of children. This can play out in everyday life, and it has also played out in a lot of research about children. Whether you're a reporter or a researcher, if you want to know what a child thinks, more often than not you ask his or her parent or guardian.

But now, in both popular sources and academic research, we see more attention being paid to what is called the agency of children—how much freedom and control they have in their own lives. For example, researchers are increasingly conducting studies where kids are not just watched in their homes to see what their patterns are; they are consulted about the interpretations of those patterns, whether the patterns relate to food choices, purposes of certain home hiding places, or feelings of safety.[8] Children are now considered a group whose voice has not been heard enough in scholarly research and theorizing, from studies that include interviews with little kids to interpretations of children's drawings.[9] This means that not only is childhood socially constructed, how we study it is, too.

Ideas about Privacy and Children's Spaces Have Changed

Private spaces for children look different from home to home. Families may have separate children's bedrooms or sleeping spaces, but not a defined playroom separated from the rest of the home. Families may have children share a room with each other or with their parents when they're little, but not when they're teenagers. A lot of this depends on the way people define the age where privacy may matter, the definition of privacy between genders, and also social class and housing type, since what you can afford and what is available can often dictate how much room you have for your family members to have their own spaces. Having less square footage in your home means that spaces are sometimes used for more than one purpose. Living in a small space with children means watching television at the kitchen counter, doing homework on a computer with annoyingly slow Internet speed at the living room coffee table, and playing with toys stored next to a couch rather than in a separate playroom.

It's no wonder there's a whole lot of storage supplies advertised that are meant to fit into adult spaces but hold kid things. (Ooh, look at the faux wood grain hutch! But don't look at the race cars and pretend plastic food that are stored inside that beautiful faux wood grain hutch!) While we still see separation of spaces for use and privacy, and more and more items we can use to store things out of sight but near in reach, we now see children's things in all parts of the house more than ever before. We see living rooms that look more like what geographer Olivia Stevenson and sociologist and childhood studies scholar Alan Prout call "throwntogetherness" than segregation by task or family role. And with this new picture of contemporary U.S. living rooms, we see parents working on the boundaries between kid space and not-kid space by purchasing elaborate storage systems, figuring out ways to handle clutter, and creating family rules (mostly addressed to children) to manage all of it.

But remember the earlier point about kids being increasingly seen indoors instead of outdoors? This has occurred because homes have been more likely to be defined today as private spaces that are separated from an unsafe world where children are rarely seen alone, and where children are defined as distinct from adults. At the same time, within these home spaces that have come to be defined as increasingly private, kids have taken over, or, in some cases, parents have had enough time, energy, and financial resources to create rules and storage solutions to keep the kid stuff invisible when the grown-ups need to use the living room. Further, family life is increasingly connected to the public world via technology, which means kids can connect with other kids without leaving their homes. Thus, the idea that kids are participating only in private life, while increasing, is not as clean-cut as it seems.

How childhood looks in terms of privacy has an interesting history.[10] Before the nineteenth century, home spaces for families that would not have been considered affluent or elite (or royal, for non-U.S. places with monarchies) were much more about shared space, multifunctionality, and not a lot of privacy. Before central heating, parents and children slept in the same room, likely the one with a fireplace into which parents feared their children may wander. There weren't many hallways or interior doors that shut to speak of. Children and adults were visible together, seeing each other and all that each other were doing. And hypervigilance (regardless of whether there was a giant open hearth in the sleeping/living/dining room) about kids' safety was not on parents' radar in the same way it may be today.

But then an increased move toward privacy for middle-class families emerged in the nineteenth and twentieth centuries in the United States, resulting in more hallways, more walls, more stairs, more specialized uses for all rooms, more separation of spaces by age and gender, and bedrooms for family members that had doors that closed (and thus, less visibility of activities that happen behind closed doors). This included children's bedrooms, and, for people who could afford it, and who lived in places where land was plentiful or basements or second and third stories were normal, this also may have included a separate space in the home for children's play. It also included, beginning in the early twentieth century, the invention of playpens (patented by Emma Read as portable *baby cages*).[11] It is no wonder that when I perused my mom's *Better Homes and Gardens* magazines and Sears catalogs in the 1970s, I saw plenty of references to rec rooms, playrooms, playpens, and even toy rooms. And I read these things in our wood-paneled basement rec room, away from the surveillance of my parents, but still inside.

Fast forward to today, and in some ways we have come full circle. We still see hallways and bedrooms, and sometimes playrooms, but we also see homes with great rooms and open-plan living rooms that make everyone in the household visible, at least when they're awake, whether they're cooking, eating, doing homework, paying bills, watching TV, or playing with toys in a playpen in the corner. Living rooms for today's young parents look far from pristine and look more like a preschool than a place where a formal front room celebration would take place. We see an increase in people's use of the living room as a more public multigenerational and multiuse space, with grown-up leisure activities like games and books now colonized by children's toys and schoolwork.[12] At least until the kids grow out of the puppet-show stage.

Childhood Is All-Consuming

Earlier I said that my living room LEGO-stepping antics were sociologically interesting because they signified that I could afford expensive toys, because I think that good parenting requires buying educational toys and abstaining from foul language in front of a toddler, and because their presence in my living room shows how intermingled kids' and adults' worlds have become in our living rooms. Regardless of which of these sounds most interesting to you, they all have one thing in common: I had to buy the LEGO bricks in the first place.

The boundary between private family life and public life is crossed every time we buy something. Parents buy things for their children. But what is bought and why can change depending on parents' views on what is safe, what is affordable, what they perceive to be good for their child, and what may make them seem like good parents to other people. So, when a choice has to be made about whether to buy that video game (or ask Grandma not to buy it even though she really wants to spoil your kid), it is never just about the video game.

Not only is childhood socially constructed, but what counts as a *good* childhood is, too. A good childhood today is one that is defined by some as protected from the harsh realities of the adult worlds of conflict and economic exchange. In this definition, children's lives are best when filled with imagination, creativity, play, and learning. This is affirmed in news stories that report concerns about children's increasing access to adult-themed media, or younger generations' attachment to brand characters in video games instead of to our natural world. In both of these cases, childhood is defined as polluted if adult themes or the marketplace (or both) enter it. And yet, parents need to participate in the marketplace even if they want to provide good childhoods, often through educational toys, extracurricular activities, or other things that cost money.

According to David Buckingham, whose work centers on how childhood intersects with the world of consumption, children are defined by concerned groups as vulnerable and innocent victims of predatory marketers and a vicious marketplace filled with things they're enticed to buy (or ask their parents to buy). Interestingly, the concerned groups who define children as powerless have political values that are actually quite varied. There are very few problems in our world that would unite environmentalists, political conservatives, feminists, and religious groups, but the effort to battle the marketers who define children as powerful and autonomous seems to be a battle that unites rather than divides. Children are indeed involved in the marketplace, whether it's wearing clothes that their parents chose for them or pressuring parents to buy the new video gaming system because their friends all have one.[13] But seeing all of this as a problem or not depends on what interests groups have in defining it that way. For many parents and critics of our all-consuming world, children are to be protected. For marketers, children are to be socialized into brand consumers, and they're probably savvier than we give them credit for. And for many marketers, the goal of making good childhoods better with products that are educational and developmentally appropriate is a good thing. So, whether something for our children is defined as a problem—even whether something is defined as *moral* or not—may depend on who is asked.

Whether buying things is seen as a problem may also differ by social class. Sociologist Allison Pugh found that all of the parents in her research in Oakland, California, have their children's best interests at heart, but what this looks like can vary by class.[14] The middle-class parents in her study who had plenty of money, but who didn't want their kids to grow up as materialists, incorporated something called *symbolic deprivation* into their parenting. They withheld buying things for their kids even if they could afford to buy them. They did this to enact and pass along values like thrift and antimaterialism to their children. For working-class and poor parents, participating in *symbolic indulgence* meant saving up money to buy a visibly expensive symbol of wealth, which was used to allow their children to maintain their dignity and fit in with their peers. New shoes and we can afford it? Not now, because we don't want to spoil you. New shoes and we can't afford it? Let's see if we can make it happen so you fit in with your friendship group and we don't look like we're struggling to others.

All of this is to say that childhood and parenting include activities and ideals that are increasingly connected to buying things in the public sphere, and that can make us wonder what others think of us as parents. Before I had my own child, I had nieces and nephews. Whenever I bought them presents, I sometimes worried whether they would be things that their parents would "approve" of. The approval, in my mind, included hoping they were fun, to be sure. But I also wanted them to be educational, appropriate, and symbolic of good parenthood. These parenting projects come with steps, materials, instructions, viewing by others, and maybe even the potential of receiving a grade of *good* or *bad*. For American parents and anyone who buys these parents' children presents, then, the project of childhood is one that needs to be managed, scrutinized, and completed quite intentionally. This can be challenging if the parents don't have the resources to buy the materials to do so, and it may even yield results that could be less than helpful for kids. So, while I might have been labeled the "fun aunt" because I bought my nephew a board game that his parents saw as perhaps a bit too raunchy, I still had to think about what the game said about me and what impact it may have on him. And for parents themselves, there can be a fear of getting a bad grade if they do it wrong with their own children.

FAMILY PHOTOGRAPHS

"Quick, let's take a family picture since we're actually all together for once and there's someone we know nearby who can take it," I say, feeling simultaneously proud for thinking of it and annoyed that I'll have to manage the thirty blurry smartphone camera shots that will be taken. After the impromptu family photo shoot, I feel immediately overwhelmed with the task of figuring out which ones to delete (my husband notoriously closes his eyes in pictures), which one to crop and post on social media (my son is notoriously private and picky about which photos to post), and where I can buy good photo paper to print one out for my mom (my mom notoriously prefers printed pictures over figuring out how to download pictures to save in an online folder). About ten years ago I bought a dozen beautiful coordinated photo albums, so that not only would our living room cabinet house precious family memories preserved on digital photo paper, but they would also look nice on the shelf. Many of these albums sit empty on a shelf in our living room, because I haven't printed a picture since 2010.

Sociologists generally agree that families are *primary socializing agents* (that means they're the first place where humans learn about their culture, their roles in it, and what people think is important). Family photographs are visual representations of the ways that families demonstrate adherence to cultural values, play out their roles, and show what they think is important. I was the one who thought of taking our family picture, and grabbed someone who would do it for us. Maybe that's because I'm fearless when it comes to talking to people, or maybe it's because I'm the mom. Taking, saving, organizing, and sharing photos of family members are ways that we act out family roles (like momhood or dadhood) and that show the cultural importance placed on preserving family memories.

A few years ago, Helen Scalise and I set out to investigate what people did to manage everything associated with family photographs— taking them, organizing them, sharing them, deleting them, all of it. We knew from past research that it is primarily women (and primarily mothers if there are children) who are socialized to be the family kin- ship keepers, and who are more likely than men to put family photos in frames and find a place in the home to display them.[15] We knew that women more often than men are charged with preserving the family history, evidenced by their greater likelihood to put pictures in albums, label the albums, and make sure the albums find their way into their children's hands. And these albums are not just placed on shelves in case someone needs to remember what happened in 1968. They are also tools that unify the family symbolically, both among themselves and sometimes, in the case of an embarrassing wedding rehearsal dinner slide show, in front of other people.[16] The interesting thing about moth- ers is that they are likely to be in charge of the family photo albums not just to keep things orderly, which women are socialized to do in homes more than men; they are also the ones who *feel responsible* for present- ing a careful image of the family to others—careful in terms of how others perceive the family's well-being.[17] Thus, mothers feel respon- sible for showing that their families are moral and good, both to them- selves and to others. And pictures are sometimes used to show this.

If mothers had different role expectations than fathers, and this could be seen in how family photos were curated, Helen and I wondered if both changing gender roles among younger families, as well as the digital revolution with photography, had impacted whether women felt like the family photo project—what is sometimes called the *curation* of family photos (like an art exhibit requiring organizing, narrating, and making viewable, or, as discussed in chapter 2, like a collection of love letters in a box stored under the bed, but that is likely to be shared with others)—was the same kind of project that parents participated in a generation or two ago.[18] We wondered if it was mothers who were still the ones who preserved the family identity in pictures more than fathers. We were curious about whether the processes surrounding the taking, organizing, and sharing of family photographs affected parents' senses of their family roles. We asked whether people felt pressure to participate in these activities in order to show an idealized version of their family to themselves and to others via photographs. After all, we can all imagine having an awkward family photo taken, but we must also imagine photos of smiling families with sadness or conflict or secrets hidden beneath the smiles in the touched-up photos. And then figure out who is responsible for curating the images of smiles to show their family to the world. The curation of smiles, by the way, is by itself socially constructed, since we know that presenting a positive image of family that hides pain or difficulty may not necessarily be normal across all social groups. We know that whether a family shows any pain they're enduring to people outside of that family is something that depends on the culture in which the family is operating.

After doing in-depth interviews with fifteen sets of middle-class parents that represented a wide range of ages and racial-ethnic identities in the U.S. Pacific Northwest, we learned, not surprisingly, that everyone felt overwhelmed by the thousands of pictures in digital folders that seemed nearly impossible to sort, edit to look perfect, and share. Our interview data showed that we have seen a shift from the rare display of family portraits to the ubiquitous, and arguably more democratic, taking, organizing, and displaying of digital photos of virtually every aspect of family life. But we also learned that both gender and age matter, and that the emotional reaction by parents to the whole family photo project tells us an important story about motherhood and fatherhood in contemporary U.S. families.

What did we find? Not surprisingly, especially among the younger people, fathers and mothers were likely to turn the family photo album into an entirely (or mostly) digital project. However, there was a gender difference in how people defined the tasks surrounding family photos, and how they *felt* about it, among all age groups. Here is where an intriguing concept that sociologist Sharon Hays coined, called *intensive mothering*, applies.[19] Intensive mothering means that mothers are idealized as the primary nurturers and caregivers of children in families. This goes beyond breastfeeding and hugs. It's all-encompassing, it's supposed to be done by moms more than by dads, and it includes kinship-keeping through things like planning family events and managing family photos. This includes remembering to take family photos at opportune moments, creating photo albums and scrapbooks, organizing photos digitally or physically, displaying photos in the home, and editing and selecting photos to share with others that represent the family (usually in a positive light to emphasize their success as mothers). This social pressure sometimes means that only certain images are selected to best align with the cultural expectations that families are supposed to look happy. If my family looks happy, then I'm doing a good job as a mother.

Despite young fathers' participation in family photo tasks (they did a lot, especially compared to older fathers), the curation of family photos, even if shared between men and women, was defined as mothers' work at every stage. Moms took more pictures than dads and felt compelled to do so. Even when dads took pictures, they described themselves as venturing into "mom territory." When people say that they're doing things that are more normal for the other gender, it seems as if we are blurring the gender lines. But actually, the lines between them become more distinct, since the tasks are still labeled as men's or women's tasks.

Women also carried the responsibility of worrying about how to organize family photographs more so than men, even if women and men both participated in downloading pictures to the computer and putting them into organized folders. The emotional burden of worrying about how to organize an overwhelming number of photographs fell more commonly on women's shoulders, which is consistent with the expectation within intensive mothering that women are charged with portraying a positive representation of the family, a representation that requires much time and energy to manage and organize in the first place. Additionally, when it came to sharing photos, mothers and young fathers were more likely than older fathers to make an effort to view digital photographs with their children on the computer. But when the sharing process extended beyond the immediate family in order to maintain kinship ties with extended family, women were more likely to take on the primary responsibility for that sharing.

It is important to acknowledge that the people in this interview study were very privileged—most had stable family backgrounds, most had a secure financial status, most had time to ponder the whole question of whether it was a burden to organize photos. But, as Sharon Hays found, it matters that the ideal of intensive mothering pervaded all social groups, even among those who could not achieve it. The focus here, then, is on the pressure that is felt, while at the same time we need to recognize that not everyone has the resources to alleviate that pressure.

A second piece of the definition of intensive mothering is that childhood needs to be protected and preserved as an innocent time—which is consistent with the earlier discussion about how modern childhood is defined as a time of innocence—and that mothers are responsible for doing so. The creation of a chronological child's photo album was most commonly described by mothers in our study as a "review" of their children's childhood, and often participants referred to it as marking the end of childhood. In our research, it was only mothers who talked about this and who worked on this as an intentional project.

The albums that the mothers in our research shared were meant to serve as reminders to their children that it is their mothers who have helped to organize their lives, and this reminder is permanently part of the children's collection of material culture. It was the mothers in our study, rather than fathers, who created these photo albums. The making of these albums preserves the ideology of nurturing and protecting innocent childhoods found within intensive mothering. These albums represent children as central to family life, and symbolize the preservation and protection of family life as women's work.

Finally, we need to recognize that there are many people, mothers and fathers alike, who love taking, organizing, and sharing family photos, and do not find it burdensome in the least. My dad was like this—until he died several years ago, it was he who spent his free time putting together family scrapbooks and photo albums, and he loved doing it. He took the pictures, had them developed, organized them, and explained to us kids the importance of preserving memories in our family. Acknowledging this kind of story as real and valuable, our research suggests that, for those people who feel a bit overwhelmed by all of the photos, it may be due to societal pressure to take on the job of portraying a family in a happy way, and this pressure is more likely to be felt by mothers. As sociologists will always say, we have agency to do what we want in our family roles, but we're still operating in systems that either put pressure on us to do things, or make us spend energy deciding not to do so.

LEGO

I am sure that my current adult self was shaped by my childhood experiences. Perhaps even more than the experiences, I'm shaped by what I remember about them. I believe that the objects of childhood, whether held in one's hands or in one's mind, can both reinvigorate and signify memories, just as youth and gender scholar Claudia Mitchell has described in her writing on how memory work, or "productive remembering," helps us understand the social (and, in her research, often gendered) significance of childhood objects such as toys.[20]

I have fond memories of playing with LEGO as a child in the 1970s, back when I wanted to be an architect. I remember spending hours in our cold basement rec room building houses and creating little neighborhoods, a prepubescent urban planner in the making who used these little brick objects to create a hypothetical community. And, while I did have little triangle evergreen trees to populate the tiny neighborhoods, I didn't have any minifigures—the little people who populate today's LEGO sets and come with changeable costumes and accessories and faces to characterize them. Thus, while I can picture holding the houses and trees in my hands even today, the neighborhood's human residents were, and still are, in my imagination.

Fast forward nearly four decades, and my LEGO memories are now accompanied by my adult sociologist self occasionally teaching and researching children's cultures in Denmark (birthplace of LEGO), and talking with Danish friends who either work at LEGO or who teach about it. I have also spent a lot of time watching my son complete sets of *The LEGO Movie* and *Minecraft* LEGO, and play video games that contain LEGO-fied characters from *Harry Potter*, *Star Wars*, and *The Simpsons*. And I peruse news articles debating whether the new

Friends line from LEGO is just giving girls what they want (this line of LEGO has "minidolls" instead of "minifigs"—small people who have larger heads, feet that can only move in tandem, and a noticeably greater amount of pink and purple in their accoutrements) or if it tells girls that their interests should remain squarely in girl-land.[21] So, while I no longer imagine myself the young girl creator of a brick community with triangle trees, I spend a lot of time thinking about why and how I played with LEGO, why and how my son played with it, and why this particular toy keeps crossing my mind as an interesting sociological object.

LEGO tells a fascinating story about how we construct childhood and parenting today. In a time and place when smartphones, video games, and laptops are as likely to be seen on children's beds as dolls and stuffed animals, it is interesting to focus on a toy that you don't plug in. LEGO has seen a recent upsurge in success, and a sociological analysis helps us see that this success is in part due to the company's ability to align with current behaviors and beliefs about childhood and parenting in contemporary society.

There are several patterns worth noting here. First, as suggested by David Buckingham, LEGO is one of the brands that encourages play in its stores, even though those stores are most often visited by kids with affluent parents. Children are increasingly playing indoors, and when they are outside of their homes they are more likely than in the past to be seen in commercial spaces like stores. In some ways, a focus on childhood as a stage that requires protection (or perhaps overprotection, in the minds of some critics of behaviors that exhibit helicopter parenting) requires closer monitoring. That's what keeps some kids indoors and pushes the need for things to do inside that are seen as good for children. Bringing a child into a LEGO store, while public, is still a form of controlled monitoring by parents.

A second sociological pattern that matters is that LEGO as a brand has figured out a way to capitalize on parents', especially in Generation X, nostalgia about their own childhoods, sometimes tied to other nostalgia-inducing markets like movies and video games. Buying a LEGO set for a child can call forth a parent's own memories of childhood. I was able to see my own little budding urban planner as he played with his LEGO bricks, even though his neighborhoods were populated with Harry Potter, Darth Vader, and Maggie Simpson instead of little triangle trees.

Finally, Buckingham says, what sells to parents today are products for children that emphasize discovery, creativity, learning, and fun. Since socializing children to be productive members of society entails preparing them for school, buying toys like LEGO is part of parents' goals to facilitate spatial reasoning, motor skills, organization, and direction-following skills in their children. LEGO is even visible in schools. From robotics to motor skill development, the presence of a commercial product in our schools that is not often questioned by many parents is notable. If the marketplace is something from which we are supposed to shelter children, we often see an exception made for products that are defined as educational. If our future engineers depend on the bricks, we will buy them to help them along in the socialization process. If we can afford them. Plus, this mind-set suggests, educated kids with good engineering skills will inevitably get good jobs in the future, which helps everyone.

Especially for middle-class parents, as sociologist Annette Lareau found in her study on how class impacts everyday parenting practices, an act as simple as buying a LEGO set with the intentional purpose of enhancing a child's educational potential can be labeled a kind of *concerted cultivation*.[22] This means that parents who can afford to do so participate in an intentional cultivating of a child's activities to align with academic achievement and future success, just as one would cultivate a garden by tending it and ensuring only good nutrients are woven in. This, of course, requires time and money, which is not available to all parents equally. If parenting is a project, one of the accessories that comes with the project is a toy that teaches skills that are translatable into future academic and economic success. Thus, while buying the latest LEGO robotics set does not directly translate into an A in sixth-grade science, it could inspire a child to enjoy learning, and it could be defined as a piece of *cultural capital* that can symbolize status and smarts, for both the child and the parents.

Communications scholar Kathy Merlock Jackson describes changes in the history and function of toys in the United States.[23] She notes that many toys exist today that have been around for decades, including Frisbee, Play-Doh, Barbie, and LEGO. The attachment of toys to brands and media characters is not new, but it's more plentiful today and in more varied media and digital forms. Jackson's research highlights how, even if individual toys have changed, the theories that academics use to understand children's play have continued to focus on the importance of toys to facilitate play and socialize children about roles and cultural values (which include getting a good education and being marketable in a future marketplace). Toys are, in a sense, vehicles used by us to pass along what we think is important to the next generation. And because playing with a pile of bricks is fun, children may not even know they're learning how society, for better or for worse, is built by playing with them.

REFLECTING ON OUR STUFF

Homes show how the boundaries between public and private matter for families. Focusing on childhood in today's society requires focusing on private life. Children are more likely to spend time indoors, thus making them less publicly seen than in the past. But they're also likely to have their things in the same spaces as those that belong to the adults in a household, making today's homes look, perhaps, similar to one-room homes from centuries ago, especially if they were built during an era when "open concept" was all the rage. Children's lives are more connected to the public world via consumption patterns and digital communications than ever before, requiring parents to monitor their children's privacy and infiltration of the public world into their children's lives in new and ever-changing ways. Childhood and adulthood are separated realms, with childhood often depicted by concerned groups as a life stage in need of protection and separation from the harsh public world of commerce and conflict. But the creation and study of transitional stages like tweens and emerging adulthood means that we're constantly playing with the borders around those realms. Clearly, then, just as the border between childhood and adulthood is constantly being redefined, the border between public and private changes, too.

Homes tell us about individual families, but also about broader social issues. Parents may like to think of their child as unique and especially talented. Sometimes those thoughts are what help parents channel patience when their child dumps out a box of LEGO bricks into their cereal. But children are born into a world that contains role expectations, buying patterns, inequalities, and values. Every time we hear someone mutter, "back in my day . . ." or "kids these days . . ." as they lament something that they believe is a problem with children today, we are witnessing the power of historical change on childhood in general, even as we acknowledge that there are diverse individual children's experiences today.

Having a child is a project, and that project looks different for today's parents than it did for parents raising kids a couple generations ago. First, parents may buy a LEGO set because they had one when they were little. They believe that it will be educational and facilitate motor skill development in their child, and because they saw that their child's future school offers a LEGO Robotics elective afterschool program. While it may not be in the fronts of their minds, they may have a latent hope that their child will think about a future career in engineering or anything that requires a perfect combination of spatial reasoning, math, and aesthetic creativity. In doing so, they may be more likely than their parents to complain about how some LEGO kits are marketed to boys and others to girls, unlike the gender-neutral LEGO from their childhood. Because they aren't sure if they can trust their neighbors, they keep their child inside to play. They not only take pictures of the child putting the LEGO set together, they also take seventeen pictures of the completed set sitting on their living room coffee table (in this case, it's the mom who takes the pictures in order to capture this stage of her daughter's childhood for future reference). After sixty-seven Likes on Facebook from the cropped picture they chose to share, they feel proud that they're doing a good job as parents. But they're a bit stressed out by the whole thing. And in their stress, they probably fail to recognize that it's a privilege to do or think about any of this. Computers and smartphones and good cameras are expensive, and so are LEGO sets. The parenting project may or may not result in good childhoods, but the ability to complete the project is affected a lot by whether parents have the resources to do so.

Homes are not only symbolic, but also shape our lives. Much of what this chapter contains is how the experiences of parents and children are shaped by the time and place in which they live. It's also important to remember that, for most of us, we live in spaces we did not build. That means that, no matter whether our home has any sort of "open concept" design or whether it even has space to play, our roles as family members are shaped by the architecture of the rooms where those roles play out. Our roles are also shaped by customs and values that we learn about from our own parents, from the media, and from other families. So, sociologists would most definitely agree that parents, in many ways, shape children. That's why we call families primary socializing agents. But both parents and children are also shaped by the rooms where their relationships play out. Sure, we build the bricks when we play with LEGO or even build an actual house, but sometimes the bricks build us.

When I walk into my living room, I reminisce about the time when my son was learning to crawl. To help me remember this sleep-deprived time, I sometimes browse our short videos, organized by date in a folder on our home computer sitting at a desk next to the living room. One video that stands out is the one where he is learning to crawl by grunting and thrashing forward all in the hopes to reach the Duplo block we have set just far enough away from him to offer a challenge.

My role as a parent is wrapped up in memories like these. These memories are facilitated by the recordings of the events that stress me out enough to get me to organize them in a well-labeled computer folder. They are also facilitated by the toys we bought to help our little project learn how to crawl in order to gain independence. Now he can reach whatever LEGO he wants, and we don't capture these moments on our smartphones nearly as often. As he sits with his smartphone next to the shelf with a dozen put-together LEGO sets that he no longer plays with (each with its own elaborate set of instructions and each with a connection to some media character he knows), I realize that it's impossible to understand what we think about childhood without looking at the stuff that comes with it. The stuff that socializes our kids almost as much as we do.

5

GENDER AND HOUSEHOLD DIVISION OF LABOR

Toolboxes and Spices

TOOLSHEDS AND KITCHENS

Turn on a decorating television show and you're eventually bound to come across the term *man cave*, a word that I have deduced from my hundreds of hours of watching HGTV refers to a space just for men to retreat from the rest of the home, often to watch sports, consume some kind of beverage that is marketed to men (remember Dr. Pepper Ten's bizarre "Not for Women" ad campaign that lasted five minutes?), hang out with other men, or just have some quiet time. Or, in recent home and garden décor news, you may have meandered down an idea path toward something called a *she shed*, a tiny house or shed placed on someone's property for a woman to retreat from the rest of the home to do whatever it is she is supposed to do in solitude, usually with a sign hanging in it carrying some kind of inspirational quote ("Dream as if you'll live forever. Live as if you'll die today. And drink Dr. Pepper Ten").[1] In both of these examples, homes are defined as places where men's spaces are differentiated from women's. This, of course, is not new. All you have to do is look at advertisements from the 1950s where women are pictured only in kitchens and men are pictured only in yards or dens (and where kids, as chapter 4 noted, were only in kids' spaces or mostly invisible).

While man caves and she sheds do not on the surface call to light political ideologies that tell a man that he needs to take back home spaces that have become too feminized, or that tell a woman she needs a Virginia Woolfian room of her own, the messages about these spaces must be placed in a larger conversation about what we think men and women should do, where they should do it, and whether any of this has changed, especially, but not exclusively, in homes where both men and women live. This conversation goes beyond individual style preferences or a personal desire for some quiet time. This is not just about feminine flowers or masculine leather; this is about how we view gender roles in contemporary society.

Gender is the set of social rules and role expectations we attach to girl/womanhood and boy/manhood. There's a lot of great conversation going on, academic and otherwise, about how gender may be overemphasized as dichotomous—falling only in two places rather than represented as a spectrum or other image that allows for more variety. The American Sociological Association, for example, advocates using multiple categories beyond *man* and *woman* when asking people to identify their gender in survey and interview research. But so many places in our world reinforce gender as a set of only two options.[2] The presence of man caves and she sheds in our decorating stories certainly fits into this reinforcement. In this chapter, the dichotomized version is used, given the evidence in our home spaces and objects that reinforce this. But at the same time, the idea of gender as dynamic and fluid and containing multiple categories is important to recognize as we think about our families and ways that we may be seeing social change in them.

Creating a good life in a home requires labor. Whether it's research on couples, families, or roommates, gender roles are always discussed in social science research on something called *household division of labor*. This is true even in single-person households (an increasingly common phenomenon), since how we are socialized in terms of gender can affect the type of work we put into our homes. So, while it may be easy to think about what "he does" and what "she does" in a household where there is a man and woman, we can also understand that there may be gender differences between households with only one gender present in each. If that wasn't the case, we wouldn't so comfortably throw the term *bachelor pad* around and assume people know what it means and what it may look like.

Kitchen and cleaning devices have made running a household both easier and harder. Yes, a fancy lime green stand mixer looks good in your kitchen and makes stirring cookie dough easier, but it's expensive and can make people feel that they need to bake more cookies and have a kitchen big enough to house a stand mixer in a corner *kitchen appliance garage*—a term that by itself makes us realize just how expansive (and expensive) people's ideals about kitchen sizes have become. It is still the case that the objects used to perform the labor in a household (that is, cooking, cleaning, lifting, disposing, building, remodeling, decorating) tend to be gendered. In other words, even though it's hard to find rooms that are used *only* by either men or women, it is not hard to find rooms that are used *disproportionately* by either men or women. The kitchen, including the appliance garage, is still primarily women's space, and the toolshed is men's, at least in homes where men and women live together. The stand mixer is (mostly) hers, the hammer is (mostly) his. Despite the fact that I do not have a stand mixer, and that I am the most likely person to use a power tool in my home, the pattern is that people *in general* are more likely to have certain tools and perform certain tasks based on their gender.

What's strange about this is that the spaces that men occupy in homes are, in most cases, the same spaces women occupy. It's not normal today to have spaces that are *entirely* off limits based on gender. And yet, some spaces carry with them gendered meanings that are still quite powerful, especially visible in how we talk about home spaces that are more likely to be labeled as men's spaces. In contemporary American homes, including those featured on lifestyle blogs, television shows, and in print, man caves, garages (for cars, not appliances), and toolsheds have come to be defined as men's spaces where women are not as likely to be found. Many of these spaces, as the photographs taken by Ken Ross in James Twitchell's book *Where Men Hide* illustrates, are defined as happy places for men that are separated from the world, from children, and from women.[3]

With industrialization and suburbanization, idealized homes became defined in the last decades as havens in a harsh world, and, over the course of the twentieth century, they also started including garages and sheds for men to participate in a burgeoning *do-it-yourself* (DIY) culture of building, tinkering, and fixing things—all so that they could spend time at home but not delve too far into the feminized interior spaces of the home (like the kitchen). These men's spaces are part of what sociologist Tristan Bridges refers to as "architectural sites for the recuperation of blue-collar masculinities that have been replaced in the post-industrial economy."[4] In other words, a toolshed is not just a toolshed. It is a historically situated home space that, like garages and basements and man caves, has come to be defined as a desirable men's space that harkens back to some idealized past about what manhood is supposed to be. So, even if a man waits tables in a restaurant, wears a three-piece suit in a bank, or stays home with a new baby, he can build or fix something with his hands to reinforce his connection with an ideal version of masculinity.

And what about women's spaces? Is the kitchen just for women? Of course not. But there is no shortage of research on how ideals about gender roles play out in the kitchen, even today. Being domestic, whether it's emblazoned in my memory of my mom's 1960s home economics textbook sense of modeling efficiency and scientific applications to household tasks like cooking and cleaning, or shown in a home that is aesthetically pleasing and clean, is still associated with traditional notions of femininity. As the kitchen moved from the hidden back of the house to a more central location in residential architecture, and as kitchen tasks became more scientific, more likely to be shown to guests, and more likely to be performed by men, the kitchen has become more like a theater with performances for many audiences to see, with many roles to portray, and with many props to show off.[5] Today, as author Winifred Gallagher points out, the kitchen has become a space with so much attention devoted to it that it features centrally in conversations about time crunches (Working too much? Buy this efficient dishwasher), consumption (Need some retail therapy? Buy this Williams-Sonoma garlic press), and parenthood (Feeling guilty that your kids don't see you enough? Put in this huge island with stools so they can talk to you while you cook).[6]

While a lot has changed since my mom read her textbook in the 1960s in terms of societal gender roles and the ways that kitchen spaces and objects are marketed to families, the kitchen performance is still decidedly gendered in many homes. It turns out that, despite that TV commercial you may have seen showing a man in a kitchen who was not a cartoon character holding an ax pictured on a paper towel roll, women still do most of the cooking, dishwashing, and counter cleaning in actual American households. In households shared by a full-time working mom and dad, according to the Pew Research Center, mothers are more likely than fathers to handle household chores and responsibilities. More specifically relating to kitchen tasks, the 2014 American Time Use Survey results tell us that men spend an average of four minutes a day on kitchen and food clean-up, eleven minutes on interior cleaning, and seventeen minutes on food and drink preparation. Women, on the other hand, spend more time on all of these tasks (eleven, twenty-eight, and thirty-seven minutes, respectively).[7] Now, I don't usually keep a stopwatch on hand to time my daily eleven-minute counter scrubbing (probably because I'm online shopping for a new Williams-Sonoma garlic press), but you get the idea here that there are still gender differences in the tasks that take place in a kitchen, especially if we look at men and women who live together.

As this discussion has shown, while women are more likely today than in 1960 to venture into toolsheds, and while men are increasingly likely to be visible in today's American kitchens, the spaces and the tools contained in them still carry with them masculine and feminine meanings.

WHAT HOUSEHOLD DIVISION OF LABOR LOOKS LIKE TODAY

There is so much historical and contemporary research out there on gender and the division of household labor in the United States, as well as on how rooms in homes perpetuate this division. I do not wish to rehash this already sophisticated body of knowledge at length, but it is important to delve briefly into three topics in order to see how home spaces and objects matter today in the work that men and women do in homes: first, as the previous section introduced, gender roles have changed, but there is much about them that looks strikingly traditional, even today; second, the work of maintaining and decorating a home has crossed into the marketplace in new ways, especially via DIY projects and home-based décor businesses; and third, our home designs are not very good at aligning with the roles that many people are experiencing, and that many would like to see, in our families.

The More Things Change . . .

I am more likely to wield power tools than many of my female friends. I can attribute at least part of this to my desire to take out my frustration by knocking down walls, and part to my socialization. My grandpa was a middle school science teacher and farmer, and every time we visited his farm, he included me, the only granddaughter, in all fix-it projects. Barn wood in need of repair? Give Michelle a hammer and teach her how to avoid hitting her thumb. Mini-bike not working? Teach Michelle how to take the engine apart and check the oil. And pray that she doesn't drive head first into the chicken coop. Which I did, but only once, and I did not injure myself or any chickens.

My grandpa was on to something. Men's and women's roles are becoming more similar to each other than in the past. Amidst the larger conversation about whether gender has two or more categories, we at least need to acknowledge that gender roles have been changing a lot. If that weren't the case, I would not have received a dark gray toolbox with a hammer, pliers, screwdrivers, and wrenches in it as a wedding shower gift from my grandpa in 1997.

But at the same time, gender is still a powerful driving force in our expectations for others. If that weren't the case, I would not have received strange looks from the older women who attended the wedding shower when I opened my grandpa's gift. I would not have received a rolling pin from my husband's grandmother on our first Christmas together. And I would not have found myself as the only mom in a sea of dads wielding that 1997 hammer at my son's Cub Scout troop's pinewood derby building party just a few years ago (his car got the ribbon for "Best Use of Color," by the way).

The story I shared about my grandfather is actually fairly unusual for contemporary American women. It is still the case that who does what in a household is noticeably different for men and women (and for boys and girls who may reside in these households), even though men's and women's roles are more blurred than they have been in the past, and both men and women are doing less housework than in the past regardless of whether they live alone or with other people. All of this can be discussed under the heading of *household division of labor*, a term that helps us research and tell the story of who does what in a home. To expand the aforementioned time-use findings, we know that, despite a decline in the breadwinner-homemaker model of households (changing gender roles that have brought increasing numbers of women into the paid work world and increasing numbers of men feeling comfortable [and in some cases, having no choice but to be responsible for] taking care of homes and children), there are still gender inequalities when it comes to household work. In heterosexual households, men, as compared to women, tend to spend less time doing it, and perform more infrequent and outdoor tasks such as yard care and outdoor cooking. Women, on the other hand, in both popular and academic sources, are discussed as being intimately connected to interior household cleaning and cooking. Even in the increasingly present households where men clean and cook more than women, women are more likely to feel responsible for presenting a clean and well-decorated aesthetic of their home to outsiders. In same-sex couples, importantly, chores are more likely to be shared as compared to heterosexual couples. We know that the divvying up of household labor tasks for these couples is based less on prescribed gender roles, who has the lower earning job, or who works fewer hours in the paid labor force (these last two lead to doing chores more stereotypically associated with women's work), and more on personal preferences. So, when sociologists look at who does what in a home, we see that someone's desire to fold towels may stem from someone's preference to do so, but it likely has at least something to do with what we learn is normal for men and women to do.[8]

What household "work" looks like depends greatly on the task, and is manifest in how we use our home spaces and objects. Anthropologist Sarah Pink, in her book *Home Truths: Gender, Domestic Objects and Everyday Life*, articulates how objects in our homes play a role in how we think about and act out gender. First, she notes how home decoration (which she calls *home creativity*) differs from housework. Home decoration includes things like painting walls, hanging pictures, moving couches, and laying carpets. These activities happen relatively infrequently and create a long-lasting arrangement of things in homes. Housework, on the other hand, occurs more frequently, and includes things like dusting, vacuuming, cooking, and washing clothes. Both housework and home decoration are defined as women's work more than men's.

We now see television commercials with men cleaning and women grilling, and dads are more visible with young children than they used to be, on TV and in real life. But, even with women working more paid hours than men, they still outperform their male partners in what sociologists Arlie Hochschild and Anne Machung called the *second shift*—the set of unpaid tasks such as cleaning, child care, and cooking that serve to maintain a household.[9]

So what can we make of this mixture of findings on gendered household division of labor? On one hand, men are doing more than they used to. On the other hand, women are still doing more than men. One way to think about how these differences still exist is to ask why people would agree to be in households where tasks were not evenly split. Here is where thinking about fairness versus equality can shine light on what we're talking about.[10]

Social researcher Janeen Baxter studied the relationship between fairness and equality when she conducted her 2000 interview research on household division of labor in Australia. Her research revealed that women (primarily) find that an unequal household division of labor (that is, women do more than men do) is *fair* even if they do more than half of it. Did you catch that? Fair but not *equal*. This belief that something that is unequal can still be fair can be explained at least in part because women may be comparing their male partners to their dads, whom they remember doing way less housework. Additionally, men doing things stereotypically assigned to women seems even more impressive to them than women doing things stereotypically assigned to men. So, a husband dusting "counts" as challenging gender roles, and thus more fair, as compared to a wife mowing a lawn. And, because dusting was never what a dad did twenty years ago, it is even more impressive. Impressive means fair. Or the women may believe that it's okay for men and women to perform different tasks, because they're talented in different areas. Or perhaps they believe that the way to have a happy marriage or partnership is to not pick battles, so believing that things are fair helps. In all of these cases, despite inequality, women sometimes view a situation wherein they do more housework as fair, because it seems better than an imagined alternative, it aligns with their ideas, or it doesn't seem so bad in light of other issues. And so, it is important not just to research what people do in the household, it is also good to ask what they think about it. This can reveal a lot about gender roles.

We would also be well served to examine closely how we talk about heterosexual couples who reverse the a traditional model of man-bread-winner and woman-homemaker division of household labor. These are referred to as "status-reversed couples," where either women outearn their male partners or the men stay at home. This is a pattern that has grown, especially since the economic recession a decade ago. Because this population has a specific name that includes the term *reversed*, it is clear that what is defined as the normal way of doing things is still pretty tied to traditional gender roles. Even in these partnerships, the men do not necessarily take on nontraditional household work, and the couples participate in something called *deviance neutralization*.[11] This means that, even if they believe that men and women should be equal, these couples engage in concealing and covering processes to lessen the chance that others may see them as deviant. This can explain why husbands whose wives outearn them may reduce their participation in household work, while breadwinning wives may try to do more housework. For both traditional and nontraditional couples, then, there's a lot of pressure out there to conform to expected gender roles, even if you're defying them in your paid work roles.

In Scandinavian countries, where I've lived and worked occasionally in recent years, there are both policies and everyday practices that demonstrate a devotion to egalitarian gender roles. As anthropologist Marianne Gullestad found in her 1992 study of Norwegian homes where men and women live together, the ways homes are designed, decorated, and arranged show this egalitarianism in visible ways. Men and women do household projects together, from buying couches to removing a wall to making a bedroom bigger. And even though in Gullestad's study it was still primarily women who were charged with turning a house into a home (both through interpersonal nurturing and aesthetic transformation) and men who were charged with being handy, home projects were shared and the roles associated with the projects were defined as equally valuable. In this way, equality between men and women was visible in how homes were arranged, at least more so than in cultures where gender roles may be more traditional.

Gullestad's findings were based on research conducted in the late 1980s and early 1990s in Norway. What about today in the United States? Are there gender differences? How do our homes and objects matter in the way that men and women perform household labor today? Here is where the work of American sociologist Tristan Bridges, especially in his "Inequality by (Interior) Design" blog, is worth highlighting. In several insightful posts, Bridges notes not only how spaces have become attached to expectations about manhood and womanhood but also that things like smell and color have become defined as having genders.[12] He says that scents have cultural meaning, from what bodies are supposed to smell like to what homes are supposed to smell like. Think about the way that body products that contain virtually the exact same ingredients are marketed to men and women. Men's body wash is in black and green and blue bottles, women's in white and pastel colors. Men are supposed to smell like pine trees, and women like the flowers near those trees. Home smells are the same, evidenced by household scents from candles or room fresheners that are often feminized with names like "Fluffy Towels" and "Home Sweet Home." Lest you think that these are not really feminine, consider that the Yankee Candle Company created a line of "Man Candles" with names like "Riding Mower" and "2x4" to assure men who burn candles that they can do so without stigma if the candles smell like the areas where they are supposed to be in a home: the yard and the garage.

Color matters, too, in the social construction of home spaces as gendered. In Bridges's research on man caves, for example, he discusses a line of paint colors that were specifically designed and marketed to men for these spaces. They were even named accordingly, with a swatch of tan called "Wolfden" that, in a different paint line, was called "Monterey Cliffs." Talk about attaching gender to the meaning of a space! Beyond the proverbial blue and pink baby rooms, then, spaces within homes have become defined with gender merely by renaming the wall colors.

With these fascinating insights from scholars looking at everything from moving a couch to choosing masculine paint colors, we see that not only is it important to look at the ways men's and women's roles may (or may not) have changed in homes, but also at the ways that home spaces and objects contribute to those roles and expectations.

DIY and the Gendered Business of Home Décor

I am in a category of people who have the privilege to be able to afford some art pieces for my home that have cost as much as a monthly car payment. When I got a work promotion a few years ago, one way that I decided to celebrate was to purchase a small painting done by a local artist. It was a big decision, not only because it was expensive, but also because I knew that I needed to find the perfect spot to hang it in my home so that it fit in with the rest of my carefully crafted interior decoration. I had done a good job painting the walls, and now I needed the work of a real artist to hang on them.

What I didn't take into consideration, but what has mattered ever since I bought the painting, was what kind of cloth, if any, I could use to dust it. *Home decoration* (choosing the painting and the wall color) and *housework* (doing the dusting) are different from each other because of their frequency and purpose. While both may make a home look nice, designing or decorating a room and dusting its contents are not the same job and do not occur with the same frequency. I bought the painting once, and I need to dust it every so often to preserve it and to prevent people with dust allergies from sneezing when they look at it closely. This means that when we think about who does what in a home, it's important to think about whether we're talking about infrequent things like buying a painting or painting a wall, or frequent things like dusting or doing the dishes. Dusting is more likely to be the subject of sociological scrutiny when it comes to figuring out what's going on with gender and household division of labor, but it's important to bring to light the sociological importance of home décor, too.

Despite their differences, housework and home decoration are connected insofar as they relate to the management of household spaces and objects, they have different expectations associated with them in terms of gender, and they both require purchasing goods that are designed to make the tasks work better than if you didn't have the products. From a magic sponge that erases permanent marker to a stud finder used to ensure that the painting is hung so that it won't fall, managing tasks that make homes cleaner and aesthetically pleasing is wrapped up in the marketplace of household products and tools. And this marketplace operates differently depending on whether the consumer is assumed to be a man or a woman. Home improvement, like housework, operates with a set of expectations at least in part based on gender.

Here's a story to illustrate. About a decade ago, I went to a local home improvement center to buy a table saw. I had used a friend's saw for a home remodeling project, and decided it was time I had my own. When I asked about the selection of table saws in the store, the man behind the counter looked me up and down, called me little lady (funny, given that I was taller than he was), and asked if I was sure I wanted one instead of having my husband come in to try it out. Of course I was angry and stunned. My grandpa would have been really mad at this guy, too. The surprised feeling wore off a bit as I came to experience episodes like this half a dozen more times over the next few years as my projects became more complicated and my tools required more sophistication. But my anger never subsided because I felt as if I was being punished for venturing into a place that I felt I deserved to go, but that others believed I should not. Here I was enacting the freedom to build something I designed, and I was constrained by somebody who thought I shouldn't be doing it.

Importantly, every time I have gone to a craft shop to buy fabric, nobody has ever questioned my place there. Fabric and femininity seem to go hand in hand. Buying the tools that are required for home remodeling or redecorating is a process where gender plays out in interactions. Add to this the fact that redecorating is a term I have heard more often associated with women's aesthetic transformation in homes, while remodeling is associated with men's, and we can also see that the vocabulary we use is part of this gendered set of everyday practices. A fun test of this assertion would be to count the number of times the word *redecorating* is used in magazines like *Better Homes and Gardens* and *remodeling* is used in magazines like *This Old House*. You can do the same fun counting project with television shows dedicated to homes and gardens, and also note the gender of hosts and workers on set and what tools they're using.

It's not a far cry from these instances to see how gender matters in what we think men and women should do in terms of paid work and home duties like housework. The short interactions I've had that challenge the appropriateness of my work with large power tools highlight what sociologists call *occupational gender segregation*—how some jobs are more likely to be done by men and others by women.[13] Cross into the other realm, and people raise their eyebrows and call you "little lady" (or perhaps make assumptions about your sexual orientation if there is no mention of a husband in the conversation). Or they raise an eyebrow if you're a man buying floral fabric, something that also brings to mind the connection between gender roles and assumptions about sexual orientation. We can see how gender role expectations play out in something as seemingly benign as home decoration and remodeling.

Even though there are still prescribed gender roles in the realm of home creativity, increasing numbers of people from all walks of life are participating in the do-it-yourself (DIY) phenomenon in the United States, with more and more tools to buy, stores to patronize, and television shows to watch to get ideas. We have seen television programming devoted to residential decorating and design gaining popularity in the last few years, with both cable and network stations introducing new shows every season.[14] Makeover shows are particularly American, and home makeover shows, like much of American culture, are, as the *New York Times* reported in 2004, "built upon the dream of transformation—the idea that through some drastic change in your material surroundings, you can take a giant leap toward happiness."[15]

Interior decoration, both in reality and as it is represented on television, is important to examine from a sociological point of view for several reasons. First, making things look better is socially constructed. Endeavors like building a new wall or choosing wallpaper are composed not just of aesthetic choices but also of social networks of artistic producers, as well as socially situated conventions that dictate the form and content of design. In other words, that Ikea nightstand doesn't make itself—it is designed, crafted, shipped, sold, and purchased amidst a whole network of people, and in the midst of rules that say nightstands should be a certain height and width in order to have people understand that they are actually nightstands. Second, taste is socially constructed, because it varies by all sorts of categories that go beyond personal taste.[16] The Ikea table may look fantastic to you, but your grandma may think it looks like it'll fall apart in five minutes. So might a dozen other grandmas who are asked. And finally, the makeover element of home decorating television can be situated in a larger cultural context whereby seeking status, change, or a better life through material transformation is a powerful ideal that can be attained only if you buy the items you think will give you status. Even though our nightstands may be hidden in a private bedroom, we may be thinking about whether people will admire our taste in nightstands if they happen to see it when they put their coats on our bed during our Super Bowl party.

In terms of home design as shown as TV, it is important to analyze this growing media genre because it shows just how much industries associated with the rapid before-and-after transformations of American homes are connected to everyday practices of people. People change their furniture and paint colors more often now, in part because there are more choices and more accessible big stores to buy them in, and in part because our media feeds are filled with the idea that frequent aesthetic change is a good thing. Some people, if they can afford it, participate in this change by filtering the ideas from television programming into their own homes. Others are more critical, protesting the perfection that's portrayed on TV shows and online sites that show off successful domestic projects. This is why we see humorous websites devoted to more realistic attempts at home décor projects, attempts that result in a finished product that looks nothing like its idealized representation on Pinterest, an online platform to share style ideas, how-to tips and, as the site says, "other inspiring stuff."

The whole DIY phenomenon is not just about the shows that inspire ideas in people's homes, it's also about people taking some of these ideas and creating their own home-based businesses out of them. With online marketplaces like Etsy, blogs about home design, and idea-sharing sites like Pinterest, the creation of a good home with good design is not just an ideal that people share with their own family members or guests when they visit. It has the potential to become a hobby-turned-business for anyone who wants to turn do-it-yourself into do-it-for-others-and-get-paid. What's interesting about this trend is that, unless you're talking about construction, large metal fabrication, and outdoor tasks, the people who tend to participate in these online sites and industries devoted to lifestyle, domestic transformation, and home crafting are women. This mirrors the gendered occupational breakdown of people in building and design sectors and people on television shows dedicated to home transformation, where engineers, builders, contractors, and architects are disproportionately men and interior designers and decorators are disproportionately women.

Do Our Home Designs Work?

Housing designs both reflect and affect gender roles of the people living in them. Some scholars have argued that traditional gender roles in household labor are encouraged by the architecture of the single-family home.[17] Yet, homes can also be designed to create more equality between men and women. Let's look at how these shifts have occurred over the last century or two in the United States. Sociologist and architecture scholar Daphne Spain points out that home spaces in twentieth-century America have become more gender neutral, demonstrating that as society's attitudes toward gender roles and responsibilities change, these changes are also reflected in architecture and interior residential design. She claims that changes in residential architecture, including the shift from parlor to great room as the locus of women's activity in the home, coincided with the increased status of women. In contrast, masculine spaces in Victorian homes (billiard rooms, smoking rooms, libraries) were strictly separated from feminine spaces (parlors, sitting rooms, nurseries). The rooms within each set of gendered spaces were carefully connected to each other by separate gentlemen's and ladies' staircases and hallways, ensuring that men and women encountered each other only in communal spaces such as the dining room. Spain explains that as bungalows replaced Victorian homes in the late nineteenth century and "as architects were simplifying housing design in line with aesthetic and technological principles, they were also reducing gender segregation."[18] Bungalows were, in turn, replaced by ranch houses following World War II, and this new housing design allowed for a number of multipurpose rooms, the most important of which was the great room, a multipurpose space designed to accommodate food preparation, dining, entertaining, and leisure. As multipurpose spaces that were shared by all members of the family became more common in American architecture, the status separations between men and women and parents and children were lessened. Especially after the 1950s.

However, even with the addition of multipurpose spaces—and hence more multigendered spaces than in the past—roles are still subtly divided and perpetuated within single-family households. American studies and architecture scholar Dolores Hayden has articulated that the detached single-family home became the most common housing type in the United States following the Second World War, as more

Americans bought into, or attempted to buy into, the American dream home ideology. This ideology reinforced gender roles that included men using home as a retreat and women using home as a place of work. The ideal goes like this: the men attempt to maintain a green lawn, a shiny new car, and a set of scrumptious hamburgers on the new grill, while women perform their domestic roles inside. And home designs were meant to support these roles. While these images seem outdated, and were not attainable for many American families even during the *Leave It to Beaver* era, the separate spaces model is still present in homes that people are living in, unless they remodel, as my husband and I did when we knocked down one wall to make our 1937 kitchen less hidden from the rest of the home and the rest of the family.[19]

The reinforcement of *separate spheres* is visible in home spaces that are meant for cooking and cleaning. The design of most single-family homes built before the twenty-first century in the United States separates kitchens and laundry facilities from living areas to hide from public view the messy tasks that take place in these spaces. Kitchens are often located at the back of the home behind doors or down hallways. Laundry facilities are tucked away on another floor or at the opposite end of the house from the rooms where the members of the household actually change their clothes. Additionally, as Hayden outlines, kitchens are often designed to accommodate only one cook. Further, neither hidden laundry facilities nor enclosed kitchens provide convenient places to multitask by watching children or performing other household tasks. When the spaces designated for the work of cooking, laundry, and childcare are small and hidden away, and when these tasks are disproportionately completed by women, the amount of time, space, visibility, and energy devoted to housework, as well as any frustrations associated with the tasks, become gendered. The devaluation of household labor is reinforced by its often hidden location within the home. The design of postwar homes thus made life harder for many women.

Kitchens are being designed now with more of an eye toward connectedness to the rest of the house, as well as partnered sharing of tasks within the space. But, of course, most people don't have new houses. The housing stock contains design and architecture that doesn't easily support the possibility of changing gender roles or shared household labor tasks. And there is no guarantee that living in a home with a great room and lots of open space will necessarily steer gender roles away from traditional places. Whether this happens depends on what the family members view as fair, and how strongly they may adhere to the very powerful (and, to some extent, changing) gender role expectations in our society.

THE TOOLBOX

Some people store a hammer in a kitchen drawer, and others in a toolbox outside in a toolshed. So what does gender have to do with all of this? About a decade ago, I found myself sitting in front of the television watching show after show devoted to home remodeling and redecoration. Of particular note was *Trading Spaces*, where designers-slash-actors would lead a pair of neighbors in remodeling a room in each other's homes. The outcome was always a reveal that included surprised (and sometimes horrified) looks on the homeowners' faces, and a few ideas for the home audience members who wanted to make changes on a budget to incorporate into their own homes.

I also looked forward every week to watching *Extreme Makeover: Home Edition*, partially because one of the former *Trading Spaces* carpenters that I liked was the host. This show had as its premise a deserving family who had experienced a hardship receiving a massive home remodel completed in a very short amount of time. I had the good fortune of being on set for one of the episode tapings in 2004, and I can attest that things happen extremely fast.[20] I can also attest that one of the female carpenter-slash-hosts on the show wielded a hefty tool belt and a sturdy work jacket. Both were pink.

Being a viewer of these kinds of shows, and then an observer of the behind-the-scenes part, and then a home remodeler whose ideas sometimes stemmed from the shows, I wondered whether other women were wielding tool belts and grabbing hammers from toolboxes more than in the past. And whether this meant that they were charting territory that had previously been occupied primarily by men. I was raising this question in the early 2000s, when television shows about redecorating and remodeling homes proliferated. HGTV viewing increased. New channels and shows emerged. Product lines associated with the channels, shows, and show performers started showing up in stores. Lifestyle media was blossoming. Now, with Etsy and Pinterest and a universe

filled with blogs about home design, we see (primarily) women participating in tasks connected closely to the home, but they're doing it in a
more public way (that sometimes requires toolboxes)—a way that can
even produce an income.

The objects we use in our homes carry with them feminine and
masculine meanings. It may seem strange to think of the hammer in our
toolboxes as "he" or "she," but we attach gender to things all the time
(just like the body wash and paint I mentioned earlier). If that hammer
was advertised to women, especially in the last couple decades, marketers would follow a pattern that pundits refer to as "shrink it or pink it."[21]
Want a woman to buy that hammer? Make it smaller and put a pink
handle on it. This kind of marketing has stopped working well, by the
way, especially among those of us who have used nonpink hammers
since 1997.

So the question becomes whether women who wield tools such as
hammers (with or without pink handles) and remodel their own homes
or sell their décor online are demonstrating freedom from traditional
gender roles, or adherence to them. Does work on homes, lifestyles,
and décor support research findings that men and women are becoming
more similar in their household tasks, or not? If a woman had a hammer, what would it mean?

This question was precisely what I had in mind when I studied
women's responses to home decorating television shows in the early
2000s with Lindsey Menard. We wondered whether the thirty-four
middle-class women (ages thirty to seventy-two, most married with
kids, most participating in the paid work world) we interviewed in their
own homes saw their participation in home decorating and remodeling
that was inspired by these shows as being progressive or traditional. We
knew that watching home decorating television means female viewers
are focused on the traditionally feminine topic of making homes look
better. But we also believed that the do-it-yourself aspect of completing
projects can be empowering. Sociologists often frame freedom to do
things and have power as *agency*, and feeling limited by others as *constraint*. The project was a way to figure out if using building and construction tools to do home decoration projects inspired by home decorating and remodeling television shows was interpreted as agency, constraint, or both by the women interviewed.

When sociologist Ann Swidler described the way we create meaning in our everyday lives as a cultural *tool kit* of materials that can be used in order to deal with different kinds of social situations or interpret different meanings of what we see, she was speaking figuratively.[22] For example, when we go to someone's house whom we do not know, we may pull out a "polite phrase" or "try not to burp" tool. Or, for example, a cultural tool kit may consist of people dressing to fit into gender norms (clothing as a tool), or even using a particular body posture to align with gender expectations (crossing one's legs or not as a tool). Our tool kits provide the tools we need to deal with our social worlds—but they're pretty abstract in the way that sociologists talk about them.

Studying the meaning people attach to ideas and behaviors inspired from home decorating television adds a whole new meaning to the concept of tool kit. Home decorating shows often provide viewers with a mental array of techniques, products, project ideas, fix-it solutions, and words that are meant to instill confidence in a viewer's ability to "do it herself." But many women who apply what they have learned also develop an actual physical tool kit, full of hammers, electric drills, and nail guns, that assists them with projects in their homes. The existence of both a literal (e.g., hammers and nails) and figurative (e.g., gender norms) tool kit both challenges and supports traditional gender role expectations, because women are taking on roles formerly reserved for men, and yet are still performing these roles in order to improve how their homes look. Just like when I got the toolbox from my grandpa in 1997—I wore a dress to the all-women bridal shower, but I wielded the hammer in my hand when I opened the present.

Women in our study felt powerful, to be sure, sometimes perform- ing new tasks with actual power tools once reserved for the men in their homes. For example, one woman said, "I like to learn how to do things. It's empowerment. I'm a mechanical kind of a person and I like to know, I like to learn how to do things. I tend to [do] fix-it rather than novels and fiction and stuff like that." At the same time, though, the women overwhelmingly felt like they needed to manage and maintain control of (and, according to some, be controlled by) the domestic sphere. This wasn't necessarily presented as a problem in the inter- views, but it did align with past research on how home décor is still primarily women's work. With newfound confidence and hammers in hand, the women are still the ones focusing on making their homes pretty. Both agency and constraint are tucked into the tool kit.

SPICES

Sugar and spice and everything nice, that's what little girls are made of. Grill rubs and tools, and a slathering of Old Spice, that's what big men are made of?

It occurs to me that body wash in black bottles and renamed tough guy paint colors for men are not the only places where the same ingredients are gendered just by naming or packaging them differently. Take spices. You know—cinnamon, pepper, ginger. Parsley, sage, rosemary, and thyme. Now, imagine you are seeing a combination of cumin, black pepper, sea salt, and cayenne. What kind of container(s) are they in? Where are they stored? On what kinds of foods are they going to be sprinkled or rubbed?

If you're imagining them to be contained in a short round cylinder with a black lid and bold font on the label, perhaps you'd refer to them as a "rub," and maybe you'd envision them to be stored outside next to the grilling tools and the barbeque. In an article entitled "Why Do Men Grill?" Jesse Rhodes uncovered the finding that the United States is unique in its attachment of manhood with the BBQ and the patio as a "men only" area.[23] American lifestyle television, books, and products relating to outdoor cooking feature all of the tenets of idealized masculinity: toughness, ruggedness, ability to control nature (or at least a beef patty and some flames), and providing sustenance for a family. This is less likely due to men being evolutionarily connected to hunting and women to gathering and more likely due to the mid-twentieth-century movement of suburban living and an increase in the expectation that dads should spend their free time with kids (and still be manly enough to be called proper men). Add to these historical trends the idealization of suburbia and the introduction of the first backyard grill in the 1950s by Weber, and it is not surprising that in a majority of American homes, barbequing on a grill is still viewed as the cooking task most likely done by men in households where both men and women are present. Despite an increase of men in kitchen cooking and cleanup, "manning" the barbeque is the most acceptable way that men participate in domestic food preparation in the United States And yet, it has only been around in this form for a few decades.

The spices that are to be sprinkled atop the meat are not only sold in places where men shop and in containers and with names that are attractive to people who grill, they are likely stored near men's cooking tasks. If the spices are in separate tall cylinders with small lids and labeled and organized alphabetically, they're probably in the kitchen spice rack. I would guess that they are also unlikely to include the word *bold* in bold font on their label. While this example may not resonate with all families, it does show us that home objects with the same ingredients can be given different names, containers, and locations, which then connects them to gender in ways that we usually don't think about.

Let's look more closely at the sociology of spices. The use of kitchen items to enact gender roles as they intersect with other identities is highlighted by sociologist Roksana Badruddoja.[24] She has researched how life changes for adult children of post-1965 South Asian immigrant families once they come to the United States. Her interviewees' families emigrated from Bangladesh, Myanmar, Bhutan, Sri Lanka, Maldives, Nepal, Pakistan, and India. She outlines how life changes are often visible in how home objects (including spices) are used. For the women she interviewed, life in the United States is filled with pushes and pulls from the countries and cultures their families left and the communities they now find themselves in.

Badruddoja talks about food as a "territory of the self" where identities played out along the spectrum of these pushes and pulls. In particular, spices found in the kitchen came up as the women discussed what to cook and eat. They also were talked about as if they were props used to show how much the families had succeeded in *acculturation*, or adoption of social patterns of life in the United States. In order to connect with what they perceived to be less traditional U.S. gender roles, the women distanced themselves from traditional notions of kitchens as feminine spaces from their parents' homelands and generation. Sometimes this meant that their husbands cooked, and sometimes it meant that they chose to cook things that required much less time than traditional dishes from their South Asian homes. Often the discussion of the time-consuming dishes included mention of particular spices that were not only expensive or hard to get in the United States but that also symbolized, to them, an elaborateness and carefulness and effort that they simply did not have time or energy (or desire) to perform. Using fewer spices from their parents' nation of origin meant less adherence to traditional roles in their families.

The stories highlight how gendered household division of labor is not just about what men and women do, it's also about how norms and expectations that connect to racial-ethnic identity, generation, and movement between geographic locations may play out in everyday use of home spaces and objects. So, while it may be that much of this chapter highlights how men's and women's roles still carry some tradition with them, these roles can change across different social groups and for different reasons.

REFLECTING ON OUR STUFF

Homes show how the boundaries between public and private matter for families. Public and private realms are becoming blurry in many ways. But they're also still divided by gender. The public world is disproportionately men, and the private world is disproportionately women. And even in the home, the notion of spaces as being hidden or secluded or reserved just for one type of person suggests that spaces in our domestic lives are defined as either mostly public, mostly private, mostly his, mostly hers. When we take the idea that men and women, despite increasing equality, are still socialized into roles that are different, this can turn into inequality. Public spaces and things are sometimes deemed more valuable, especially economically and politically. So, continuing to label private home spaces as feminized not only fails to capture the experience of families with non-traditional gender roles, it also results in women continuing to have less access to valuable resources than men.

Homes tell us about individual families, but also about broader social issues. Social researchers find it important and interesting to analyze what happens when people cross over into a different gender realm, as with status-reversed couples. What happens when I start drilling holes in the wall, or when my husband starts baking cookies? The fact that I am the one in our household who shops for power tools can be understood as not too big of a deal because women are more likely to have power tools than in the past. But it also needs to be considered in light of the fact that it is still unusual. And when things are unusual, they end up highlighting what's normal. My having power tools, as long as that's deemed unusual by the man working at the home improvement store or anyone, reinforces the notion that men are more likely to have power tools. And this can translate not only into strange looks in a hardware store, but unequal access to life experiences that are divided unfairly by gender. While stories about power tools seem not too serious, they can symbolize other parts of family lives that show how power may make family dynamics not only unequal, but also really problematic. Our real lives are often filled with ways that we cross boundaries, including with gender roles. But there are so many ways that our decisions surrounding home spaces and objects are subject to a marketplace and a set of societal expectations that reinforce these boundaries as quite distinct.

Homes are not only symbolic, but also shape our lives. Sarah Pink has said that "the agency of the house [is] sometimes a constraint to the agency of the individual."[25] While we may see our homes as places of refuge and locations where we can act freely, they can simultaneously do things that constrain us. From people who require home remodeling so that they can fit their wheelchair under a kitchen counter to do the dishes, to those who want to keep up with their neighbors by cooking an elaborate meal on a subpar 1970s range, our individual freedom is sometimes limited by the houses we live in and the objects in them. In order to think about whether gender roles are changing in the household division of labor, we also need to think about how home spaces and objects can serve to allow or constrain our desired roles. So, as we go about our days cooking, cleaning, building, sewing, mowing, dusting, decorating, and grilling, it is important for us to think not only about whether the roles we occupy to complete these tasks suit our goals as men and women, but also whether our homes shape how well we are able to meet those goals and fulfill those roles.

6

HOME AND PAID WORK INTERSECTIONS

Work Bags and Calendars

HOME OFFICES

Imagine two partners who share a workspace. Can you picture it? What does it look like? Where is it? What kind of work are they doing? What objects do you see that facilitate their work?

Now, take a step back and think about the two people in that space. Are you imagining the word *partner* in that scenario to be a synonym for *work associate*? Or are you imagining it to mean a marital or lifelong committed partner? What if it was both?

Finally, think about whether the workspace is in a home or apart from one. In this chapter, I delve into the sociological significance of home offices, including any spaces in a home where paid work tasks are done, to highlight how family and work roles and experiences can be seen in the use of space. Since a home office specifically is used for both home and paid work tasks, it is a particularly interesting place to visit. While it doesn't include work tasks that are more likely found in the service, manufacturing, and other job sectors that require specific tools or interaction in specific places or with specific people (it's hard to dig a trench, give a pedicure, or fly a plane from home), the idea of how much work creeps into home and home creeps into work, in terms of experiences, spaces, and objects, is salient for every family. And these experiences can become really interesting if we consider instances when members of the same family perform paid work together (and I'm not talking about running the homestead from two hundred years ago, though that'd be neat to think about).

Depending on the source, we can estimate that 20 to 25 percent of U.S. homes today have rooms dedicated as home offices, most often found in the homes of affluent families, baby boomers, and/or people with college degrees.[1] However, many small businesses are run out of homes, making the notion of a home office more applicable to more families than in the past. And, of course, we know that, even if a home does not have a designated office, the ubiquity of technological tools to conduct work from anywhere (what geographers Jean Andrey and Laura Johnson call "teleworking") means work tasks are often done in many parts of the home.[2]

Architecture scholar Frances Hollis, in her book *Beyond Live/Work: The Architecture of Home-based Work*, breaks down some important facts about the growing trend of home-based work (defined as doing paid work either at home or at a workplace where one lives, for at least eight hours a week).[3] First, buildings that combine home and work (what Hollis calls the *workhome*) have existed for thousands of years, from farms to shop houses. Before the industrial revolution, home *was* work in many cases, thus rendering these two realms as simultaneously public and private; and now the need for dual-use spaces is increasing with the growth in home-based workers.[4] Second, contemporary home-based workers fall into different categories, including live-in workers, people with at-home businesses (e.g., web-based selling, home-based hair stylists), students, artists, and professionals. And third, most homes and workplaces (and neighborhoods and zoning laws) are not designed to accommodate dual use, suggesting that our living spaces do not work well for the changes in our work-home patterns and practices.[5]

The U.S. Census Bureau's American Community Survey reveals that nearly 85 percent of U.S. households have a computer, with three-fourths of Americans accessing things online with an Internet connection.[6] And so it seems as if, despite some lack of access particularly for people who cannot afford a computer, digital access to our work worlds, especially if they're located outside of our homes, is highly available in our homes.[7] Whether you're filling out an expense report, checking a shift schedule, searching for cheap plane tickets for your next conference, or figuring out the cost estimate for the special-order cedar panels your client needs for the home siding job you're doing, you can do this with a laptop on a couch in the living room. Or in your designated home office, if you have one.

There is a great body of research on teleworking and the intersections of paid work and family life, often pointing out how home and work seep into each other with this increasingly common type of home-work arrangement, how they are still kept separate by some people and types of jobs, and how the boundary between them is impacted by technologies that allow for their intersection. In terms of research explicitly on the spaces where home and work boundaries collide, geographers and architecture scholars have done a great job talking about the increasing need for multipurpose spaces for people to perform paid work tasks at home, including findings from a case study by Jean Andrey and Laura Johnson that the location of a home office in the "epicenter of family life" lessens the ability of people to focus on their work because home tasks leak into work tasks.[8] In this sense, while home and work boundaries seem to be getting blurrier in contemporary life, separating them as realms when they're both taking place in a home is functional for many. Similarly, communications scholar Donell Holloway found that technology items that may help someone do their work anywhere in the home actually serve as tangible symbols for separating work from home tasks.[9] As in: the work computer goes over here in a room that we're calling the office, but not where we eat or watch TV. Or: no smartphone use to do business at the dinner table—it has to stay in your pocket.

My favorite research on home and work stems from interviews by sociologist Christena Nippert-Eng, who in the 1990s talked with people about how their use of objects and spaces (among other things) showed how they saw themselves along a spectrum that ranged from integrationists (home and work are totally overlapping) to segmentists (home and work are separate realms with clear boundaries between them). I applied these concepts from her book *Home and Work: Negotiating Boundaries through Everyday Life* to my own research in the late 1990s, but added a twist when I interviewed married couples who worked together in the same workplace, occupation, or both.[10] I figured that if couples have a literal overlap of home and work by virtue of them occupying the spouse and colleague role simultaneously, this would yield interesting results for their home-work boundaries.

I limited my interviewees to people who worked in higher education and in legal fields, since these groups were more likely than, say, veterinarians, to do their work at home. Like Nippert-Eng, I got to see lots of briefcases, purses, keychains, calendars, and living rooms with piles of work on the coffee table. And yes, I saw some home offices, including the insides of file cabinets with files labeled "home improvement" adjacent to files labeled "pay stubs." One way to have home and work intersect is to do work at home. But this intersection can be made a little more formal, and a lot more segmented, if there is a designated work space in a home where work activities are performed and where other activities are not. Even if people think of a home office as seamlessly connected to the rest of the home, the fact that it can be declared on taxes as a business expense suggests it is a unique space to think about home life intersecting with other life realms.

My research uncovered some interesting findings in terms of how people use home offices to either segment or integrate their work and family lives. Married couples who worked at the same workplace were more likely to have their own home offices or separate home office spaces in different rooms than those who worked at different places, especially for those who shared occupations, too. This is interesting because there was very little variation between occupation groups in terms of actually *doing* paid work at home, but there was a difference in the kind of *space* delineated in which to conduct that work. Clearly, the notion that working within the same space at work as their spouse necessitated more of their own spaces at home for the potential to do that work. They wanted more symbolic privacy for ownership of their own paid work. These people did not want to share everything about their paid work with their spouses in terms of workspace. In this sense, not only do people need to manage whether and how spaces are separated in their homes between home and paid work tasks, demographic patterns (e.g., spouses both in the paid labor force) may affect this separation.

HOME AND WORK IN CONTEMPORARY U.S. SOCIETY

What things should we think about when we imagine the importance of home spaces and objects as they matter for home and work boundaries?

Below I discuss three areas that show how people's arrangements of spaces and objects in homes tell us about contemporary patterns of paid work and family life. First, it is important to think about what is meant by the term *boundary* when we think of home and work, and how that boundary can be defined as blurry or solid, depending on how we use spaces and objects. Second, we need to examine how the expectations in the increasingly "greedy" paid work world have changed historically. And third, the construction of boundaries between work and home has to be situated in a family's experiences in terms of demographic factors such as type of job, employment and economic status, gender, parental status, and race.

Home and Work Stages, Props, and Boundaries

If you've ever been an actor or seen a theatrical performance, you may have heard of the term *the fourth wall*. This term refers to the imaginary border between performance stage (the three-sided box) and audience, and it helps both performers and audience members suspend disbelief and pretend that all have entered into the world of whatever theatrical production is happening. It's also the place where the audience gets to view the world of the stage, like a one-way mirror within the wall. There is no actual wall, of course, but, as I recall from my high school days of playing the part of the Fairy Godmother in Rodgers and Hammerstein's *Cinderella*, both performer and audience work to maintain its existence in order to enjoy a normal theatergoing experience. We know people put the wall there, because when the wall is knocked down, say, by a phone ringing in the audience, we feel a little uncomfortable and have to work to get our brains back into the imaginary world of the performance.

There are literal walls around a home, but it can be fun to think about ways that we construct some invisible walls (or tear them down) through our actions and beliefs. Saying the home is a private space seems easy enough to do, since we can close our door and pull our curtains and hide things from the rest of the world. But as soon as you count the ways that other realms enter in, and ways that family life ventures out, it gets complicated. With changing patterns regarding the ease of doing some forms of paid work from anywhere, it's easier to bring work home than it used to be. With more people (especially women) performing paid work (the U.S. Department of Labor reports that 70 percent of women with children under eighteen participate in the labor force)[11] and with increasing attention to the importance of benefits for working families and self-care, it's easier to allow family and personal responsibilities to impact work than it used to be. How families experience work and family increasingly includes blurry and permeable boundaries, even as the value of the privacy of home and the publicness of paid work lives on in our policies and practices.

As Nippert-Eng discusses, the work associated with putting up a boundary, crossing it, poking a hole in it, or moving it is called *boundary work*, which is the way that we work to create or maintain the overlap (and sometimes separation) of our work selves and our home selves. We perform boundary work when we see home spaces occupied by work objects, work spaces occupied by home objects, and spaces in either where you can't tell which is which. The work comes when we have to decide how much we want these realms to collide. It takes work to keep them separated when they so easily lend themselves to integration, as with the invisible theatrical fourth wall discussed above. And it takes work to integrate them if they're defined as quite separate (for example, it'd be hard to bring your baby to the construction site where you're welding). The result is that even the way we think of ourselves can change depending on how we use the props and stages of home and work. If all the world's a stage and we're merely actors, as Shakespeare said, then our acting roles include navigating which props to use on which stage, figuring out which stage to move toward and when, and even managing both stages in one spot or at one time. The more we integrate, the more props we carry back and forth and the less it matters to us if the props of different realms commingle on the same stage. The more we segment, the less likely it is to find our front door keys in our work bags and our work appointments on the calendar stuck to our refrigerator door.

Greedy Workplaces and Technology

Laptops and smartphones make working anywhere there is electricity and wireless access possible (and even expected). The intermingling of work and home realms is increasing, not decreasing. Much of this has to do with the fact that technology makes the intermingling easier, but it also has to do with what our workplaces expect from us.

In the February 28, 2016, issue of the *New York Times Magazine*, a bulk of the articles were about contemporary work life, noting that "we do often work at home. But we also work at work, before going home to work more. The office has persisted, becoming even bigger, weirder, stranger: a symbol of its outsize presence in our lives."[12] We have seen an increase in the proportion of workers who work at home (some or all)—from 19 percent in 2003 to 24 percent in 2015. Additionally, the amount of time people who are employed spend working at home has recently increased by forty minutes per day.[13] At the same time, work hours in total have not decreased. Workplaces have become greedier, and we are increasingly required to devote emotional energy to managing our work selves even at home.[14] Technology facilitates the spillover of work into all life realms and during any time. This is not true just for the home-based workers discussed earlier—it is true for an increasing number of jobs, especially ones that can be done using portable technology.

Take a laptop computer, for example. Being able to carry it back and forth between an office and a dining room table means not only that the work is portable, it also means that the person using it to do work at the dining room table has to think about whether it may impact, or be impacted by, interactions with others in a home. I have a home office, but I prefer to bring my laptop to the dining room because the space has more natural light than my office and I can get a snack more quickly. As I write this chapter on my laptop in our dining room, I'm waiting for my son to wake up, at which point he'll talk to me and I'll have to pause my writing and switch gears to participate in a home-related interaction. Once he sits down to have breakfast, I can return to my writing while I listen to him make chewing noises with his cereal. In this little scenario, you can see how the boundary between home and work can be represented by an object—a computer (and cereal, actually)—and how it can be made more permeable if I easily move back and forth between writing and talking with my son, or less permeable if I choose instead to ignore him and put headphones on so I can remain in work mode. My work self and my home self, in that instance, are in negotiation with each other. And regardless of which self takes the stage in that particular moment, my work expectations are large enough that I need to do them at home outside of normal work hours.

Inequalities and Work

As just discussed, the boundary work we have to do to manage home and work selves seems to be increasingly devoted to managing the ease with which our paid work can enter our homes, both in terms of our literal objects and spaces and also in terms of our roles and how we think of ourselves. This means that how much we segment or integrate our home and work selves through the use of objects and spaces can be constrained by factors outside of our control. This includes the type of work we do as well as factors like gender, race, parental status, and social class.

When discussing how home and work intersect in family lives, it is important to first acknowledge that not all adults have the kind of employment that allows them the ability to have a laptop, bring work home, or even, as American sociologist Matthew Desmond's vivid 2016 ethnography *Evicted* shows us, afford their rent. Among the entire population of people who are of working age, nearly 60 percent are employed, with blacks showing a lower ratio than whites and Hispanics. But many people are unemployed or underemployed, just shy of poverty, a status disproportionately experienced by blacks, Hispanics,[15] and Native Americans and Alaska Natives.[16] While half of American adults live in middle-income households (earning between $42,000 and $125,000 a year in 2014), this proportion has declined in the last decade, and that income range is very wide. Nearly a third are below this, and the gap between the wealthy and the poor is growing.[17]

While numbers fluctuate, the unemployment rate has not decreased below that from the Great Recession. Sometimes working less or not at all is by choice, often by those who wish to stay home with children or who opt to stay home because it would cost more than they earn to pay for child care. But not working at all is sometimes far from a choice. The unemployment rate in the United States fluctuates depending on how strong our economy is, and varies between racial-ethnic groups. Recent statistics show us that whites experience lower rates of joblessness than blacks and Hispanics, at 6.6 percent, 12.6 percent, and 9.4 percent, respectively.[18]

When people do have jobs, the kinds of work they're doing have changed over time. The sectors where we've seen the largest increases in employment in the last several years are health care, service and retail industries, and social assistance. The greatest decline has been in specialty trade contractors and construction, as well as manufacturing, education, and government.[19] When we think about how home spaces may or may not be suitable to perform certain kinds of work tasks, keeping in mind the growth in certain more and less portable jobs is important. Not everyone has an office or a laptop, let alone any space to personalize at work. Not everyone can do their jobs at home.

In terms of gender, while women represent nearly half of the workforce in the United States, they are more likely to adjust their jobs and careers (taking time off, reducing hours, quitting, or turning down a promotion) for family reasons, including taking care of young children. Sometimes this is justified by heterosexual two-parent families because women are likely to make less money than men (something at a larger societal level referred to as the *wage gap*). But often it is defined in these families as a preference or in terms of gender roles that prescribe women as nurturers. Interestingly, most Americans believe that women should not return to their traditional societal roles. However, 70 percent believe working full time is the ideal situation for men with young children, while only 12 percent believe the same for women. While a generational shift may be coming, with millennial men and women equally saying having a child may slow down their careers, millennial mothers are still more likely than millennial fathers to find it hard to get ahead at work as a working parent.[20]

Nearly half of families with two parents have both of them working full time, so it will be crucial to monitor how work and family expectations look for men and women over the coming decades, too.[21] It is important to note, as family researchers Jennifer Glass, Robin Simon, and Matthew Andersson found, the gap in happiness between parents and nonparents in the United States is wider than it is in any of the twenty-two countries included in their cross-national study, due in large part to inadequate workplace policies that allow balancing work and family responsibilities without penalties like stress, decreased pay, and promotion loss.[22]

What we know about paid work and family life is that, first, not everyone has a paying job. For those who do, not all have one where they can actually bring work tasks back and forth, and access to these kinds of things is affected by one's demographics. White picket fences and white-collar work with fancy laptop cases and good pay and policies that allow for a family to have a child are not available to most people. These ideals are reminders that not everyone has access to spaces and objects that signify a high-status job and/or one where a person has autonomy and control over time, space, and objects associated with that work.

WORK BAGS

I go to a lot of conferences where paying the registration fee comes with a name badge, a thick program, and a canvas bag with the conference logo on it to hold the program and local restaurant recommendations. I probably have about twenty of these bags hanging from a hook on my office door (let me know if you need one). I once met a professor who used her bags as a filing system: one bag for each research project, all lined up on her office floor in order of completion status. I have always thought this was a brilliant way to use the bags instead of waste them, but I am far too picky about how clean my office floor is, and I don't currently have twenty separate research projects going on. As Tammy Schotzko, Certified Professional Organizer, has said, if you want to keep things tidy, "you need as many bags going out as you have coming in."[23]

I am also picky about the bags I buy to hold the other stuff I buy. I'd rather have a nicely lined soft leather bag with no logo than a bright red canvas bag with itchy straps and the words "XXII Conference of the Society for Awesome Social Scientists (SASS)" on the side. For my work, a bag needs to hold a laptop, a power cord, a keychain with just my office keys on it, a stack of papers, and some pens. And it needs to be easy to carry, fit over my shoulder no matter how thick my coat is, and not drag on the ground when I hold it from my long monkey arms. It is nice if it can also hold a quart-sized clear plastic bag full of three-ounce toiletries for when I have to travel to a work meeting by airplane.

For other kinds of work, a bag that is used to transport work items could include carpentry tools, a stethoscope, a work uniform that needs to be washed, or a note about which shifts to work next week. Depending on the commute, a work bag can be a backpack that works well for bike riders, or a briefcase that sits securely on a lap during a train ride. And sometimes the bag used to bring work items home is really just a purse or wallet (or even the trunk of a car) where we put work items until we find time to put them elsewhere. In any of these cases, what we use to transport items back and forth from work to home (or perhaps from a home office to another part of the house, for those who work entirely at home) can symbolize a liminal, or in-between, space where we are not quite sure whether what's inside is entirely located in the work realm or in the home realm. When you put a piece of paper with your boss's new e-mail address on it into your bag, it changes definition. It moves from more public to more private. When you put your son's latest school picture in your purse, it is private until you display it at work where anyone walking by your work space can see it. If we have a home self and a work self, then bags we use to transport items back and forth between these realms are fascinating sociological shuttle buses for the self.

Just think about the action of taking a work task object out of a bag at home—this is both a physical and a mental process. I move the item from the bag to the desk, and I switch to thinking of myself as a worker in a home space. The same thing can be felt if we turn on a computer at home and open a work file, suggesting that increasingly the "bag" we use to transport "items" back and forth can be digital or physical.

So, what's in your wallet? Some of my favorite moments in Nippert-Eng's book are when she discusses the wallets, purses, tote bags, brief-cases, backpacks, and laptop cases. She calls these *identity kits*—objects we use to contain ingredients that define who we are. Usually these are more likely to be containers that bring work items home, and less often the reverse (though certainly items can stay in the bags that represent our identities as nonworkers [e.g., food, personal hygiene items, pictures of family members]). Because of this, it's interesting to look at what's in people's purses and bags and wallets to see how much work stuff is in there that will end up crossing the boundary into home. Nippert-Eng found that, even though our workplaces are often greedy and we can access work in more and more places, we are usually expected to carry around mostly personal items in wallets and purses. But perhaps this expectation differs now that we have elaborate work bags and technological access to all of our life realms at any moment (remember that her research was in the 1990s). She also found that differ-

ent kinds of bags signified different identities, as when the female scientists she interviewed carried backpacks to and from work but purses
to and from the grocery store. This pattern shows that gender displays
differ depending on what is expected in different realms. According to
the interviews, being a scientist requires downplaying femininity, but
going to the store does not. Different occupations may matter, too. As
you can imagine, if your job is to carry around papers, your bag will look
quite different from someone whose job is to carry around house paint.

I was inspired by Nippert-Eng's work on wallets and purses, but I
wanted to answer a few more questions. So I interviewed twenty-six
married couples who all had children still at home about how much
they brought work to home or home to work in terms of dozens of
objects (including, as I mentioned earlier, whether they brought items
into home offices or not), with specific focus on what I called "work
bags" like briefcases and backpacks rather than purses and wallets. I
interviewed people who worked in academia and in the legal profession.
In addition to seeing if a more specific type of bag mattered, I wanted
to see if spouses who work together at the same workplace may have
had different kinds of objects and boundaries than those who did not
(that's what happens when you marry another sociologist and want to
understand your own work-home dynamics). I wondered about this
because if you work at the same place as a partner, you already have a
lot of "home" at work, and you may have to work harder than others to
avoid having a lot of work stuff at home (especially talk).

What showed up in these spouse/colleagues' work bags? I found that
couples sharing a workplace were *more* likely to integrate *work into
home* than those not sharing a workplace, often indicated by items such
as computers and files carried from work to home in a bag. Sharing
workplace thus translated into more integration in the direction of work
items being brought into the home in bags of some kind.

But what about bringing home into work, especially since we know
that workplaces are greedy and some bosses frown upon bringing home
responsibilities to work that look like they may hinder work performance? What kinds of home things do people bring to work in a bag?
And does it matter if members of their family work at the same place,
thus blurring the boundaries between home and work just by being in
both places? My interviews revealed that those couples who shared a
workplace, while more likely to bring work home, were *less* likely to

integrate *home objects into work spaces* than those who did not share a workplace.

Why? One possible explanation is that, when a family member is already present in person at the workplace, it becomes less urgent to have symbolic reminders of family and home in a work space. People did not need a substitute when they could have the real thing down the hallway or at least in the next building. From a more critical perspective, though, respondents talked about avoiding the display of objects that represented home life in the paid workplace (even if it was just in the bag used to transport work items back and forth—a liminal space) because of their perception that coworkers or bosses may judge them negatively. Calling to mind potential accusations of nepotism and workplace identities too closely connected to a spouse, people wanted to be seen as workers and not have their family connections highlighted. For these workers, any visible reminders that family members were present in the workplace *because* they were family members, whether true or not, could have been perceived as negative by coworkers. For this reason, bringing fewer personal or home-related items in work bags to work was a more common strategy of action among those who shared a workplace. Interestingly, this was especially true for women who got their jobs after their husbands did—a finding that indicates that even symbolically, the perceived identity of "trailing spouse" (now more often referred to as "accompanying partner") calls to mind both the legitimacy of someone's work status and the puzzle women face in general about fearing the perception that they're more dedicated to home than work. Deemphasizing home items in work bags, then, helps people establish independent work identities that show dedication to the workplace rather than to home.

I saw this process play out most vividly when the interviewees talked about their children's artwork. Was it brought to work in a bag and then attached to the wall? Was it less permanent, as would be found on a dry-erase board in an office? Of all of the pictures of kids' drawings in offices, only couples who worked at the same place had their children's drawings on chalkboards and dry-erase boards, as opposed to on paper that was taped to a wall or mounted in a frame, initially brought to work in a work bag. In other words, children's art was temporary, erasable, and easy to remove for people who shared a workplace with a spouse. This was most likely true for two reasons. First, these people were more likely than different workplace couples to have their children physically present in their offices, which meant that drawings could be done at parents' workplaces. Second, perhaps if same-workplace couples wanted to avoid symbolic representations of their families in the workplace for reasons mentioned above, the temporary nature of kids' drawings on chalkboards meant that they were not visible on the walls, they were never found in work bags, and they could be quickly removed.

In contrast, different-workplace spouses had numerous home objects in their work spaces that were brought to work in their work bags, including kids' drawings, as illustrated by one man's reflection:

> Sometimes it's nice when I talk to people with whom I have a little more than just a professional relationship . . . the family artwork creates some bridge, like a straw to hold onto sometimes when there is need. Sometimes work can be overwhelming, and if there is a window through which to notice another world that's out there and that is relevant, too, it can be a refuge . . . my role as a father and a husband, I think, is also accepted by most people at work, and so I don't shy away from showing symbols that reveal that other existence—they mean something.[24]

With this example, the fact that his spouse was not at the same place meant that other workers had to be reminded of his family members. But more than that, perhaps he had to be reminded of family because he was not able to see the in-person versions of family during the paid workday. The substitutes were there to bridge the worlds, and make him feel better about why he was working so hard in the first place. Further, he did not need to avoid showing signs of family members, because he already had an independent workplace identity separate from his spouse. Nepotism and special favors to family members in the office were not issues for people who did not share a workplace. Further, as is clear from the above comments, home was seen by respondents as a refuge or a joyful place, while work was a demanding necessity. The greedy workplace was already so present in people's hectic lives that they wanted to point the directional arrow from home to work to remind them of other parts of their lives, but only if their coworkers were not their spouses, too.

CALENDARS

Life is hectic, perceived to be due in part to the demands of paid work, and also because of how busy our family lives have become. So many appointments on the calendar, so many work tasks spilling into the evenings. All of this busy-ness suggests we may have less free time than we used to. Or do we have more?

The answer to the question of more and less is actually yes, to both. But how can that be right? On one hand, studies that ask Americans to track their daily tasks in diary form find that we have more free time than in the past, and that we do not have a shortage of leisure time. It's just that the leisure activities tend to be located more at home than in the past. At the same time, though, in study after study, work hours seem to be increasing and families perceive their lives to be increasingly hectic and busy, with each day requiring way more than twenty-four hours in it to get everything done. While being busy affects all families, this is especially true in single-parent families, as well as in dual-parent families where both parents perform paid work.[25] What this tells us is that what families actually do and how they perceive it may be mismatched. Additionally, how people perceive free time and how social scientists measure it may be different. Add to this the fact that many of us cannot distinguish work from family time if we are multitasking, and the answer to all of this is just plain puzzling.

Think about time. Do you have enough of it? How do you measure it? What segments of time are most meaningful to you and why? Do you ever define time by type of task or quality of the moment rather than number of minutes? As a sociologist, I think of time as socially constructed. That means that how we measure it, whether we think we have enough, and how much we think we need for certain tasks are defined by us. And even the tools we use to track time have sociological importance, since our perceptions can be affected by our exposure to reminders of time (every ding from our smartphone ringing like Pavlov's bell), as well as by the people whose lives we intersect that demand our time (every shared calendar invitation for that work committee you really dislike; every calendar marketed to moms who are tasked with managing the entire family's busy schedule). Our lives are increasingly complex in terms of logistics, and our (and our children's, if we have them) lives are increasingly managed and structured.

It may be that we are actually busier. Or it may be that managing all of the complexity and structure that defines our time may be the ingredient that pushes people to perceive their lives as more busy. Even if we have more free time, much of it is interrupted by scheduled activities, and some of it is spent thinking about (and reading social media stories about) how to manage all of it. That makes it feel less free. At the risk of downplaying important research that uncovers real differences in amounts of time different groups spend performing certain tasks (see chapter 5 where I talked about the number of minutes women spend scrubbing a kitchen counter as compared to men), it is the case that, while the actual amount of time spent matters, so does the perception of the way that time is organized in our lives. How often we look at the calendars on our smartphones may be more important than what day it actually is.

And so, I turn to the calendar—besides the clock, the object we most often use to manage our time. As with briefcases and other work bags, calendars can be objects where we make concrete how we think about realms of our lives as segmented or integrated. Having one huge calendar with everything on it for every person in a household represents a highly integrated family life: picture a dentist appointment written next to a job interview, just above the meeting with a child's teacher. But some people prefer separate calendars, each dedicated to a different life realm. This can be represented by two distinct physical calendars (e.g., a wall calendar in a home for family things and a desk calendar at work for during-the-work-day appointments), or it can be represented by using different colors in the same electronic calendar (blue for family events, purple for medical or other personal appointments, green for work, pink for dog grooming appointments, etc.). In both of these instances, life realms and time segments are treated as mutually exclusive categories.

As Christena Nippert-Eng found in her research on home-work boundaries, the more we integrate items on our calendar, the more we are aware of what's going on with all realms of our lives. No wonder we feel busier—the ever-present calendar always visible on our smartphone means we can schedule a doctor appointment while we're on a conference call at work, and we can send a text about our child's track meet while we're at the grocery store. We can look at our time in days, weeks, or months, depending on how much detail we want to see. Even if we want to segment our life realms and think of ourselves as different people in different places, it's getting harder and harder to do so. In the blink of an eye, one look at my calendar calls to mind my role as a mom, wife, professor, writer, friend, traveler, community volunteer, daughter, music enthusiast, dog owner, medical patient, and a person who made it to a total of one yoga class before she gave up.

My sister-in-law recently sent me a picture of her family calendar—an antique French door with multiple separate glass panels propped up against their hallway, each panel filled with inked details on scheduled activities for each family member. In my family, we have a family wall calendar, but we always forget to write on it because both my husband and I share an online calendar that we can reference by pulling our smartphones out—smartphones that are also our clocks. And, each of the activities that my husband, my son, and I are involved in has a separate paper calendar, so our hallway bulletin board is plastered with music, sports, and club schedules on separate sheets, all nicely pinned next to an empty wall calendar we use to remember what month it is when we look at the other calendars. Even though my in-laws write their stuff down on a large physical door calendar and we type ours into a pocket-sized piece of technology, the events, tasks, and appointments in both cases are written down, shared, and sometimes even color coded. And our looking at them affects how we think about time.

Where families keep their calendars have been called "logistical command centers," and families seem to have no shortage of calendars these days.[26] Research from anthropologists at UCLA's Center on the Everyday Lives of Families on Los Angeles homes shows an average of more than five calendars per household examined (each household had parents and two or three children with at least one between the ages of seven and twelve). And this was in addition to the pieces of paper attached to refrigerator doors that contained sports schedules, work and social events, and day-by-day school lunch menus. While a lot of past research centered on the kitchen as the hub of family scheduling and logistical arrangements, the infiltration of smartphones and shared on-line calendars has permeated family lives, making the location of a family calendar (if there is one) less likely to be found in a singular physical "command center" in a home.

My research on calendars as tools to either segment or integrate work and family roles adds to this discussion.[27] When I interviewed married people who shared a workplace, occupation, or both, I found that spouses who shared workplace *and* occupation (e.g., both lawyers at the same law firm) had the highest level of work-family integration along one important symbolic measure: the use of calendars. Most people I interviewed used calendars of some sort—pocket calendars, appointment books, palm pilots (this was a few years ago), wall calendars, computer calendars—for a variety of reasons, from simply knowing what day it was to writing every detail of work and family life in a highly organized day planner.

Those who shared occupation and workplace intimately commingled work events and reminders on their home calendars (usually in the kitchens) and home events and reminders on their work calendars. These people were likely to have one "master" calendar that had everything on it—as one interviewee said, "every work commitment, every personal commitment, every child's appointment or school activity, and addresses." For couples who didn't share both workplace and occupation, the most likely cross-realm items on home and work calendars were those things that had a direct impact on time spent in the other realm. For instance, a doctor's appointment was listed on a work calendar when it was scheduled during the paid workday. A work trip was noted on a home calendar so the family could see when that parent would be unavailable during "nonwork" hours.

How we think of time is affected by how we think of home and work spaces. And we use objects to assist our management of both time and space. If a family member is also a coworker, this whole process gets complicated. But it also shows us that our home and work selves are not mutually exclusive. These territories of the self are overlapping, sometimes invasive (especially in the greedy workplace-to-home direction with the assistance of technology), and important locations for us to enact our family roles.

REFLECTING ON OUR STUFF

Homes show how the boundaries between public and private matter for families. People who integrate their work and family lives, either via work bags or calendars, have few boundaries between spaces that are easy to see, and easy movement between them. When we blur the boundaries between work and home, people in both realms get to see what we're doing. For people who keep these realms separate, we see an increasingly challenging task given the way that technology pokes holes in any boundaries we build to keep work out of home or home out of work.

We live in a time when our workplaces get greedier and greedier, and when our home lives are more and more likely to be the subject of public social media spaces. With more fences being taken down (I can work from anywhere!) and more cameras capturing every movement of life (I can share my kid's Halloween costume with people I don't even know on Instagram!), more conversations about the value of privacy spring up. What this tells me is that, despite evidence that the realms of work and family are becoming increasingly integrated, we are thirsty for some space to sort out things we deem private. And research supports this thirst.

Homes tell us about individual families, but also about broader social issues. Sometimes boundaries between work and home are created for us, as with rules about sharing confidential work information with family members or limitations at work on whether we can plaster our cubicle with pictures of our dog. And sometimes we do the boundary work and create the boundaries ourselves. In either case, boundaries between our life realms are not reducible to individual choices or how easy it is to reach our computer bag or calendar; they are socially constructed. The mental and social boundaries we create, or that are sometimes created for us, can be represented and reinforced by physical boundaries between spaces and objects, whether via a door to separate a home office space or via a different color on someone's smartphone calendar app.

One of the intriguing things about boundaries between work and home is that they affect how we think of our identities. My work self may be different from my home self. It may be the case that I have chosen these different versions of self because I have a lot of discretion over when and where I do my work. But for many people, this choice is limited, depending on their employment status, type of work, and ability to control their work spaces. Having a home office is a luxury and is associated with a particular kind of work. Having the luxury of autonomy and access to work that allows for movement of ideas and papers and e-mails needs to be contextualized in terms of gender, race, parental status, type of work, and socioeconomic standing.

Homes are not only symbolic, but also shape our lives. We notice how much we integrate our home and work lives when someone points it out or forces us to switch between realms. (Hold on, my son just asked me a question. Okay, I'm back. But now I've lost track of what I was writing, so I'll just move on to the next paragraph.)

When I walk by my basement home office, I cringe a little bit when I'm feeling as if I'm not getting enough work done. Little does this lovely room know how much boundary work it makes me perform. Or perhaps it does know, and takes pleasure in serving as a visible reminder of a greedy workplace. Of course, no matter how many times I walk by my office, my inclination is to be drawn upstairs instead, into the sunlight in our dining room, so that my basement-phobic dog can lie at my feet and my snacks can avail themselves to me. Of course, situating myself in this beckoning work space, while seeming like a lovely choice, also means I get interrupted by dog snores and afterschool questions about snacks. I am visible, so I am available. The public definition of our dining room acts upon me. My work has leaked into my home, but the interruptions that come with a pet and family mean my home life leaks into my work too. It is no wonder that current workers' mental energy is often spent thinking about how and whether to separate home and work, even though both are increasingly looking like blobs that just make up the space of life.

7

SEPARATED FAMILIES

Sofa Beds, Laptops, and Cell Phones

TWO BEDROOMS IN TWO HOMES

I am fascinated by research that uncovers the meaning of children's drawings. Today, if I were to take a sample of drawings of homes from the kids in my son's middle-school class, surely there'd be some depicting a pointy-roofed house with a mom and a dad, a kid or two, a dog, a pristine fence, and a tree. And there'd also be these images: a home with a fence tipped over, no dog, and grandparents but no parents; an apartment with a child and a dad (who's only there when he's not working nights); a farm with horses and cats, two moms, and an auntie; and probably more than a handful where the child needs to decide which of two homes to draw because she spends time with each parent in separate places since they split up, or since one parent lives here and the other lives in the country from which some of their family emigrated.

This last example—where a child shuttles between two homes—is increasingly common. Because of demographic shifts, changing norms about what counts as a family, and increasing geographic mobility, we need to revise the image that may pop into our heads when we see the phrase *childhood home*. Gone are the days of the ubiquitously drawn pointy-roofed house. In fact, those days have never really existed for people who could not afford a roof, or who could not live under the same one. Children spend time in multiple households for all sorts of reasons, and they always have. Today, though, the reasons may look a little more varied as compared to a few decades ago, and we're probably talking about it more. Maybe their family moves to a new home every few years because a parent switches jobs multiple times. Maybe they spend all of their weekends with grandparents. Maybe one parent is in another country, either working or receiving financial help from a parent in this country. Maybe they are homeless and couch surf with friends and cousins. Maybe their parents live in two different homes because they've split up or never lived under the same roof. While this chapter focuses primarily on families where parents go from living together to living apart, and the experiences that children have as a result, the types of families that experience living under two roofs are quite varied.

Common with parental divorce and separation is having a child move back and forth between parental homes per a custody arrangement. This means the child has two sleeping spaces, and must move his or her things back and forth between two homes. For children and parents alike, home objects can change meaning over time and between household members, which is especially visible during and after the emotional negotiations over possessions during and after a divorce. From music collections to wedding rings, for the adults in a relationship that has dissolved, the objects of the marriage transition into the objects of divorce, and it is during this transition that the objects' meaning changes to express the shifting identities of partners or spouses into exes. Identities change during a divorce, and so does the stuff that represents those changing identities. In the deliberation about who gets what, these objects become symbolic of identities, sometimes as a couple and sometimes as an individual. Managing the objects is part of the relationship dissolution process.[1] Although children do not divide the spoils in quite the same way as their parents after a divorce, the displacement, loss, and division of their personal possessions between two homes has implications for changes in their identity, too. Spending time in two sleeping spaces, and either bringing things back and forth or having two sets of their possessions can show us how kids experience their daily lives after their parents' divorce.

The following quote helps to make vivid how children's experiences living in two homes play out. It is a compilation of children's words in family therapist Isolina Ricci's 2006 book *Mom's House, Dad's House for Kids*:

> What makes a place feel like home to you? Some kids say, "My parent is there, so it's home." "My siblings are there with me." "My stuff is there." "A bed that's mine." "I have a spot that's mine." "Furniture and things from my old home." "I helped pick out things for it."[2]

These are words from children Ricci has counseled as they've experienced their parents' divorce. The book is designed to be a self-help guide for children, and there's a companion book for the parents. What's interesting about these quotes is the mention of the importance of home spaces and objects in kids' definition of home. Having a "spot that's mine" is listed alongside being with family members in these children's understanding of what counts as a "home."

Psychologist Judith Wallerstein, known for her decades of research on the effects of divorce on children, once said that divorce can sometimes turn children into "mere property," as if the conflict between parents yields a division of all that is theirs, where not only does the bedroom set need to be divided, the children do, too.[3] We know that children have opinions that affect their desire and willingness to go to a parent's house, opinions that include not only their relationship with their parent, but also the condition, location, and features of that parent's home. But the children, Wallerstein says, are often excluded from the deliberations about custody, which means they don't get much of a voice when it comes to choosing where they'll spend their time.

In light of Wallerstein's nod to the finding that children care about the features of a parent's home, I believe that we also need to talk about the *property of children* if we want to understand the divorce experience more fully. The stuff of childhood (its objects and spaces), as chapter 4 discusses, tells us about how we think about children—what they're capable of, where they should be seen, what they need to thrive, and what we do or don't buy for them in an attempt to have them have "good" childhoods. The divorce experience for kids should be part of this discussion. Bringing digital music players or a favorite stuffed animal back and forth to parents' places, choosing a specific type of bag used to transport clothes and toiletries between parents' houses, being involved in the decorating of a bedroom at one parent's house but not the other's, transporting a laptop computer to do homework in two homes, and wanting to be at the parent's house who has faster Internet—all of these examples demonstrate how home spaces and objects (even virtual ones) can symbolize the transitional spaces and identity formation for kids of divorced parents. Further, these objects and places of divorce can demonstrate how parents relate to their children via their stuff.

Sociologist Thomas Gieryn posited in his article "A Space for Place in Sociology" that attachment to a space brings with it personal benefits, and the loss of that space can have consequences. Space can help define an identity (both individual and collective), facilitate a sense of security and well-being, nurture a feeling of belonging, evoke or stabilize memories, and/or embody history. This is what it means to turn a *space* into a *place*. As anthropologist Anat Hecht noted, homes are "private museums of symbolic roots."[4] Whether we're talking about moving homes, being homeless, or moving back and forth between homes, people often feel as though they have lost an individual or collective identity, memory, or history when they lose a space, or that they are missing the sense of security that came with that space. It follows, then, that a loss of place, of home, even if it is just for a portion of the time, as it may be for kids whose parents get divorced or separated (sometimes referred to as *family dissolution*), is likely to affect people who experience that loss. In the case of divorce, it is possible for family members, and especially children, to feel a sense of loss because their home spaces change, or can even go away. This may make their own private sleeping spaces even *more* important to them, since these are more likely to be spaces where children have at least some control. Earlier in the book I said that when things disappear, we are more likely to think about them as being important. We don't know what we've got until it's gone. If a child changes spaces, it takes some adjustment to figure out what the space means (or meant) in terms of his or her understanding of what feels (or felt) like "home." This isn't to say that it's all bad. It's just to say that it takes some energy to figure out what the spaces may mean if they change.

If people move to a new environment, turning a space into a place usually requires meaningful objects. If objects are taken, lost, moved, or labeled unnecessary, people may have a harder time doing this. And then, if a place goes away, objects with memories and meaning attached to them can become even more important. In the case of divorce, feelings of insecurity or unfamiliarity can accompany a change in or lessening of an individual family member's control over his or her stuff. For a child whose parents divorce, the transition may be easier if she is able to make a place for herself in two home spaces by surrounding herself with security objects that help her construct or reinforce her identity on her own terms. And even if this doesn't happen, or may not need to happen, her stuff and her space(s) can help tell the story of how she is experiencing her family life during a transition such as a divorce.

FAMILIES IN SEPARATE PLACES

In order to understand how spaces and objects in the case of family dissolution or separation matter, it is important to discuss three big issues that matter in contemporary family life: the changing nature of family composition, the importance of understanding the divorce experience for kids, and the role that life stage (and spatial) transitions play in our understanding of families.

A New Architecture of Families and Family Spaces

The old blueprint for what families look like, who is included, and where they live has been replaced with multiple new plans. Social psychologist Bella DePaulo, in her book *How We Live Now: Redefining Home and Family in the 21st Century*, unpacks just what's behind this new set of blueprints as she shares numerous stories of families who are creatively reshaping how we think of family, from groups of single neighbors who form tiny house communities and created families, to married couples who choose to live apart. In a nutshell, how families live now is as varied as the architectural styles of their dwellings. When families change membership, the spaces may change. What these changes look like today is not uniform. DePaulo attributes this variation to the value of choice—people are creating what she calls *do-it-yourself lifespaces*.[5]

What might make someone have two bedrooms or sleeping spaces in two different homes? Certainly the separation of parents due to divorce is a logical subject to discuss when making the point that families can often be found living in more than one space. But other family experiences are relevant, too. The more family life changes to include parents who never live together, communal living, transnational families with members living in two different countries (this happens for military families, too), combined families, commuter partnerships, and people who are partnered but live apart (as mentioned earlier, referred to as LATs—living-apart-together couples), the less we ought to rely on one kind of image, or one dwelling, to represent home.

Another example where adults have more than one sleeping spot is in a new kind of parenting arrangement, both increasingly practiced and present in popular television shows such as *Transparent*, called *birdnesting*. This family form is when parents separate and share custody of children who stay in the home. The parents rotate in and out of the home per the custody arrangements, often to create a sense of stability for the children and sometimes to save money because the nonresident parent space does not need to accommodate children and can therefore be less expensive.[6] More common in cases where parents split up and share physical custody, however, is the movement of children back and forth between two homes.

Families, like homes, can be reimagined, remodeled, and renovated. Like other parts of a home, family relationships sometimes break, sometimes need to be repaired, and sometimes end up being stronger afterward. Part of the process of splitting up is a remaking of the spaces and objects that are part of the family's experiences. New photos are hung that may exclude one parent. New toothbrushes are placed in a bathroom. New bedding is used in new beds. Or, perhaps, nothing new happens and one of the sleeping spaces for a child of divorce is part of a newly defined multiuse space.

Are the Kids Alright?

Research is mixed on how children fare after parents split up. Some researchers point to concerns about children's ability to do well in school, stay out of trouble, or even have successful relationships later in life. Others point to how divorce brings kids out of bad situations that could be more damaging than splitting apart.[7] Sociologist Constance Ahrons's important 2004 research[8] finds that there are plenty of *good divorces*, in which family connections and success are preserved even as a marriage is dissolved. In some cases, family members are able to figure out effective communication and coparenting practices that may end up serving the children well in the long run. But these divorces are rarely discussed because they call into question the nostalgic image of the traditional American family.

While most research, when looked at in aggregate, points to impacts that are rarely always harmful or always helpful, there is not a lot that investigates how spaces and objects help us understand the divorce experience for kids. As Judith Wallerstein finds, the divorce or separation experience allows children to gain skills such as time management, organization, feelings of independence, a willingness to take risks, and an ability to deal with diverse social situations and difficult people. These may be the result, in part, of having to spend time in two places and manage two sets of possessions.

Having two childhood bedrooms or sleeping spaces matters not just for people interested in divorce outcomes, but also for those interested in how *room culture* matters for children and adolescents.[9] How children identify themselves and what they think about their family relationships can be seen by looking at what they include, how they decorate, and what they do in their bedrooms. It is important to study how kids use, modify, and talk about their private spaces because very little public or private space is deemed theirs in today's society.[10] Sociologist Jill McCorkel called these spaces *critical spaces*, which can nurture young people's ability to create identities, to counter claims of adults, and to feel safe.[11] Without access to critical spaces like bedrooms, children and adolescents may find it more difficult to construct identities that resist the identity demands of adults (which is a normal part of the growing up process, or so I'd like to claim to justify how annoying I must have been to my parents in my teenage years). So, if the divorce experience for kids includes them changing their individual identities as the family identity changes, and if we can see changing identity by looking at a child's use of space and objects, then researchers need to pay attention to the spaces where this process takes place.

As I found in my own research discussed in more detail below, children can feel displaced after a divorce, or, in other words, they can feel as if they're not sure where their "home" is anymore. This feeling of displacement often results from a family being split in two, having to move out of the home in which they had lived (at least for some of the time), and feeling like they no longer have a center or a home because their family does not live under one roof anymore. Often, in order for children to feel *emplaced*, to feel as if they have a home, is to ensure that they have social connections to help them feel supported. These can come in the form of friends, teachers, and siblings. In today's families, these connections can also be maintained by using smartphones and laptops to communicate with others who may not be in the home. The maintenance of social connections can help children whose parents split up feel as if they have multiple sites of support. If they are old enough to talk with others using communication technology, they can also feel as if they have some control over this virtual space.

Where a child lives after a divorce depends on custody arrangements. It is still the case in the United States that mothers in heterosexual couples are more likely to get legal and physical custody of children than fathers, but custody matters for both moms and dads, and regardless of whether the parents are heterosexual.[12] When parents, sometimes with the involvement of a mediator or judge, plan custody and visitation schedules during and after a divorce, they often are intricately planned out, including rotation of certain weekdays, weeknights, weekends, months, and even years. Winter and summer vacations are sometimes broken up into equal halves and these schedules often rotate on even- and odd-numbered years for each parent. Holidays often present a quandary for divorced or separated families, and parents or courts often draw up complex plans including the hour and day children will switch houses to certain parents depending on whether it is an odd- or even-numbered year.

Many divorce experts call out to parents and clinicians to recognize the importance of the child's preferences and needs when setting custody and visiting schedules, as well as reviewing and revising these schedules periodically as the child's circumstances and developmental stage change. As the rest of this chapter outlines, listening to how kids talk about their spaces and objects can be an important part of the conversation, too.

Transitions between Life Stages and Spaces

If you move into a different home, you are likely more aware of how space matters to you compared to when you spent your everyday life there. Changing, losing, or switching between spaces matters in how we think about families, mostly because these transitions actually make us think about the importance of space and things more than we would otherwise. Jackie Goode articulated this well in 2007, when she wrote,

> When a marriage breaks down, what has been "taken up" and what "projected" is laid bare and becomes subject to competing claims of "how it was." Here, contested claims of ownership of items . . . , made while "dividing the spoils," render the organization of social, cultural and aesthetic relations more visible. [13]

This chapter, to some extent, is about being transitory, being unfixed, being perhaps unsure, and seeing oneself as identifiable not with one particular home. Like the college students' decisions to bring or leave at home their childhood stuffed animals discussed in chapter 2, going through a life transition can bring to light how someone identifies him- or herself.

In cases where parents decide to split up, the consideration of children's things does not go away. In fact, it may become even more present in the minds of the parents and children. When you divide a household, you have to decide who gets what things and who gets what spaces. For children whose parents divorce or split up, their stuff gets defined differently. It is divided between two homes (some clothes here, some clothes there), transported between them (a favorite stuffed animal), or sometimes purchased twice so it can be available in both homes (two toothbrushes).

Sociologists know that times of transition sometimes help us understand our social world more clearly. This is true for individuals, families, and even large communities. We learn about ourselves when we are forced to change. How we deal with change tells us a lot about what we value, what we fear losing, what we keep, and whether we agree or disagree with other people regarding the change. Divorce transitions help us see how individual children's relationships with either parent play out, and they help us see how children spending time in two home spaces matters in those relationships. As I discuss below, I researched this by analyzing lengthy interview data from young adults whose parents had divorced. Turns out, their bedrooms and belongings mattered a lot when they talked about the whole experience. The fact that they went through a life transition by spending time in two homes meant that they became more aware of the importance of spaces and objects in their understanding of family.

A SOFA BED

Family life consists of transitions, and so might the rooms and the furniture in our homes. Years ago when someone I know remarried and bought a house with his new wife, I remember his young children telling me how they couldn't wait to have me visit, since they got to decorate their own rooms at their dad's new house. Before this time, their dad had primarily lived in rental houses, so the only way they could claim bedrooms as theirs was through their things, not by painting a wall. Their dad and new stepmom had told them that they could choose the wall and bedspread colors. And so, when I showed up and saw their rooms, I was delighted to see the boldest wall color combinations that, in my estimation, had ever been featured in a suburban bedroom. What this showed me was that the kids in this new combined family valued the ability to control their new spaces. Sure, they had rooms to sleep in at their mom's house, where they spent the most time, but now that they felt as if the rooms in their dad's house were actually *theirs*, perhaps (wished their dad) they'd want to spend more time there.

It was this experience that inspired a line of interview research I conducted a few years ago with Caitlyn Collins.[14] After talking with twenty-two young adults whose parents had divorced (and looking at pictures of their rooms), we learned a lot about their sleeping spaces—the wall colors, the favorite objects, the things they brought back and forth between two homes. But more important, we learned how the definition of where they slept, what they slept on, and their control over these mattered in terms of how they talked about their relationships with both parents.

There are innovative furniture companies that are capitalizing on the creation of two households after a divorce, especially when one household may have limited space. One website articulates, "Insofar as changing the furniture is concerned, two prominent instances of home transformation come to mind: the office by day and children's bedroom by weekend, and the living room by day and bedroom by night."[15] And the site continues:

> How happy the divorcee is by day needs to match the ease by which day converts to night and vice versa. The trick is the conversion and multifunctional furniture helps pull this off! Like magic, sofas transform into beds, coffee tables into dining tables, ottomans into storage boxes, bookshelves into nightstands, console tables into desks, chairs into ladders and so on and so forth. Creating adjustable spaces helps take an ostensibly difficult time and turn it into a fun and flexible environment. Maintaining a balance between having a "family" home by weekend and a "single" home during the week is made possible through the use of transforming furniture.

These pieces of advice, to some extent, make sense for parents who are labeled as "part-time" or "weekend" parents. And sometimes the ideas are presented as if the default room configuration is a child's sleeping space rather than a living space for the parent. For example, one website advertises the Ikea Stora lofted bed, or the Brekka twin bed that has drawers underneath and looks like a bed but can convert to a sofa when the child is with the other parent.[16] Of course, only some people can afford a large enough space for new furniture, or furniture that transforms from a sofa into a bed that is even a little bit comfortable. So, acknowledging that parents who divorce cannot often afford two homes that have the same amount of space and type of accoutrements as the pre-divorce home, what do children make of ideas like this?

Our research shows that kids do not care how big their sleeping space is or how fancy the furniture is. They only care that they have control over it and that it is theirs more than anything else. This means that a spot in one parent's home that serves a purpose beyond the child's needs is seen as undesirable. Take a sofa bed. This signifies a temporariness to the space in terms of calling it someone's bedroom. Children's feeling as if they have control over a space, and a space to call their own (even when they're not there), may be more important than having a large spot that serves purposes beyond their stays with one parent. A feeling of permanence, rather than transition, is what the kids want.

If the post-divorce arrangements include a plan for one parent to use a space for more than that dedicated to the child (even a tiny space), the child may feel as if he or she is a transitory guest in a home that is not theirs. A sofa that's also a bed means it's not just a child's bed. For parents who may wonder how best to accommodate children given limited resources, our research reveals that at least having a conversation with a child about the importance of the control over space (and its single or multiple use) would be helpful indeed. Kids can't always get what they want, and families can't always provide the things they want for their kids, but having an honest conversation about how a child thinks about her or his space, and control over it, should be a helpful part of divorce conversations more generally. This is because space and objects represent concrete parts of the identity transformation process that kids go through when their parents split up.

LAPTOP AND CELL PHONE

Communicating with friends and family members is more and more likely to include digital communication devices, from video chats on a laptop or smartphone to messages shared with family on social media platforms. According to the Pew Research Center, nine out of ten Americans across a wide variety of geographic areas and demographic groups have a cell phone, and three-quarters have a computer. The number of laptop owners has risen particularly fast, up to 45 percent from just 3 percent in 2010.[17] Laptop and tablet computers, as well as smartphones, are increasingly popular because they allow for the portability of work and other tasks, and some versions are more affordable than in the past. In terms of home use, if someone spends time in two different family homes, whether because their parents live in separate homes, or because they work in a different geographic location than where the rest of the family lives, the use of a laptop or smartphone could be instrumental not just to do work or send an e-mail because they are portable, but also in order to see and hear distant family members via audio and video chat platforms. So, these pieces of technology allow for the portability of tasks in the physical presence of others in two different spaces, and they allow for the portability of family members (at least their faces and their voices on a screen) who are located in two different physical places.

In terms of children's experiences living in two different homes with separated parents specifically, a laptop and cell phone may travel back and forth, especially if the child is old enough, in which case it may be used for logistical communication and/or schoolwork. Research on how communication technology in divorced or separated families is used by parents after they get divorced shows us that its use is impacted by the quality of the parental relationship. For parents who have a good relationship with each other, they can use technology to more effectively share coparenting duties and information with each other. Planning is easier for these families. But in families where divorced parents have a poor-quality relationship, technology may be used to avoid face-to-face or telephone conversations and in attempts to control or judge a partner's parenting decisions.[18]

My own interview research with Caitlyn Collins on young adults whose parents have divorced helps us see how digital communication technologies matter not just for parents, but also for the kids themselves.[19] Many of our twenty-two interviewees talked at length about their use of computers, Internet, and cell phones. In addition to participants using technology, particularly television and computer/video games, as a means of entertainment, they also referenced the use of technology to personalize a space at a parent's house. For example, a number of people used the music on their portable laptop computers (this was before cell phones were also likely to be portable music devices) to personalize their space wherever they went. When asked if she brought any favorite items back and forth between homes, one person commented, "It's like a connection to my life, I *love* music . . . because it's mine, I try to make it, I don't know, my area, my space." Another interviewee articulated that "music, it's basically music that has always connected me between places."

All of the people we interviewed discussed the importance of computers, the Internet, and cell phones in communication. The latter proved to be particularly important to people in our study because they had a need to be in contact not with one parent, but two, since they did not live in the same residence. One woman explained the importance of this technology in aiding with transportation, custody, and visitation arrangements: "Once we had cell phones it was a lot easier . . . my dad would call from like the halfway point or when he thought he was half an hour away and then me and [my sister] would quickly pack up our stuff." In some families, this communication not only allows for efficiency but can also mean that parents who do not get along need not meet face-to-face for the kids to move between households. This can be seen as fostering independence in the children. But it can also be seen as problematic because it fails to foster the opportunity for parents to productively interact with each other face-to-face.

Respondents also stressed the importance of feeling connected and reachable. The lack of this connectivity at one parent's home or the other often resulted in feeling bored, annoyed, and lonely. One woman explained that at her dad's house, "I would just feel kinda stuck, especially with no Internet, I just get really antsy there unless I go there specifically to hang out but otherwise I think I'm like, 'there's nothing to do.'" Conversely, respondents seemed satisfied when their ability to connect was equal at both houses, evidenced by this quote: "Well, we had Internet at both houses, thank goodness. I don't think I'd be able to live without Internet. I'm a twenty-first-century girl." When asked if he had any favorite items he brought back and forth between houses, one man said, "Well, my computer because it's my life . . . the laptop's easy, because I take it wherever I go." Another interviewee got a laptop so she could easily do homework at both houses: "I started to need to type things up and write papers and they were on different computers and there were times when I would, like, need to work on a paper and realize it was saved on the computer at my mom's house and it was at Dad's house and it was due the next day." Technology was used, then, to help respondents feel more organized and connected, but only when it was available. If it wasn't equally available, the kids were more likely to note how it impacted their everyday lives.

Generally, children were more willing and interested to go over to a parent's house if they had the phones, Internet, and other pieces of technology that made it comfortable, convenient, and home-like to them. This shows the striking differences in the eyes of children of each parent's affluence or provision of certain expensive items. One person, for example, explained that she never spent the night at her father's house as a young adult because "I need to be using the phone and the Internet and the car every day and I think that it's those that aren't available to me there. . . . [At my mom's the] Internet is here, my clothes are here, the car is here, yeah, it's just a lot of stuff that is really useful for me to use. There's a phone line here, there's not a phone line at my dad's because we both have cell phones." For another woman, her father's refusal to get a cell phone or use the one she bought him resulted in her seeing him less often because he was so hard to contact. Another person explained how the technology at his mother's increased his desire to be over there and actually shifted the time spent proportionally at each house:

> It probably became 60–40 in effect. . . . The faster Internet was over there, so when I was always doing homework and everything like that, it was better, and because it was—this was shallow and superficial of me—but I was in middle school and high school, because it was the "nicer" house and the "richer" house, it would be what I wanted my friends to see or people to see.

Remember when I mentioned that transitions can sometimes help us see what we value? When we don't have something, we realize we want it. Along these lines, respondents who had very little to say about the significance of technology in their lives as children growing up in a divorced family were those whose houses had no discrepancies in the amount or types of technology. Their awareness of the role that technology played in their relationships with both parents after a divorce, as well as their awareness of how that technology affected their everyday freedom to use their time as they wished, was more likely in cases where the two homes had different levels or types of technology available for their use. One woman, for example, had an equally nice computer at each house: "It was never like, 'I need to stay at Mom's this weekend because I need to write a paper' type thing, we could always just take that to the other house and work on it there. And just take the floppy disk it was on, you know." Oppositely, one man explained that it was a big inconvenience and source of discomfort that there was a disparity in the computers at his parents' homes:

> Because the computer at my dad's house was like the family computer and it was also a lot slower and the Internet worked sparingly, I couldn't do schoolwork on it, well I could do schoolwork on it of course, but it was trying and took way more time and all sorts of stuff like that. So, yeah, during a lot of high school, one of the big things I would say is, "I'm going over to mom's house to work on a report." . . . And he'd say, "Why don't you do it here?" And I'd say "um . . ." because I didn't want to say "the stuff over there is nicer."

The language used by these respondents is different than those who had similar technological capacity at both homes. They often discussed their homes not as "mom's and dad's" but "mom's versus dad's" (or in a few cases for those with same-sex parents, "mom's and mom's"), thereby seeing the difference between the two as an inequality. Even though the quotes above are about desktop computers that are not transported between houses like laptops are, and even though they are stories from older kids whose families had enough resources to provide computers for schoolwork, they both highlight the importance of technology in the divorce experience for kids and they show how differences in access to technology change their impression of both homes. As with the aforementioned idea that life transitions can help us see what we value more clearly, seeing differences between two home spaces in terms of technology may make people more aware of the importance of that technology in their everyday lives.

One may be tempted to conclude from these interview excerpts that getting better technology may make a parent-child relationship better after a divorce. But this would be the wrong conclusion to draw. Importantly, for many interview respondents, the relationship quality with a parent *preceded* the desire to spend time at that parent's house, regardless of how fast the Internet connection was. It is not as if the parent with the better technology won. Rather, a discussion of technology is often a tangible way for young adults to talk about their past and present daily lives, especially if, as noted above, technological tools for everyday life are more available at one parent's house than another's. Technology becomes a tangible representation of how differences between the objects available in homes can highlight differences in how kids see their connection to these homes. For younger children, these connections may be a little harder to figure out.

REFLECTING ON OUR STUFF

Homes show how the boundaries between public and private matter for families. There's the private divorce and the public divorce. The one that the family experiences, and the one that results in friendships being divided, social media accounts being blocked, kids' friends being either supportive or not, and a legal record. The spaces occupied and the objects that fill them are meaningful in the divorce and separation experience to be sure, not just to the individuals who may attach meaning to them, but also to the larger world. This is because sofa beds, laptops, and a gallon of brightly colored paint used to remake a sleeping space are part of a larger system of economic exchange. This marketplace contains buying and selling of things that matter in particular for families undergoing divorce or other splitting. For example, divorce-as-commodity is ever-present in places such as *Divorce Magazine* (divorcemag.com), which has created prepackaged advertising options for attorneys and financial planners whose services may be useful for couples undergoing a divorce. Controversial advertising images used by divorce lawyers to attract clients are being discussed on law marketing blogs.[20] Finally, the high divorce rate in many countries is sometimes placed in a long list of societal ills that relate directly or indirectly to other societal ills, including heightened stress, increased individualism, and an increased need for immediate gratification. (In the United States, the projected likelihood for couples to divorce is still hovering around 50 percent, but the divorce *rate* has been declining for several years and is now at fewer than seventeen divorces per 1,000 married women who are at least fifteen years old.[21]) Thus, while home consumption (buying stuff) can be affected by changes in household formation (e.g., deciding whether to buy a twin bed or a sofa bed for a child who sleeps at two different homes), the culture of divorce itself is subject to consumption practices that go beyond private households and help to tell the story of larger public values and economic practices.

Homes tell us about individual families, but also about broader social issues. Children whose parents get divorced undergo identity transformation, sometimes related to the spaces they occupy and the items they choose to bring back and forth between two homes. This is especially important in light of the fact that kids are more likely to be found indoors today than in the past, and they need spaces to feel safe, free, independent, and perhaps even free from adult control. That's how growing up works. When parents get divorced, it is not necessarily a precarious situation, but it does carry with it change and negotiation. Involving children in how time, space, and objects play a role is important in this negotiation.

The divorce experience is not only different for adults and children, it varies depending on the family's access to financial resources that allow (or disallow) for a second home, new furniture, communication technology, or transportation between homes. Add to this the fact that individual parents often have different socioeconomic standing after a divorce, which means that any views that children have about whose home has better "stuff" must be couched in terms of that parent's ability to get the stuff in the first place. Reliable Internet is dependent on demographic factors such as social class. So is the possibility of a separate room for sleeping. Because of this, the stories that children tell about their sleeping spaces in two homes shed light on the inequalities that may be operating in society as a whole.

Homes are not only symbolic, but also shape our lives. It would seem strange to place too much importance on something as mundane as a toothbrush. But when one toothbrush has to move between two homes, and a child who is used to a toothbrush in one spot needs to remember to pack it every week, not only does the toothbrush serve as a hygiene tool, it also reminds the child of the transitional nature of his or her family life. Seeing a backpack or duffel bag in the entryway packed for a trip back and forth between parents' homes is a reminder of that transition, of the changing definition of family, and of the identity work that the child must do in two family spaces.

Imagine a woman who marries a man with a teenage daughter. It would not be surprising if she was nervous to have them move into her home and eager to see her new stepdaughter's reaction to the bedroom space that she'd be getting. Of course, the two of them could have a conversation about the significance of this life-stage transition and new family formation, but let's say, instead, she silently shows the girl the room and watches her eyes light up as she gives her dad a "thumbs up" gesture. In this scenario, the space acts on all three of these people without a single word. Of course it is important not to overemphasize the importance of spaces and objects in creating relationships (buying presents or spending oodles of money to redecorate a room for stepchildren is not necessarily an advisable way to strengthen the bond), but this scenario shows us that, at the very least, it is important to understand all of the emotional and identity work that goes into the simple act of sleeping in two different spaces, both for children and for any adult who may enter a family as a stepparent. This understanding can help us recognize how kids' views about their spaces during a big life stage transition should be included in the conversation about the changing architecture of families.

8

BEYOND SINGLE (NUCLEAR) FAMILIES

Dining Tables and Dishes

DINING ROOMS

Imagine you are at a big table with enough food on it to feed a dozen people. All are gathered around the table for a celebratory feast. Who are you imagining at the table? Are they related to each other only by blood or adoption? Are there neighbors or friends? How many generations of people are there? How about first cousins? Or third cousins, twice removed? Would you call all of the people at the table members of your family, and how would you know? What kind of occasion is it? And, isn't it great that Cousin Gus made the effort to come to one of these feasts?

Perhaps you spend all of your free time making *genograms* to figure out how many times removed your cousin Gus is (genograms, by the way, are the fancy family tree diagrams with connecting lines to signify how people are related, shapes to signify people, and special markings to show broken relationship lines, specific health problems, or people no longer alive. You know, genealogy stuff). Or perhaps you spend time just calling Gus your favorite cousin without checking some strange linear family tree diagram to see if he's actually related. In either case, Gus is your cousin, he got invited to the feast, he actually showed up this time, and now you need to find an extra chair.

In the first chapter, I said that homes and families are often connected, sometimes made synonymous. In addition, big feasts like the one I just described are often associated with holidays, rituals and events that mark life stage transitions (e.g., bat mitzvahs, weddings, graduations, funerals), or maybe, for some of you, a weekly tradition. How frequently this feast occurs, where it occurs, and who shows up at the table are all important considerations in our understanding of what different kinds of families do in their homes. How we define family depends on who we are imagining at that feast, and whose home is host to the feast.

When you imagined the table earlier, did you picture it in a room dedicated to eating? If your extended family is like mine, when there are big gatherings, there is no single room big enough (or table long enough) to hold a dozen people. Usually these meals are set up in multiple rooms where at least two wobbly card tables are slid next to Great-Grandma's old wobbly oak table with six leaves precariously placed between the two pull-apart halves. Atop these tables are plastic tablecloths that don't match each other, but that have colors and designs that represent whatever season or holiday is being celebrated, and that cover up the seams between the tables. At the tables are mismatched chairs, sometimes including a piano bench and a lawn chair that needs to be dusted off. It's amazing that more people in my family don't spill all of their food in their lap, what with all the wobbles and gaps and chairs of all heights.

What about meals that occur more frequently, have fewer people, and are more mundane than feastlike? Growing up in a family of five in a ranch-style home that was plenty big but not big enough to have a separate dining room with four walls, most of us ate our everyday dinners at the little table by the refrigerator while my mom leaned over the pullout cutting board on the other end of the kitchen to eat. We would have eaten together at the larger table in our living/dining room space, but it was usually covered with our homework, my mom's work, or travel brochures that my dad was always trying to get around to showing my mom.

Maybe in your family, you have a huge stunning dining room table with matching chairs situated perfectly in a large and ornate dining room that can easily hold a dozen people (preferably dressed up like the lords and ladies of *Downton Abbey*). Or maybe you just eat at a coffee table or lean over a counter while watching *Hoarders*. For special occasions, maybe you meet up with everyone at a park for a picnic and hope that someone remembered to bring the tablecloths because those park tables are known for being targets for birds flying overhead.

Whether we have tables with extension leaves or large extended families, TV trays or a spot at the table for the cat, dining rooms are a great place to think about how we define families, how that definition is changing, and what impacts these changing definitions may be having in our family rituals and use of objects and spaces. This is true whether we're thinking of the tangible tables and spaces where the tables are situated, or if we're thinking of more intangible things, like how family meals are valued because they can promote communication and interpersonal connection.

And what counts as a dining room? Architecture critic Edwin Heathcote said that all it takes to turn a table into a dining table is a cloth. He also said that the dining room is a construction of social class norms and politics, arguing that there is no universal need for a dining room at all, since any surface can be used to eat upon. The dining room is "absolutely pivotal to the idea of the bourgeois dwelling and simultaneously completely dispensable," which means it is not really a functional necessity, but can be a really useful symbol of wealth if people need to show it.[1] The dining room is something that has had its heyday in royal times and places, and during times when the preparation of food was supposed to be kept separate from the eating of it. But really, it's not needed in order to have a home or a family. In contemporary society, we often define the dining room as both a location for hospitality, especially if used for dinner parties with non-family or extended family guests, and a space for individual family connection. But only if they're all there at the same time, and eating.

Today, what we would call a dining room may actually be better named a dining space, which is now more likely to be found in a large open space in an open-concept home (so we can see each other and see what's cooking), or in smaller spaces in older dwellings that are used for multiple tasks. In both cases, family members can perform multiple roles and tasks without being in isolated spaces. Importantly, a dining room is relatively new and frequently only found in places where people can afford to dedicate a separate space for eating. As sociologist Lisa Wade has articulated, dining rooms were not that common in North

America before the 1700s, and now, when older homes within neighborhoods that are being gentrified are remodeled by affluent people,
dining rooms are among the spaces that are commonly added. As Wade
says about home remodeling in New Orleans after Hurricane Katrina,
"The rejection of the traditional floor plan in these remodels—for being
too small, insufficiently private, and un-dining-roomed—hints at a turn
toward a richer sort of resident."[2] Where we break bread is sociologically interesting, especially since breaking bread is one of many tasks done
at a table, and the likelihood of having a dedicated dining space is
dependent on whether people can afford the space.

When my older brothers went off to college, our family meals sometimes consisted of my parents and me gathered at the kitchen table. But
more often than not, I had basketball practice, my mom had evening
work, and my dad had meetings, so a realistic picture of our busy evening dining consisted of me eating my Big Mac in front of the TV while
I did my algebra and my parents eating leftovers at the kitchen counter.
If we add the notion of time to our discussion of dining, then we also
see that whether family members eat with each other may depend not
just on space, but also on whether they're in each other's presence for a
meal at the same time.

BEYOND NUCLEAR FAMILIES AND
SINGLE-FAMILY DWELLINGS

Ever since I began studying families in an academic sense, I have seen
the term *nuclear family* countless times in research and popular writing. I started learning about families around the same time as the Cold
War was ending, so the term *nuclear* always carried with it multiple
meanings for me. The term *nuclear family* is used by social scientists to
refer to a family form where there are two generations, usually consist-
ing of two adults who are parents, and children whom people recognize
as theirs. For years and years, this family form was defined as the most
basic and elementary (and often functional) form to have. Today, the
term has lost favor among many, and among others, its definition has at
least been amended to allow for more flexibility than its past iterations,
where the parents do not need to be married or heterosexual, where
there needn't be two parents, and where the kids can be biological,

adopted, or socially defined as belonging to the adults in other ways. And for still others, the nuclear family with a mom, dad, and two kids is still preferred.

While I began learning about different family forms in sociology and anthropology courses, I began to wonder whether the term *nuclear family* referred to the scientific analogy of an atom nucleus, which contains protons and neutrons and has a boundary around it to keep out the other parts. I always wondered if parents were the protons and children were the neutrons, and I wondered whether grandparents or neighbors or pets were the electrons floating outside the nucleus in a metaphorical cloud. Or maybe, I pondered, the term referred to, and emerged out of, the historical era during which both radioactive threats and in-school war drills were as present as ideals about the family that excluded everyone except Mom, Dad, Dick, Jane, and Spot. Or perhaps, I contemplated, in light of years of critique of the mythical idealized *Leave It to Beaver* family, the word *nuclear* referred to the caution we should use when we want to examine a family form that was both unusual and potentially problematic for many who were in its nucleus. As in, Stay away from that—it's nuclear.

My daydreaming about this term eventually led to a more useful realization: how we come to understand our own families stems from our understandings of the past. How we remember the past happens in our own minds, through the stories told by those who lived it, and in our collective memory through venues like movies, TV shows, and news stories. But in order to understand how families are today, we have to unravel some of what historian Stephanie Coontz calls *nostalgia traps* of the past and look at what families were actually like. This section looks at three things: some of the past myths that matter for understanding families and homes today; the impact of an aging population on family forms; and the ways that creative housing options represent changes that come with demographic shifts and changing (or just more visible) values.

FAMILY VALUES, FAMILY VALUABLES, AND THE ALLURE OF NOSTALGIA

The discussion later in this chapter is about whether and how things that are old ought to be passed down to the newest members of families. This brings to mind the necessity of looking into the past to see whether what mattered then still matters now. As with an antique piece of china, which may contain lead and cannot be put in a dishwasher, it is easy to look nostalgically back at past families with rose-colored glasses and neglect the fact that there may have been hidden (and even toxic) problems that were not easy to get rid of. A lot of political and religious rhetoric hearkens back to a time when things were simpler, family life was somehow better, and there were fewer problems. And, according to Certified Professional Organizer Tammy Schotzko, different family members have different value they place on certain items. Grandma may think a wobbly old oak table is both monetarily and sentimentally valuable, but her grandson may prefer to shop for a new table at Ikea.[3]

But, of course, looking back in time, as is the case with both individual and collective memory, is always flawed and often mythologized. This is the spirit in which historian Stephanie Coontz has written about our erroneous conceptions of past family lives in her book *The Way We Never Were: American Families and the Nostalgia Trap*.[4] Coontz, in all her work, covers multiple myths about family life worth debunking, from gender roles to parenting, from ideals about marriage to norms about sexual deviance. We learn that there has never been such a thing as a normative perfect white picket fence suburban family with no problems. We realize that racial and class inequalities have meant that ideals are just that—idealized images of what is desired, but likely not what is achieved by many families. We come to know that *family values* are highly variable and dependent not just on what people want, but more accurately based on what they are able to achieve. Ultimately, Coontz says, if we trap ourselves in myths of the past, we won't be able to successfully deal with real problems in families today, and we'll be stuck with feelings of guilt and blame that will lead us nowhere when it comes to making family lives in America healthy and strong. It'd be like using glue from 1978 that you found in the back of a junk drawer to fix a brand-new platter that you accidentally broke. The glue won't stick, it probably didn't work that well even in 1978, and the plate will still be broken.

In my work on people's saving and storage and display of family photos and love letters, as discussed in chapters 3 and 4, I got to learn about how people use home objects to remember the past and preserve the present for an imagined future audience. Who knew that something as benign as an old photo album with new pictures saved in a cedar chest for your son's eventual home could incorporate the past, present, and future all at once? But the task of preserving memories is not just a way to preserve what may have actually happened. It can also be a way to preserve what we'd *like* to remember happened (even if it didn't). Just as with a studio family portrait, how a family is represented, either in popular stories or in our minds, is not necessarily how their lives actually play out. And when we're interpreting the past stories of our family life, whether it be through a letter, a photo, a table, or even a news story, it is crucial that we take a step back and remember that we're looking back with today's glasses—glasses that may not always provide a lens into what happened in reality. Or that may not have happened equally for different groups of people.

When it comes to home objects and spaces bringing up memories of the past, it can be really hard to let go. As we go through life, we accumulate possessions. There is no shortage of self-help books and lists of home organization professionals who advocate reducing the number of things we have, especially as we move into later life. Online bookstore shelves are lined with titles like Vicki Dellaquila's *Don't Toss My Memories in the Trash: A Step-by-Step Guide to Helping Seniors Downsize, Organize, and Move*, or Marlene Stum's *Who Gets Grandma's Yellow Pie Plate? Workbook: A Guide to Passing on Personal Possessions*. Not to mention Marie Kondo's popular book *The Life-Changing Magic of Tidying Up: The Japanese Art of Decluttering and Organizing*. We are told constantly to buy things, and now we are told to find a way to manage all of the things we've bought (or inherited).

This plethora of advice exists because it takes work to manage our possessions—where to keep them, how to use them, and what to do when we don't have room for them. And getting rid of them can sometimes require as much effort in the good-bye process as parting ways with a person can. This holds true whether we're eighteen-year-olds deliberating about setting our childhood stuffed animal aside, or an

older person downsizing in order to move into a smaller residence in a
retirement home.

Sometimes it can be hard to get rid of an object entirely if it is from
someone you love who is no longer with you. Before my dad died he
gave me a really ugly and obnoxiously loud telephone with a big Elvis
Presley figure on top. Because I am an Elvis fan, my dad figured that I'd
be giddy every time Elvis's hips moved when the phone rang to the
tune of "Hound Dog." But the hips never worked, even when Dad
bought the phone. They were attached haphazardly with a rubber band
to the mechanism that was supposed to move them. Since a haphazard
rubber band was my dad's usual fix-it-all solution for anything from
canopy beds to boom box battery compartments, each time I looked at
Elvis's broken hips I thought about my dad. Elvis currently lives in a
basement closet, not being used. But I just can't throw it away. Correc-
tion: I just can't throw *him* away. That rubber band reminds me too
much of Dad. Also, it's hard for me to throw anything with Elvis on it
away.

If you turn on an episode of the television show *Hoarders*, you will
see that home objects and spaces can be visible indicators of someone's
well-being. The accumulation of certain amounts or types of things tells
the story of the owner's conception of self, often defined as unhealthy if
there are too many items or too much of one kind of unhealthy item. If
you have dealt with a deceased family member's cherished possessions
by sorting through them with fellow grieving and competing family
members ("No, I get Dad's rifle; you take his teacup collection"), you
know that home possessions are more than just things. They have
meaning. They have memories attached. They connote their owner's
identity. They call forth relationship dynamics between siblings, parents, and children. They serve as reminders of loved ones even after the
loved ones are gone. They may even be more about a nostalgic image of
the loved one from the past, a bit romanticized or idealized, to cover up
any negative images or pain. They are physical reminders of what material culture scholar Therese Richardson calls *continuing bonds*.[5] Intentionally saving objects can even give them a kind of sacredness. And
because of this deep meaning in objects, family members can engage in
battles over stuff—conflict over who gets it, what it's worth, and who
finds it most meaningful.

AGING AND PLACE, AND AGING IN PLACE

There are lots of reasons why we might get rid of an object—maybe it's worn out, or we don't use it, or we stop liking it. For people in older age, though, more reasons come into play: the objects have been around longer and therefore may have deeper meaning attached to them; the people who have the objects may not be able to manage having them because of health concerns; and family members have a greater likelihood of caring what happens to the items.[6]

If there is one element of family life that has undergone vast demographic change in the last century, it is the simple fact that people are living longer than in the past. There are plenty of millennials, to be sure, but there are nearly as many baby boomers.[7] Just think about what it means that the average life expectancy is now nearly eighty years old for Americans, which is decades more than it was even a century ago.[8] This has implications not only for larger population and resource concerns, but also for family life. Now we see greater variety in family arrangements and behaviors, from more visibility of active grandparents with their grandchildren (sometimes with multigenerational living), to more diversity in couples' living arrangements (Coontz notes that staying together "'til death do us part" is a much longer time period than it used to be; while older adults are more likely to be married than in the past, there is also a growing proportion of them who are divorcing, living with a partner without marriage, and remaining single). And with these changes, we also see massive amounts of research (and its accompanied funding) on *gerontology* (the study of aging populations), retirement, health, and generational differences in attitudes about everything from sex to political candidates.

We've also seen changes in how families work in terms of intergenerational relationships. Greater geographic mobility and technological innovation allow multiple generations of family members to keep up with each other's lives via social media, digital album sharing, and video chats. Additionally, what used to be called the *sandwich generation*—parents whose kids and aging parents simultaneously need care from the generation between them—has been complicated because aging parents are living longer. It is more usual than in the past for a person who is already a grandparent to need to care for his aging parent. Acknowledging that there are great disparities in health outcomes for individuals, often based on class and race, the sheer fact that people live longer on average means that caring for them extends longer in the lives of those who succeed them.

With an aging population, living arrangements for aging adults have become a focus for growing industries relating to care work, retirement and senior living building projects, and assisted living options. Enhancements in health care and longevity mean aging adults, grandparents included, are living post-retirement lives in home spaces that may not be anywhere near the family home, or, if they are nearby, they may be in sections of a home such as a mother-in-law suite or, as discussed below, a *granny pod*. They may also be in the form of senior living centers and retirement communities, which are interesting locations for studying the concepts of home and family. It is in these locations where a family dinner is in a communal room with other residents who are not necessarily related in traditional familial terms. But even if the dining is communal, the dining room is nonetheless situated in a home.

GRANNY PODS AND COMMUNAL LIVING: FLEXIBLE HOME CONFIGURATIONS BEYOND THE NUCLEAR FAMILY

Think about all of the kinds of living spaces that incorporate the word *home*: group homes for individuals who require living assistance, nursing homes, retirement homes, townhomes, vacation homes, children's homes, mobile homes, foster homes, tiny homes, and the HGTV Dream Home.

If family lives are getting increasingly diverse, and if the definition of family has widened and changed, and if we see more of the diversity of family lives that have actually always been around but are more visible and accepted now, then it follows that the places families live have changed, too. With a changing definition of what counts as a family comes a changing definition of what counts as a home. For example, in addition to rural farmsteads that often contain multiple homes on one property for multigenerational living (not necessarily a new idea), we now hear much of mother-in-law or secondary suites in urban and suburban communities, where adults who are shopping for a living space include an aging parent in the search, suggesting that three-generation (and even four-generation) living is increasingly visible. Emerging in this genre of multigenerational living are also ideas such as granny pods—small homes situated on the property of an adult child's home for his or her parent to live independently but still be close (perhaps that is most similar to the floating electron in the nuclear family metaphor). In legal terms, these configurations are more accurately labeled accessory dwelling units, or ADUs, which, as the AccessoryDwellings.org specifies, can be basement apartments, above-garage apartments, or tiny homes on the same property as the primary dwelling.[9] In addition to multigenerational living, we also see more home designs with two owner's suites, sometimes used by adult siblings and their families in order to expand the definition of household to include extended family horizontally (e.g., cousins in the same home) rather than vertically (grandparents in the same home as grandchildren).

The flexibility of living spaces and family arrangements can also be seen in communal living situations such as *cohousing*. Cohousing, as defined by the Cohousing Association of the United States on their website, is an intentional neighborhood designed by its residents in order to share some tasks otherwise performed by people in separate homes, and that are often motivated by environmental sustainability and a desire to enhance family lives with social and community support. Cohousing is a unique and relatively new type of community form, borrowed from Scandinavia and introduced to America in the late 1980s. In the United States there are nearly two hundred of these communities established or in the planning stages, and the size of the communities varies from a handful of residences to dozens.[10]

From tours and conversations with residents in cohousing communities in the United States and Denmark, I have learned that, while they vary in size and goals, these communities are made up of individual household units and extensive shared facilities, usually including a centralized common space where members share frequent community meals. This shared space, often called a Common House, is usually a centralized building that contains mailboxes, a kitchen, a dining area, recreation areas, and sometimes laundry facilities. Most cohousing communities share common meals three to five times per week, with every adult cooking only a few times a month.

Cohousing is not just a collection of individuals or families with pooled economic resources (which is what cooperatives are), it is not entirely communal (as with communes), and it does not necessarily have sustainable living as a primary goal (like in ecovillages). Unlike members of communes or co-ops, the members of cohousing communities own or rent their own units, but also have some investment in the shared common spaces. Further, many cohousing communities are technically set up as condominiums because banks are more familiar with this model and more likely to finance it. The major difference between condominiums and cohousing, however, is that the members of cohousing communities design their own communities and are devoted to using their shared spaces to interact with their neighbors. Cohousing thus represents an in-between space that intentionally sets out to redefine family and community roles and responsibilities, and that fosters a part-public and part-private way of living and dividing up resources and responsibilities. As you can imagine with residents in a retirement home with communal dining, cohousing residents may dine together at one big table or in one big room, but they return to their private spaces later on to have a bedtime snack (with just their immediate family).

DINING TABLE

A table was sometimes where we dined as a family when I was growing up. But the busier we all got, the more we ate in dispersed locations (me in front of the TV, my dad in the kitchen, my brothers off at college, my mom, as I mentioned earlier, leaning over a pulled-out cutting board in the kitchen). Dining room tables are not always present in homes, nor are tables always used to dine at. To have one requires a space dedicated to dining. And so, for the purposes of this chapter, I define the dining table broadly to include any surface where household members eat. And I define household as including single nuclear families, as well as intergenerational families, collective communities, and created families made up of what some social scientists call *fictive kin*.

Tables can be made out of many materials, from a door placed on cinder blocks to a large circle of glass on brass legs, from a low surface without chairs to a bar-height counter with stools. This aesthetic variation reminds us that it doesn't matter what the table looks like, as long as it provides a horizontal surface. But tables are also sociologically interesting because they are surfaces that see a multiplicity of tasks and serve a multiplicity of functions—eating, to be sure. But doing homework, crafting, working, gift wrapping, bill paying, letter writing, dish stacking, and game playing can all take place at a table. I suspect that if we all counted the number of activities taking place on any given surface in our homes, the table where people eat (or are supposed to eat) would yield the longest list (though the bed may come in a close second, especially for those of us who sometimes eat in bed).

Tables are sociologically interesting even if they are reserved for eating because food brings people together, and types of food served (and utensils used to serve and eat it) represent tastes, cultures, and resources a family has. Etiquette rules about bodies, communication, and group statuses emerge depending on whether the table has elbows or smartphones on it, whether they are set next to paper plates or fancy dishes, and whether everyone is required to wait until Dad sits down before picking up a fork. Whether there is a separate table for adults and children tells the story of how age matters in family rituals. Even the quality of family relationships has been studied by researchers who look at dinner rituals (Do we sit at a table or not? Do we eat together or not? Do we allow texting or not?).

Most research points to the idea that families spending time eating together at a table, at least on a semiregular basis (and not just for an annual feast) strengthens family bonds, enhances effective communication, and makes kids feel safe and secure.[11] A table, then, regardless of its location, size, and cost, can anchor a family through regular eating rituals. The family that gathers at a horizontal surface to eat together, stays together. Or, as a sociologist would say, that family is more likely to develop habits that increase the chances of strong family cohesion, though this is by no means a guarantee.

Beyond a family residing in a single-family dwelling, dining tables also reflect changing eating practices, housing types, and definitions of family. In terms of retirement and cohousing communities, for example, dining is collective. It may include sub-units of people that may consider themselves family (although, if you interviewed diners at a retirement home or cohousing communal dinner, I'm not sure all of them would say their neighbors are part of their family; but the notion of dining together under one roof is a family activity, which makes this worth playing with).

Imagine when you get older that you will move into a residential community for people in older age (or, if you are already in this position, think about your surroundings), where the meals are served communally and the dining tables are not the possessions of any resident. Researchers Jane Kroger and Vivienne Adair noted such a transition in their 2008 study on aging and cherished possessions. They wrote that a person's shift to an elder care home meant a shift in social status, represented by one person's feeling of loss when her large table was sold. She was formerly the host of large family gatherings, and she was now a "guest at a table where another presided to serve the meal." Another resident's story was different:

> She had brought a big farmhouse table to her residential unit, against her family's wishes, because she believed that she could not maintain her interests in entertaining others, sewing, and jigsaw puzzles without it. The table had been an important gathering place at the family farm and remained a cherished symbol of the previous status the participant had held as organizer and hostess of family gatherings. [12]

In these cases, the dining room table is not just a functional object, it is a part of the owner's identity and status, most noticed during life transitions when roles and spaces change.

A few years ago, Lindsey Menard and I conducted a survey of U.S. cohousing residents. [13] I also studied and visited with students in a course I was teaching on the sociology of the family at a cohousing community in Denmark, participating in communal dinners, touring both shared and private spaces, talking with residents, reading their history, examining their website, and asking questions about what dining together meant to them. Below I discuss our survey findings, my informal observations from the Danish community, and ideas from recent research. All of what I discuss here is connected to the notion of communal dining, either at one big table in a cohousing common house, or at many tables where family units intermingle for meals. The ideas can be applied to communal dining in a community for older adults, too.

The first time I visited the Danish cohousing community just outside of Copenhagen, our tour guide, a mother of two, asked quite loudly how individual families could possibly survive when they had to pick kids up from school, get groceries, and make dinner every night—all while working outside the home, too. She asked this because evening meals were made by a rotating team of residents so that people would only need to cook dinner a handful of nights every month. My students and I got to eat with the residents, so we could see (and participate in) the team effort at play. In class discussions after our visits to the cohousing community, my students and I discussed how the parents who entered the dining room with their children helped set up high chairs and worked with their kids to choose a spot to sit, but they seemed relaxed. They didn't have to cook or clean the tables. They could eat and talk with each other.

In our U.S.-based study, Lindsey and I surveyed sixty-eight current residents (ages twenty-nine to eighty-seven, about two-thirds women) of cohousing communities across fifteen states. Most were married and had kids. Of all of the tasks that were shared within their cohousing communities, cooking common meals was most frequently noted. While this finding is more about the kitchen and division of labor, it includes the task of serving the food and cleaning up the communal tables. It was more likely that women were in the kitchen cooking the shared meals while men were at the tables at the beginning of the meals eating with the children. The community-shared tasks lessened work for women than would have been the case if they lived in a single-family dwelling, but the women collectively still did more than the men in these tasks, and they were therefore less visible at the start of meals in the communal dining room than were men.

Importantly, though, for many cohousing residents, a shared meal over a communal table lessened feeling overwhelmed with work and family tasks. For example, one new mother wrote,

> Before moving to [our community], both my husband and I had jobs and so housework was evenly divided. Once we moved, I stayed home and did the housework, but recently our situation has changed dramatically, in that we now have a newborn baby. This has put a lot more housework on my husband, who also works a full-time job. The main aspect of housework that now falls to the community is meals. We rely on common meals to simplify our lives much more now that we have a baby.

The communal meal, then, was a time- and energy-saving ritual that allowed this family to feel less overwhelmed.

How much were residents aware of the importance of the communal table? Although space is a difficult concept to discuss, the members of cohousing communities may be more aware of the effects of space because they have rejected the housing forms available in mainstream America and most of them have been involved in the process of designing their communities. They are on the front lines of understanding how plans for organizing communities require much work to make ideals and realities mesh. The intentionality of cohousing communities to create spaces that foster certain kinds of social interactions suggests that their residents know well how to talk about how space affects social relations, and how being seen and interacting are facilitated by spaces and objects like common houses and the dining tables in them.

One may wonder whether people in cohousing communities, because of their heightened awareness of blurring boundaries between public and private, have a broader definition of family. Perhaps it could include the entire community, an identity reinforced by communal dining. Interestingly, in a 2014 interview study of residents of one cohousing community in the northeastern United States, sociologist Heather Sullivan-Catlan found that residents defined family and community as mutually exclusive, made most evident by how they talked about mealtime.[14] Clusters of tables, dozens of people, and loud chairs in a big space—commonly cited images of communal evening meals—were seen as hectic, connected to finances (since meal costs had to be calculated and people had to pay to eat), and too public. Family meals, on the other hand, were quieter, sacred, and at times at odds with communal meals. In the quote from our research and in my students' and my observations in the Danish cohousing meal, the common dining experience seemed to lessen stress for families. But in other research, dining at a communal table is seen as loud, hectic, and public—which is pitted against the model of the single family as quiet, calm, and private.

To say that cohousing communities are *like* families may make sense, since they provide social support, tasks are shared, and people work together to socialize children. But this is not the same as saying they *are* families, at least in the minds of the residents. Research about cohousing in the United States seems to point to the notion that single-family units are preserved as sacred and separable amidst communal living and dining experiences. As with the resident of a retirement home who mourned the loss of her own table, pitting the family dinner table against the communal table reinforces the boundaries between public and private, and between family and not-family, even in communities where these lines are meant to be intentionally blurred.

INHERITED DISHES

My friend Amy Bates is the head of a large cleaning company with hundreds of homes to clean. I asked her whether she had any clients who talked about possessions in their homes that were "cherished," and, if so, how she knew they were special objects. I also asked her if there were any particular groups of people who were more inclined to point out these objects to the people cleaning their homes. As in, "Don't touch this! It's really important to me!" I was interested in these questions because one person's sentimental object may be a $1,000 painting, and another's may be an inexpensive antique salt and pepper shaker set with only sentimental value. Different groups of people have different access to economically valuable objects, even though any of us can attach sentimental value to any object, expensive or cheap. I figured that demographic factors may matter, such as social class, age, and era in which people grew up, since what is deemed valuable or scarce in a time period of great wealth may change in an economic recession. For any of us who have had grandparents who never threw anything away because they grew up during the Depression, this all may sound familiar.

The way Amy measured the presence of cherished objects in the houses that her company was hired to clean was by labeling any objects that had sentimental value to the homeowners as "not to be touched" in written instructions for the housecleaners. Interestingly, regarding the question of who was most likely to identify these kinds of objects, she noted that it was among older adults where this happened the most. Especially breakable items such as teacups or porcelain dishes, which were often the objects that had been around for a long time, seemed to have the most sentimentality attached to them. This was probably because they had accumulated more stories than newer objects, and because the owners wanted to have their legacy passed along to the next generation to preserve those stories. The self, for older individuals whose houses got cleaned and objects left untouched by the cleaners, was so deeply attached to their objects that they would have felt a tremendous loss of self if they had been broken. For younger people whose houses her company cleaned, there was less concern with sentimentality, and more concern with getting rid of stuff so as not to accumulate too much. The attachment of meaning to our stuff, then, depends on what stage of life we are in, what generation we are from, and whether we grew up during a time period when people cared about scarcity.

What happens if a parent has saved four hundred cherished teacups, all of which need to be divvied up after that parent downsizes or passes away? To keep a whole lot of these items is seen as a burden on older individuals (and on the younger ones who have to manage their possessions along with aging parents' possessions), thus reinforcing the cultural messages that getting rid of things, preferably before death, is a good thing. It helps with daily life of older individuals, and it saves time later for their children. But keeping items to remember a spouse or partner who has died, as well as to pass along stories to the next generation, is also valued. So, the paradox is that we are supposed to get rid of stuff to live a better life (four hundred teacups is too many to handle), but keep some of it—the five teacups with the most meaning—to pass along our stories to others. The work of figuring out what has the most meaning is a lot of work.

Take a set of dishes meant to be passed down from one generation to the next—they don't have to be a matched set, but a group of dishes that go from one person's possession to another's. These can be everyday dishes, or dishes reserved for special occasions and that may be stored in special boxes or displayed in a cabinet. Or they can be dishes that used to be everyday but, because they're antiques, are now reserved for special occasions. These are cherished possessions for many families, and these kinds of objects have been the focus of some great research on family stories and relationships. Even if everyday dishes are passed down, for an object to be given the label of "cherished" or "heirloom" requires that they are more than just used for functional purposes. Some people are often unwilling to get rid of things that are cherished, and if they do get rid of them, whether sold at a yard sale, given to a child, or donated, the preference is often that they go to someone else who will attach another family story to them or find them useful.

Despite this important set of meanings attached to our stuff, and the work it involves, the acts of preserving and disposing of cherished objects are often left out of research on family relationships between generations, life transitions such as selling the family home and moving into a smaller dwelling, and even how to handle the death of a family member. Illustrating this point, researchers David Ekerdt and Julie Sergeant interviewed adults about their process of preserving or getting rid of possessions.[15] One of their participants said, "My dad brought these dishes from Maine on a plane and I don't know what you call them, but there is a name for them. They were his mother's. So my grandmother on my dad's side collected those dishes." This person elaborated about how nice it was to have the set of dishes together, because it told a more thorough story of his family than if they were separate pieces in different places.

In contrast, Ekerdt and Sergeant also included the story of a set of siblings who divided up a set of collector plates once their parents had died. The set was taken apart so that the memory and stories of the parents could be carried into multiple homes, thus increasing the odds that their story would be preserved. Some of the plates were not wanted by any siblings, so they were sold. But the selling of these was only done after people chose the ones they wanted, thus enacting respect for their parents in the process of choosing and disposing of the plates.

Once dishes are inherited, the new owners need to decide whether and when to use or display them. To use the dishes animates the memory of the events when they were typically used in their past life. So you remember past feasts and the people at them when you set the table. This doesn't just preserve the memory, it shapes it anew every time it's used, and it acts out the connections family members have. When people inherit cherished possessions—whether they're dishes or collectible figurines or linens or guns—they see themselves as members of a family that has existed for generations, and would continue into the future because they're holding on to the items. For example, one respondent from Kroger and Adair's research, referring to a ceramic plate, said, "Well, I think about my mother, and my mother's side of the family. . . . I was very attached to this side of the family. My mother was a wonderful person and I love having this plate to keep me company."[16] The plate, as a keeper of company, served as a substitute family member, or at least a reminder of one.

The dishes may also be stored or displayed once inherited. Housing scholar Rachel Hurdley, in her study on what people display on their mantelpieces, says that when we display things in our homes in spaces where nonfamily members visit, we are performing our family roles and showing what we value.[17] Family relationships play out using props. This is true when people are alive and when we preserve their family role after they die by using, keeping safe, or displaying their former possessions.

When someone dies, remaining family members are more likely to be interested in money and land than small things like dishes. And yet, the small things are most likely to yield competing interests in why and whether they should be preserved; they're harder to divide fairly because they're all different things (as opposed to money or land). Whether they're kept as a set or not matters with things like dishes (though research is thin on this part). Also, with smaller objects, as opposed to land or money, the net of people who have an interest in them is wider (e.g., a neighbor who says he gets the lawnmower).[18] In some ways, then, when a family member dies, the disagreements among surviving members may get more heated with divvying up plates than with divvying up the farmland.

Most of what I've said so far about inherited dishes situates them in the hands of their new owners—a son or daughter whose parent has passed away. But the importance of cherished objects for people in later life matters beyond just how they think of what will happen when they die. As early as the 1920s, Erikson, Erikson, and Kivnick interviewed late-life people living in a residential facility about their possessions, finding that "supportive continuity that familiar objects can offer us as we age, can, of course, be a solace and a pleasure."[19] Recent research in gerontology supports this and adds that holding on to cherished possessions in late life transitions, such as moving to an assisted living facility, can help people maintain their sense of identity at a time when lots of elements of the self are fading away.[20]

And then, when a cherished object is meant to be saved for the future, passing it down to the next generation can be an important symbol of identity connection and continuity across time. A story from Kroger and Adair illustrates this well:

That's a [china] tray. My grandmother brought that out in the 1870s and it went to my mother when she was 21, and then to me when I was 21, and then to my eldest son when he was 21. But I'm keeping it for him now because he's in Japan and couldn't take it with him. He came out here recently to check on me, and I said "take the tray." And he said, "Oh, no, Mum. I won't do that—you get so much pleasure from it." [Interviewer: When you look at the tray, what kinds of things do you think about?] Well, my mother and grandmother and all the family in generations past.[21]

These stories and sentiments all suggest that something as simple and small as an inherited set of dishes can serve as a message from the past into the present, igniting memories and helping with identity transitions, and continuing the family history into the future either through display or use.

REFLECTING ON OUR STUFF

Homes show how the boundaries between public and private matter for families. When residents gather together in cohousing communities to assign tasks often reserved for individual families to the entire group, they have as a goal to save time and use resources more efficiently. Joining together multiple generations of family members in one home or serving a large group of people in a senior residential community changes the concept of a family meal to one that is expanded beyond the nuclear family. While having a grandparent live on the same property as their children and grandchildren is still within the confines of a private family, this living configuration calls to mind the notion that boundaries around family dinners are constructed depending on who gets to be included or not, and whether the inclusion is dependent on rituals such as weekly dinners or holidays. Add to this a mix of private ownership of dwellings and collective management of shared spaces as with cohousing and retirement communities, and the everyday task of eating together becomes an interesting location for examining public-private boundaries within and between families. By studying these kinds of communities and living arrangements, we can all evaluate the underlying assumption that families can, and should, conform to an ideal of nuclear families living in single-family homes with relatively fixed boundaries around nuclear family units. When we look at a dining table that can hold sixty instead of four, we can uncover whether the definition of family ritual can change depending on how the boundaries around family are drawn.

Homes tell us about individual families, but also about broader social issues. If we buy a new table or inherit an old one, that table is part of our story. The things that we may buy or receive after a family member has died are not just objects. They are part of our social fabric, and they connect to different groups depending on that group's values and norms. Age is one of those group markers. Older people, when discussing their home possessions, are more likely than younger people to note their importance in terms of past stories or passing along stories for the future. Objects like a set of inherited dishes have a history and a future. For younger people, the importance of things tends to be more about their current use and value.[22] So, for Grandma, the china set is about having her grandson remember his ancestors when he sets the table for a feast. For Grandma's adult son, his new dishes that all finally match is more about how they are part of his life today.

How families deal with objects and home spaces tells us how interactions work within that family. Take inheritance practices. When a family member dies, whether we inherit anything first depends on whether there's anything to inherit. Its value can be economic, sentimental, or both. In addition to its value, how inheritance works is tied to the interactional processes in our families, and to expectations about who gets to be included in the definition of "our family." Who gets what is related to family members deciding who seems most deserving based on demonstrating commitment to the family member who has died, fitting larger societal norms about passing on property (e.g., gender, marital status, and age of children), and being able to negotiate decisions as a family that can often carry with them a certain amount of conflict.

Even in happier times, family interactions can be shown as people gather around a dining table, as with etiquette rules associated with eating and family meals. Pulling out Grandma's good china for a large family gathering means not only that after dinner all of the dishes will need to be hand washed. It also means that behaviors around the table may include things that are not necessarily part of everyday eating practices for a family. Maybe this time, a prayer is said. Maybe this time, people dress differently. Maybe this time, children are expected to behave more formally and try not to tip over the lit candles. Whatever a family defines as important behavior for a gathering around a dining table, either every day or on rare celebratory occasions, is part of the process of learning what it means to be in that family.

Who sits at a table for a family dinner depends not just on what kind of table it is, but also on how the family is defined. Some people get included and others excluded. More than just a way to define a separation between public and private life, inclusion can also relate to access to resources that allow some families to have large tables set with ornate dishes in elaborate dining rooms, and others to not have a dining room at all.

Homes are not only symbolic, but also shape our lives. When family members disagree about whether it's important to save something left behind after someone's death, it's not just about the thing, or about whether keeping things is good or bad, necessary or frivolous. It's also about the meaning people may attach to the thing's representation of the person who's no longer present. It's maybe even about the power of the thing over us. In one small conversation about a teacup, a brother may proclaim that saving it preserves a mother's memory; a sister may doubt that claim and say a teacup doesn't matter and they should get rid of as much stuff as possible; the same brother may interpret the comment as an insult about the mother; and the same sister may find it more honorable to get rid of things and preserve a memory in stories about the mother rather than in the stuff the mother left behind. The disagreement is not just about stuff. But it is the presence of the teacup that calls forth someone's preferred form of honoring of a lost loved one. The teacup is not just a teacup. It pushes the brother and sister into realizing what they value, and how they wish to preserve a memory of a mother.

Objects have lives just like people do. They have transitions, careers, entrances and exits.[23] The practice of deciding whether to give a cherished object to a loved one, or fight over it once someone has gone, shows that objects themselves symbolize the attachments we have to our family members. Our possessions also accumulate stories—stories that are part of our lives and part of how we define ourselves and our values. It's as if the items we inherit are family members themselves. Or at the very least, proxies for family members who have gone but whom we'd like to remember. Therese Richardson, in her study on widows and widowers and their attachment to the possessions of their deceased spouses, articulates this well when she outlines how possessions can be *metonymic* (meaning they substitute for the person rather than just serve as metaphors or symbols):

> A bond can connect a widow or widower with their spouse via something that stands for them, as in metonymy. Unlike a symbol, which represents a person or thing indirectly through a metaphoric association, a metonymic stands as if it is them. . . . This means that while the deceased spouses referred to in the study had flesh-and-blood bodies when alive, now they are dead in their leavings, in the form of possessions, skills and personal attributes, form another type of body. Thus it is that a person can be represented by their "corpus," or "body of work," or possessions. [24]

In this way, something as simple as a ceramic plate or a teacup can act as if it were another person, keeping us company even after someone is no longer living.

Remember the wobbly old oak table I talked about at the beginning of this chapter? This table started in a dining room in a huge house on a farm in rural South Dakota. It made its way to my parents' basement rec room, where I spent countless hours doing art projects. After being refinished (farmhouse rain damage and too many misses in the coloring books), it then moved upstairs into the dining space in my parents' home, occasionally made larger and wobblier with six leaves for family feasts. In 2009 it made its way across two thousand miles to be in the dining space of my mom's condo in the town where I live—a condo she bought after she sold the farmland she inherited after her parents passed away. She bought the condo in order to visit us for longer stints of time, but recognized that having her own space during long visits would allow her to watch her Lifetime television shows in the evening in peace. She sold her condo recently, since she had been coming a bit less often (something about a new boyfriend who was occupying her time), which means Great-Grandma's table is now my dining room table. No extension leaves are in the table, since there are just three of us who eat at it every day as we talk about homework, the weather, and the next time our son will see his wonderful grandparents. But it is in a separate dining room, a luxury my husband and I aimed for in our home-buying search as shiny new professionals. And sometimes, on special occasions, we dim the new-lamp-that-looks-old that sits in the corner of our dining room, and we set the table with the special-occasion fluted midcentury goblets my mom gave me after my dad died—cherished inherited celebratory family heirlooms amidst some new things and woven into my little family's dining rituals.

When we're not using these goblets, they're stored in a glassed-in cabinet next to four things: the tiny porcelain Italian chocolate set given to us as a wedding present from my grandfather-in-law's first cousin who never had kids of her own but relished the love of her cousin's offspring; the hand-painted candlestick from my childhood neighbor in Germany who I will always think of as a grandmother; an old birthday card from a friend who I will always think of as Auntie; and a tiny watercolor painting from my best friend who I will always think of as a sister. What a lovely created family of cherished objects, all of which tell my family story from a little corner near my dining table, probably better than I can. These are not just things. These are mementos of my family story, all of whom are welcome at our table anytime.

9

FAMILIES, HOMES, AND SOCIAL CHANGE

Toilets and Showers

If you want to measure the spirit of the times you have to look to the bathroom. That is where the new things happen.[1]

The toilet is in many ways a barometer of civilized values.[2]

BATHROOMS

Brushing teeth. Showering. Using the toilet. Reaching for a tampon. Shaving. Applying makeup. Taking medicine. Looking closely in a mirror at that strange rash. Finishing level 158 in Candy Crush. I could craft a narrative about how the bathroom should serve as a metaphor for a last book chapter, because, after all, it is a departure point. A last stop. Or where all the you-know-what goes. But instead I want to make the case that the bathroom is the perfect room choice for the end of this book, not only because it showcases how times have changed in terms of technological innovation, global differences in access to resources that affect our everyday lives, and environmental sustainability, but also because it best highlights how spaces and objects impact families in terms of changing definitions of public and private. If this were not the case, then people who decide to live together wouldn't have to go through the mental energy of deciding whether they are comfortable peeing in front of each other.

The bathroom is a place where lots of things that are defined by many as private are stored, enacted, and sensed, often behind one of the only interior home doors that can be locked. Bodies. Medicine. Illness. Waste. Dirt. Smells. Nudity. Bacteria. Bathrooms are the most vivid locations to see (and hide) this stuff. It is the most private space in a home, exemplified by singer Alicia Keys when she said, "If I want to be alone, someplace I can write, I can read, I can pray, I can cry, I can do whatever I want—I go to the bathroom." This quote is so powerful that the popular book *Residential Design for Aging in Place* places it at the beginning of the chapter on bathrooms.[3] Another powerful quote comes from my best friend's dad (the one married to the best friend's mom referenced in chapter 1): "Things start breaking down when the number of bathrooms in a house exceeds the number of bedrooms. People don't have to interact anymore."

If it is the goal of sociology to uncover what is behind walls to know what's really going on in our families (including all of their interactions, in and out of the bathroom), as the first chapter outlined using a plumbing metaphor, then why not look at the room where the most is hidden? Let's make the invisible visible. The intimate known. The familiar strange. Might it make us a little uncomfortable to talk about the stuff we want to keep to ourselves? Probably, but that feeling itself tells us interesting things about how we view the boundary between private and public, and what we consider to be appropriate things to talk about. Bringing private things into the public is uncomfortable. But keeping them hidden means we are removed from understanding how our everyday family lives operate. And it means we are not able to deconstruct the notion that only clean and controlled bodies are "civilized" ones.

To uncover how this all matters in private bathrooms, let's start with public ones. In 1976, Alexander Kira wrote a book entitled *The Bathroom*, in which he said that when we enter public bathrooms, our feelings about privacy, being clean, and eliminating bodily waste become magnified, mostly because making these things public violates the territory that we have come to collectively define as private.[4] In other words, pooping in public makes us feel a little nervous because we define all that pooping entails to be a very private thing.

Bathrooms, especially public ones, have made the news a lot recently, mostly in terms of who has the right to use them, what their nomenclature and visual symbols should be, and what this all says about which kinds of people are defined as scary or harmful.[5] Bathrooms are also the location of research on greedy workplaces that disallow workers the right to relieve a full bladder while at work.[6] Who has the right to go into which bathroom and when is something that is a public issue, but contains values and judgments about things that feel very private. The exclusion of people from being able to do what our bodies are supposed to do is problematic, to say the least, which is why bathrooms are as political as they are personal.

What one does in a bathroom can feel so private that it can take a lot of mental work just to feel comfortable doing one's business in a public place. In fact, clinical terms to refer to shyness with numbers one (*paruresis*) and two (*parcopresis*) exist, lending support to the notion that traversing boundaries between what feels private and what feels public has real consequences in people's lives.[7] That makes sense in a psychological sense, since it involves mental work. But this is all sociologically interesting, too. A classic work in sociology by Erving Goffman discusses how life is like a theatrical performance.[8] There are props, roles, audiences, and a stage. That people act differently backstage and frontstage is not just true in the theater. It is also true in life. This is why, when I worked in a restaurant, I would have been mortified if the customers knew what I was saying behind the wall separating the eating area from the kitchen, and why I felt as if I had to "act" friendly so that they'd have a pleasant experience. My front-stage self was different from my backstage self.

All of this is to say that how we act in bathrooms, and how we think about ourselves as we're using them, are not just creations in our minds. They are part of the set of values and norms that govern our society. The bathroom door is not just a door that separates the public world from the private one, it is also the location that divides our public self from our private self, our front-stage self from our backstage self.[9] And we create that door, both literally and figuratively.

But what here may matter for bathrooms that are in private homes, where much of life is already deemed backstage?[10] Of course it matters that, for many, including those who reminisce not-so-fondly about using the Sears catalog as toilet paper in a colder-than-cold outhouse, we think of bathrooms as being *in* the home, rather than outside of it. But they're not just in our homes, they're in particular locations in our homes. Bathrooms are in the backstage of our homes, which is why the activities we do there have come to be defined as unacceptable in other rooms. While the public politics of who is entitled to use which bathroom are less applicable here, the sociological implications of bathrooms are just as relevant. I'm always struck by how much sociological research there is on public bathrooms, but very little on private ones. Like with other home spaces, social researchers have ended up prioritizing nonprivate spaces as their focus, further rendering places like homes in the devalued realm of research. Part of this is because it's hard to study private and hidden things. The only time people's private bathroom use becomes visible is when it is located in public places, or when the practices they perform require buying things in stores or tending to in doctors' offices.

We need a stronger foundation on which to stand if we want to understand the symbolic importance of bathrooms (and their hidden objects and practices) in our homes. To start, they are locations where *socialization* takes place—where we learn the rules and roles that our family and our society deem appropriate. From potty training to tooth brushing, and from learning at what age it is okay to be naked in front of people to whether to discuss scatological topics, children are taught from a very early age the socially defined right and wrong ways to use and take care of their bodies in bathrooms. As a bonus fun fact, we also know that disagreements about which way to hang a toilet-paper roll connote group differences in terms of values and views about household rules, hygiene, and household work. All of this is part of the socialization process that teaches (or trains, perhaps) people what the bathroom norms are in their households.[11]

In addition to being sites for socialization, home bathrooms are places where inequalities play out. Bathrooms are status symbols, with affluent homes showcasing heated floors and customized light fixtures, and less affluent homes containing prefab cabinets and plastic towel bars. Even where the extra toilet-paper rolls are stored (visible near the toilet, or hidden in a hallway linen closet only possible in homes with this kind of space), or how soft the toilet paper is, can symbolize class status. Cleanliness, too, becomes extra meaningful in private bathrooms, with smells and sights like bleach and mold connoting status not just in terms of social class, but also in terms of morality. The attachment of morality to cleanliness is something that has historically been part of gendered construction of household labor, too. Women are still seen as the authority on bathroom cleanliness, from striving for a dirt-free tub, to striving for dirt-free pores. The value of good hygiene can even govern the rules of a household for whether a toilet-paper roll is hung outward or not, since unrolling against a wall increases the chances that hands will come into contact with bacteria on the wall.[12] We still live in a world where powerful messages connect moral values of cleanliness with home spaces, and with certain roles within the home. We still learn that a clean home is best measured by how clean the toilets are. And we still are told that cleanliness is next to godliness, especially for women. If you don't believe me, just try imagining a TV commercial for a bathroom cleaner where the voiceover says, "It's okay if there's soap scum and dirt in between your shower tiles because, well, nobody's perfect and dirt is good for you anyway. Right, ladies?"

And so, home bathrooms (and all of the rules governing how to hang the toilet paper and beyond), while not talked about as much as other home spaces, reveal fascinating sociological patterns that are worth unrolling—patterns that help us understand socialization, status, and the social attachment of values and morals to our bodies and our family roles.

CHANGING FAMILIES, CHANGING HOMES

In many ways, this chapter is about changes, which necessarily means it's about future homes and families. What do we need to think about if we are to imagine the homes of the future? And here I'm not just talking about whether there'll be robot maids or spaceship parking docks just outside the front door. I'm talking about real issues that are already part of how family lives and home spaces have been changing (though here I acknowledge that "robot maids" already exist in the form of circular vacuums that traverse the house to pick up dirt without a human to push them around). Many authors have covered the history of bathrooms in thorough and interesting ways.[13] Here I focus more on contemporary issues, with a nod toward their origins. The three areas I focus on include changing technologies, which has surfaced in various parts of this book already. Woven together with technological change are two other areas that help us understand how our family lives our changing: global differences and environmental concerns. In more ways than one, the often-smallest room in the house shines a big light on how technology, globalization, and environmental sustainability are part of changing family life in the United States.

Technological Change

Beyond any blueprints, our lives and our homes are situated in a three-dimensional world. Edwin Heathcote, in *The Meaning of Home*, notes that time serves as a fourth dimension necessary to any understanding of homes. To elaborate, if we want to understand anything about our homes today, we need to understand their histories, since they are "perhaps the last repositories of a language of symbol and collective memory that ties us to our ancestors, to profound and ancient threads of meaning." We need to know how our built environment has changed over time, because it has shaped our family roles just as our family roles have shaped innovations in building. This is why there have been so many wonderful writings about how the history of the bathroom has been precisely the history of our society, from status differences based on who has indoor plumbing and a separate place to bathe, to cultural definitions of privacy that have allowed and disallowed certain combinations of people within bathroom spaces over time.

But now, Heathcote says, we have to take into consideration a fifth dimension—cyberspace—that "allows us to be connected to everything everywhere simultaneously."[14] This is why, when we want to understand anything about homes, home objects, and family lives, we have to incorporate questions surrounding technology beyond the discussion of porcelain, grout, mirrored glass, and nails.

Throughout this book, there have been moments when the impact of technology (especially digital, information, media, and communication technologies) on family life has been easy to spot: smartphones and romantic communication, online dating apps, video games and childhood, digital family photo management, and work-family blurriness with laptop use, to name a few. In all of these, technology has not only been impacted by changing family roles, it has also served to alter those very roles and has even changed the definition of home life as entirely private. But it is in the bathroom where we see particularly interesting ways that technology matters in our construction of homes. Geographer Maria Kaika has written that "technological advancement (plumbing, central heating, air conditioning, etc.) made the exclusion and control of natural elements [like sewage] more efficient and sophisticated than ever before."[15] In this way, technology has mattered not only in how we live our lives in all parts of our homes, it has also mattered in the definition of home as a place where bad (dirty, public, unsafe) things are supposed to be invisible.

In an interesting way, bathrooms carry with them very old technologies that, like many of the objects we may find in our bathrooms today that are meant to get rid of "bad" things, are not terribly visible to us in our everyday lives. For instance, Greco-Roman baths had spouts where cleansing water came out, which serves as the model for showerhead designs today. Today, while the technology behind the spout is totally different from centuries ago, the design of showerheads includes a devotion to cleaning off all of the bad things any given day may bring. If we move beyond the basic showerhead design and include biomedical, information, and communication technologies in our broader understanding of technology in bathrooms, then our discussion of bathrooms today can show tremendous change. This is illustrated by the increased use of smartphones in bathrooms, the inclusion of media communications in bathroom remodels, the focus on composting toilets and other sustainable design ideas, and the invention of digitally controlled multiple showerheads. At least for those who can afford them. So, even in our most private places, our homes and families are impacted by technology.

Global (and Local) Differences

Beyond the bathroom, it is important to understand that what happens to family lives locally is both impacted by, and impacts, more global forces. Global flows of money and ideas and people matter in our understanding as much as our understanding of the flow of water in and out of our homes does. Where we buy things, where they're made, who makes them, how we define families and childhood based on our geography, what our children learn about the world, where we go, and which popular design aesthetic crosses borders into our own homes are all parts of our family lives that must be placed in a context of globalization. When I discuss abstract ideas like "global flows" in my classes, the conversation turns toward the all-important concept of *globalization*. Whether it's being able to buy a Barbie in Taipei, or manufacturing computer parts in Tulsa, the main factor motivating global exchange seems to be economic. Many political decisions that cross national borders center around trade, money, and availability of human capital. If that weren't the case, we wouldn't see countless news stories about the ubiquity of smartphone use worldwide, the variations in how the use of phones is (or is not) regulated by government, and the trials of making them in places where workers are working in unsafe factories.

The impacts of globalization are visible not just in factories and phones—they are also visible in our bathrooms. Even a routine shopping trip for a new toilet may introduce a consumer to brands like American Standard, but also to high-tech Japanese supertoilets from Toto. A discussion of global differences in bathrooms also contains reference to norms about privacy and bodies. Every time friends travel internationally, inevitably the conversation turns toward bathroom observations. Whether there's a toilet, whether there's paper, whether there's privacy, whether there's water to wash hands, whether one squats, sits, or stands. Doing a search for current research on the terms "toilets and sociology" in research databases reveals hundreds of articles on health, disease, sanitation, and housing conditions in different national locations, suggesting that the meaning of the bathroom and its concomitant social and health attributes are not just an issue for U.S. audiences. In fact, bathrooms are an important place for us to see how unequal resources are distributed across the globe. Perhaps more important, a discussion of bathrooms can show us how definitions of cleanliness, safety, health, family roles, and even morality are wrapped up in global constructions of privacy, bodies, and biology. While it is hard to argue against efforts to eradicate disease, it is worth noting that what bathrooms are for, who goes in them, what happens there, and whether any of this is defined as a problem are all socially constructed.

While U.S. homes being built are increasingly likely to include more than one bathroom, and are more likely than in the past to have customized features like steam showers, multiple vanities, saunas, TVs, fireplaces, and elaborate sound systems, bathrooms around the world (and within the United States) show striking differences that vary based on families' access to economic resources.[16] To illustrate this, consider a story a friend of mine told me about when she was a nanny on the East Coast for an affluent American family. She got to know a neighbor who hired someone to travel to Europe to search for and then buy real and reproduction antiques to house their things. Globalization is indicated by the increasing ease with which we can buy and sell things across national borders, such that nineteenth-century Swedish armoires can find their way into Connecticut en suite bathrooms to hold twenty-first-century Egyptian cotton towels. Consider this story in light of recent research by sociologist Matthew Desmond, whose ethnographic work reveals the squalor that exists for an increasing number of American families whose lives are met with unsafe housing (including toxic levels of lead and mold in places like bathrooms where kids spend a lot of their time) and precarious days spent wondering if they will be evicted from their apartments.[17] Or consider the recent debacle in Flint, Michigan, where governmental missteps meant that thousands of families were exposed to high levels of lead in their household drinking water.[18] To be sure, there are global inequalities when it comes to sanitation, disease, and infrastructure relating to water, but it is important to make visible the huge disparities in these things within our own borders.

The story about the East Coast wealthy people is unusual in that there are few people who could afford to pay for someone to travel to retrieve a Swedish armoire, let alone purchase an armoire that costs four times more than a month of rent. But it illustrates two things: first, that we are seeing more and more border crossing when it comes to the movement of ideas, aesthetic preferences, money, and bodies. And second, that there are vast inequalities in what resources are available for homes across the globe, including those homes in our own communities. Because bathrooms are increasingly sites for opulence for the wealthy and health concerns for the poor, they serve as important spaces for understanding these global and local inequalities.

Environmental Concern

The bathroom, more than many other rooms in a home, brings up our bodies and our biologies—the parts of our lives that we most often associate with being part of nature. As anthropologist Marianne Gullestad said, in reflecting about how different parts of the home are viewed as having different functions and definitions, "Preparing meals, sleeping, sexual relations, and going to the toilet are seen as being more closely associated with nature than is entertaining friends."[19] There is something about what goes into our bodies and out of them that connects us more to nature, it seems, than watching TV, walking through a hallway, playing with LEGO, or putting a love letter in our underwear drawer.

When we think of what it means to take care of our environment, it is easy to think of behaviors that are public and that occur within large social institutions, such as the work done by the U.S. Environmental Protection Agency or Greenpeace, or by large social movements such as the protest against the North Dakota oil pipeline project. I remember that recently, when wildfires threatened my town's watershed, the discussion about environmental causes (e.g., climate change) and effects (e.g., air quality) was ever-present in the news, both locally and nationally. But environmental concern lies within the walls of our homes, too. From recycling to sewage treatment, the often hidden or private parts of our everyday lives that we see as close to nature—what's behind walls or in bins—are as important to highlight as more public spaces and objects where environmental issues play out.

In terms of the connection between family lives and environmental issues, researchers have produced numerous studies about things like the toxicity of household chemicals (including plastic toys and flame-retardant beds and pajamas),[20] the location of low-cost rental homes in places with high rates of environmentally caused illness,[21] the movement by some toward downsizing and tiny homes to save money and use less energy,[22] and people's purchase and display of household products that carry with them status in the eyes of those who have environmental concerns.[23] The concerns are plentiful when it comes to how environmental issues intersect with our home lives. And this is true in our bathrooms, too. When we think about whether our toilet paper is compostable, whether our toilets use too much water, and whether our toilet bowl cleaner is toxic, we are thinking about ways that environmental concern matters in our homes. If we have children and we think of these things in terms of their health, we're also considering how environmental issues affect our everyday ability to have a healthy family, and our family's ability to create and maintain the next generation.

Beyond consumption of products and access to healthy spaces, homes are particularly intriguing sites for looking at environmental concerns because they spatially represent our values about nature. And they do this in an intriguing way. To clarify this, Maria Kaika notes that a house becomes a home precisely when undesirable natural elements and processes (like dirt and bodily waste) are spatially and socially excluded from the confines of the home space.[24] As the Western bourgeois home came to be, only good parts of nature—purified water and conditioned air—became part of the definition of a good home. The pipes that move bad things—dirty and polluted water, air, and sewage—away from our house are, paradoxically, required for us to maintain the idea that our homes are safe, familiar, and filled with good things. Nature becomes "other" and yet, in defining it this way, we come to rely even more on the "production of nature" to believe that our homes are safely contained as separate from the harsh and germ-filled natural world.

Specifically, the complicated path of pipes that carry treated water in, and pump bad water out, is invisible. Yet, the clean water that comes out of our taps and showerheads is required in order for us to think about our homes as separate from the bizarre world of bacteria-ridden nature. Kaika calls this both need and denial. We need clean water and we need to get rid of dirty water. But we don't want to see how we get it or how it is taken away, and so we deny that the process that takes care of all of this is quite a large presence in our everyday lives. This is why looking at bathrooms is particularly useful to understand how we view nature and what paths we may take toward environmental sustainability. This is why it's important to look behind the walls in order to better understand how our family lives are operating. If we don't know where the water and waste go, we don't really know how our homes have come to be defined the way they are. Keeping the plumbing invisible helps to perpetuate the idea that family life is supposed to be private, protected, and preserved as somehow separate from a harsh outside world. Making it visible calls this into question and reminds us that we are the ones who decide what we make visible and invisible.

TOILET

What happens to the body may feel private, but etiquette surrounding everyday bodily acts such as removing waste is part of a larger system of control and rules. How toilets are designed and marketed is wrapped up in cultural values about what parts of the body should be clean, what smells are permitted, and what parts of other people's waste we are comfortable seeing. Children are socialized to understand the rules that surround toilets, from whether to sit, squat, or stand, to learning about what parts are feared, if any, to be filled with bacteria that are harmful. And parents learn what products to buy if they want to keep the parts that may be touched by tiny hands clean. By seeing the toilet as a location where there's a lack of cleanliness (unless deodorized and contained), people learn what it means to be proper and accepted. This learning, theoretically, then leads to a relatively orderly society where people know what to do when they encounter a toilet, both in their own homes and in the homes of others.

Many authors have written extensively about the history of toilets, but my favorite story is the one my mom tells, about the magical day her parents had an indoor bathroom put in.[25] Gone were the days of cold treks to the outhouse with a Sears catalog in place for wiping. And no sink. Now we see toilet seat warmers, catalytic deodorizers, and built-in massage bidets with electric washing mechanisms (with display panels and remote controls!), and other features that are a far cry from a hole in a wooden bench over a deep trough. I have a friend who told a story of a trip to a new restaurant in New York, where the toilet in the bathroom had so many features that it took fifteen minutes to figure it out (and then, when it was figured out, it took fifteen minutes to enjoy the many features). While there is not enough room here to cover all of the new bells and whistles that modern toilets (and bidets) have, suffice it to say that the features that exist are all associated with the ideal of being really clean, feeling comfortable, and avoiding germs. These ideals are collectively agreed upon, and they play out in everyday homes, whether it's someone teaching a young child not to touch a toilet seat or pee on the floor next to it, or someone shopping for a new toilet that not only has a padded seat, but also has separate flushers for numbers one and two to conserve water. In this sense, cleanliness features are situated just next to ones that express larger political ideals like environmental concern.

Toilets are not just toilets. As researcher Allen Chun said, they are a way to domesticate "the savage body in a changing domestic space."[26] Children who have not yet been socialized to know where to aim and what not to touch, as well as individuals who may have incontinence and/or require assistance in using a sit-down toilet because of bodily differences, are defined as these "savage" bodies, in that they violate the ideals associated with staying clean and controlling where one's waste goes, and thus controlling one's own body. There is *stigma* (a negative label) attached not only to seeing and smelling what goes into a toilet, there is also stigma attached to those who cannot properly use it. Another common topic of research on the sociological significance of toilets is how people could maintain dignity *even if* they could not use a toilet in the way that is expected. Thus, the toilet is not just about biology and sewage treatment. It is about the social construction of acceptable bodies, which brings with it the inclusion of some types of bodies and the exclusion of others. For families with members whose bodies do not conform to the accepted norms, this can prove challenging. For this reason, what is considered a proper and ideal body is reinforced by how we think about something as benign as the shape, accessibility, and cleanliness of a toilet.

For family lives at every stage, the toilet plays a prominent role. Looking back on some of the topics included in previous chapters, the toilet can serve as a symbol for whether couples who are intimate are willing to include their bathroom behaviors in the category of what they'd like to make visible to a partner. Parents and children enact socialization when the children go through toilet training. Members of a household lay out a division of labor in terms of who cleans the toilet and whether leaving the seat up or down matters in a family's estimation of rules. And, as family members age, it is in toileting practices where bodily change and stigma can be seen, sometimes requiring a crossing of the boundary between private and public when one needs assistance with a task that was formerly entirely private.

SHOWER

Water is a natural thing, but it has social meaning. If, as Maria Kaika discussed, the home is a place where we simultaneously need to get rid of dirty or "gray" water, and have access to clean and controlled water, then taking a shower is an act that entails both good (clean) and bad (dirty) water.[27] Bad water, just like with dirt and bad smells, is socially defined as damaging to the body, and good water is cleansing and healthy. Anyone who can't remove the dirt and bad smells (noting here that "bad smells" are subjectively defined) can come to have their bodies socially defined as excluded. Bathing rituals as part of the rules and roles that govern our homes are part of the socialization process whereby children learn what counts as "good" and "bad" smells, and learn what they need to do in order to prevent being socially excluded. To be included in the acceptable norm of cleanliness can be seen in stories about communities setting up shelter for homeless individuals, often with the goal of providing a place to shower in order for residents to maintain dignity in a social world where cleanliness is valued. Regular bathing has become an expected practice within homes, necessitated by norms surrounding exclusion and dignity.

We shower more frequently than in the past. While the basic design of the shower has not changed much in centuries, it has become easier because electricity and water heaters make heating up water more efficient than when people had to carry water from one place to another in order to feel it splash on their heads. In part because it is easier to shower in hot water than in the past, showering has come to be defined more as a need than a want.

The shower is a sociologically interesting home object (and space, really), because it tells the story of family roles and relationships in vivid ways. As research by sociologists Martin Hand, Elizabeth Shove, and Dale Southerton has uncovered, showering routines not only have environmental impact (an increase in showers taken means an increase in water used), they also have come to be defined as an almost entirely private activity.[28] Something that was an infrequent luxury is now seen as needed and individualized. And even though family members may shower or bathe together, the practice of showering is most often represented as a solo act.

The use of showers by individuals is, in part, due to the aforementioned technological and infrastructural advances, which have occurred alongside changes in domestic architectural design that now feature as standard shower-baths with overhead outlets. Additionally, the cultural construction of the body has influenced the favoring and frequency of showers. Specifically, bathing has been defined as part of self-care, where everyday practices are part of regenerating the body from exposure to harsh things. In addition, regulating the body in terms of cleanliness is part of civilizing society, sometimes at the expense of groups that cannot access the resources to be clean. And finally, since taking a bath is now more associated with childhood and/or relaxation, the speed of a shower has come to be associated with able and adult bodies that are able to move quickly. Get up, take a shower, and go to work. Saving time by showering quickly is part of an increased focus on cramming more and more things into our day. To deal with hectic work-family lives, families opt to shower to save time, at least if the shower is short.

And then there are those who take long, hot showers. Thomas Berker, in his research about whether Norwegian people are energy-conscious when they take long hot showers in the mornings (remember, it's cold in Norway), talks about people as *end-users*, where, despite the invisibility of a lot of the impacts of individual energy consumption, they actually sense energy on a daily basis in the form of heat and light, and even in the form of paying electric and gas bills.[29] In this research, Berker discovered that bathrooms are increasingly represented in visual portrayals of interior design magazines, and they are increasingly likely to be idealized if they are expensive, large, and full of warmth (from the water to the heated floor tiles). Bathrooms have become more likely to be discussed publicly than even a few decades ago. And they have come to include functions that go beyond hygiene and bodily waste. They have come to be defined as places where you can sit and relax, as if they are extensions of the other living areas in the home. But all of this, despite the claim that people are aware of their energy use while they are taking a hot shower, may have larger implications about how sustainable energy sources are if bathrooms are getting bigger and costlier and warmer. So, the next time you take a long, hot shower or see a TV show featuring heated floor tiles and fifteen showerheads, pause and think about how all of this matters sociologically. And not just in Norway.

REFLECTING ON OUR STUFF

Homes show how the boundaries between public and private matter for families. As Maria Kaika wrote, our private homes always need to let in the outside world, and "the outside always remains in a certain way inside."[30] At best the boundary between our private homes and the public outside world is porous. We selectively allow things in from the outside, like water (or, dare I say, toys or people or even ideas), but they have to be transformed and made pure in order for us to consider them safe for the home. And the bad parts of nature—our own waste products—are removed from the home via an invisible network of pipes that are hidden even from view outside our homes. In a weird way, it is our lack of awareness of how the water is piped in that helps us feel like our homes are clean, safe, and homelike. Seeing how the natural world is socially defined, and how the boundaries between public and private have come to be socially defined, is an important seeing. And it is a political seeing. Clean water and access to resources that help people be healthy—these are located in our private homes but are public goods. This means that when kids get a drink of water from the kitchen tap and then get help during potty training, they ought to learn about the pipes that bring them their drinking water and the ones that carry their pee away.

Christena Nippert-Eng's book *Islands of Privacy* reminds us that studying the private world actually reveals a lot about our public issues. Public bathrooms have made the news lately, and the private actions and feelings we have in those places highlight the boundary between public and private very well. This matters because public bathrooms are locations for tasks and body parts that are often defined as private, which brings to the forefront issues relating to trust in strangers. Also important are spatial and object designs meant to accommodate privacy even in a public space, often in the form of doors separating people from the bathroom space, and doors within the bathroom separating stalls (for the ones with stalls). But bathrooms in homes highlight the public/private boundary, too. Even within the walls of a home, there are places that are more or less private. If this weren't the case, people (besides babies, whose "bathrooms" are wearable until their bodies are "trained") would do the same things in each room.

Homes tell us about individual families, but also about broader social issues. If it is the case that "the toilet is in many ways a barometer of civilized values," as one of the chapter opening quotes says, then we must ask who gets to decide what the values are, and what happens to people who do not have many resources that would allow them to enact those values. The study of bathroom practices makes us think about elements like cold, dirt, sewage, and the harshness of the world outside of the home in important ways. But it also makes us realize that our homes are intimately connected to that world. And how we think about that connection is shaped by our values about nature, bodies, cleanliness, and even morality. The western bourgeois home is constructed as separate from nature, but it is deeply connected to it. We produce nature before it enters our homes as clean water, and we produce nature when we treat it as it leaves our toilets. Because there are stark differences and inequalities in this production and access to clean water, we come to realize that private bathrooms are really about public issues and inequalities.

How we behave in bathrooms, whether it's with family members with whom we share more private things than others, or whether it's when we compare how fancy our toilet or water filtration system is compared to those with less money, it is clear that our home spaces are about interactions and inequalities, perhaps more than they are about our individual preferences for a supertoilet with multiple washing and flushing features all handled from a smartphone app.

Homes are not only symbolic, but also shape our lives. When our toilet is plugged or our electrical power is cut, we become aware of how reliant our homes are on maintaining the boundary between private and public. If we see the water overflowing, or the darkened room, we are being impacted by objects and spaces that affect our behaviors and our beliefs. Our homes are intimately connected in a network of pipes and wires and other moving pieces to the outside world. We only become familiar with this network when a pipe bursts and parts of the outside or bad water are made visible inside. Seeing the network when something bad happens makes us feel vulnerable. During a plumbing crisis, we are forced to reflect on our (and our home's) relationship to other people, places, and things.

Who knew that a toilet and a shower were so important in our understanding of how we think about the world? When my son was a toddler one of his favorite shows was one where the workings of a sewage treatment plant were uncovered. Recently I asked him if he remembered the name of the show from a decade ago. He did not, but simply said, "I probably liked it because I thought poop was funny when I was little." I realized that I liked it because it unveiled the invisible ways that something works. Something we use every single day, made into an intriguing and mysterious thing. Poop is funny. And mysterious. And laden with symbolism about what we consider to be dirty and important to control, wash off, and keep private—sometimes private from people outside our families, and sometimes private from family members themselves.

Sociologists try to do what that sewage treatment show did: render the invisible visible. Discover what's weird about the everyday things we rarely think about. Follow the paths toward places that may even make us a bit uncomfortable to discover. What happens within our walls matters for what's outside of them. Understanding the implications of what happens inside the pipes, as sociologists like to uncover, matters as much as, and perhaps more than, understanding what's visible. Without knowing how the pipes work and impact us without us even knowing, without acknowledging that our desire to hide the pipes is socially constructed, and without figuring out how to make the pipes better instead of just choosing a beautiful showerhead—without these things, we would not recognize that private family life is precisely about public life.

And so, as we move forward with our families in tiny houses with composting toilets cleaned by robots, we will inevitably need to pay more attention to the local and global impact of waste and unequal access to resources that maintain health and happiness. But we need to first look inside the pipes to see how our home worlds actually are.

EPILOGUE: SPATIAL, MATERIAL, AND SOCIAL BOUNDARIES FOR FAMILIES

Fences and Pathways

The home and its contents connect to the world beyond family lives. Just as with plumbing pipes and drains, the pathways and fences that lead, meander, include, and exclude offer useful symbolic points about the interconnectedness of our family lives with the rest of the world.

Whether someone grows up with a fence around a yard depends on where they grow up, how much privacy they want, what materials are available, what neighborhood aesthetic is popular, and, of course, whether they have a yard to fence in. I grew up in rural Minnesota, and I can count on one hand the number of friends' backyards that had fences. Even the front yards had very few sidewalks and absolutely no gates. If you drew a line of my path of play every summer, it'd be a bunch of straight lines from house to house, rather than a bunch of U-shaped paths from door to gate to sidewalk to next gate to next door. Our dog had the run of the neighborhood, too, meandering down a block's worth of midcentury ranch homes without concern or knowledge that one heavenly patch of grass was ours or someone else's. The only thing that separated my childhood home from the rest of the world was an overgrown hackberry bush, a slightly different tint of green from the grass seed my dad planted near our neighbor's property line to cover up the spots where our dog had ruined the grass, and lilac shrubs that bloomed for about five minutes each year.

At various points of my life and in various locations, I have seen different ways that properties were either divided clearly or made to look like they overlap. Perception that crime was likely meant more fences, sometimes made with materials that block out all visibility or would rip your pants if you tried to climb over them. Some neighborhoods are gated, suggesting that the only people who are allowed to traverse within their boundaries are residents and vetted guests. Some regions and countries where I've lived prize fences more than others not because of safety, but because of norms associated with privacy, noise, or ways to show neighborliness. And the materials that the fences are made out of vary depending on taste, how much money the people living in a particular neighborhood have, and regional resources. There is, after all, more wood for fences in a forest.

I saw fences everywhere when I moved to the Pacific Northwest, including in the backyard of the home I still live in today. Shortly after we moved in, we added a new fence to replace the rotting one. My husband and I felt the need to talk with our neighbors, whom we adore, to make sure that our building a fence taller than the previous one would not somehow suggest that we didn't like them. Removing a three-foot fence and replacing it with a six-foot fence seemed un-neighborly to us, or at least worth explaining to people whose opinion mattered. They had no concerns, and we ended up coming up with a fence design that included multiple openings in the top two feet to ensure we could find spots to have conversations across our yards with each other. But we had more privacy, too. And our dog and their dog could only have the run of their own yards. And now, it doesn't matter whether there's a gap in the fence for visibility or not. We just love each other and each other's families.

A few years after we built our backyard fence, a seventy-foot-tall spruce tree fell into the front of our home during a windstorm. The uprooting of this tree left a new blank canvas for front yard reconstruction, not to mention a lot of holes in our roof. Since we live on a corner, our yard is bordered by two streets, and our home sits at an angle such that it is unclear which street should be the starting place where people approach our front door. To eliminate this confusion, we remade our front pathway to curve more toward one street than the other, to clarify which street we viewed as part of our neighborhood. And we widened the path, in the hopes that it would seem more welcoming to visitors.

Once they visited, we could bring them into our private backyard for a barbeque.

In these stories, a fence and a pathway served to change how my family thought of the boundaries between us (our family and home) and others (our neighbors and visitors). A lot of the ways we think of a home make sense of how it is or is not separated from the rest of the world. This matters in terms of how welcoming and private our homes feel, but it also matters for how we think about other realms of our lives that are situated outside of our home spaces—realms like schools, work-places, stores, places of worship, and even realms that are more ever-present but hard to locate geographically such as media and online communities. How separated or connected we think a home is to the rest of the world matters for children who go back and forth between a school and a home, carrying their pencils and papers in backpacks that always seem to be plopped in the middle of heavy-traffic home entry-ways. Or it can matter in terms of parental control of what media messages are allowed to enter a home (yes, even deciding to remove a cable TV box so that kids cannot access certain shows is an act that separates home from elsewhere). Or it may matter for those who are seeking to find a dating partner, and opt to use an online platform on their smart-phone rather than go to the local bar. Or, objects and spaces can serve as ways to integrate or keep separate the realms of paid work and family life, as with our calendars.

All of these examples show us that family lives and borders around them are never constructed in isolation. Influences of greedy work-places, technological access to information and faraway people, and news stories about violence and injustice prevent us from ignoring the ways that other parts of our lives find their way into our homes. This happens no matter how many fences we put up. In fact, sometimes the injustices that we talk about at the dinner table happen precisely be-cause of the fences we put up as a society.

ONE LAST LOOK THROUGH THE WINDOW

What our families are like shows us what our homes are like. What our homes are like shows us what our families are like. Home spaces and objects can tell us a story about our identities, statuses, and larger cultural values. Sometimes these have permanence, as when we use an heir-loom to remind us of our family's past and preserve it for the future, or we take time to get to know neighbors. But sometimes they can be less permanent, as with the plastic crates seen in so many college residence halls on move-in day and near so many trash bins on move-out day, or with the picture we have propped against our wall that we have yet to hang, or with those moments when we opt not to introduce ourselves to neighbors because, well, we're all just living here for a few months anyway.

We live in a time when people move more often, when our connec-tions are more and more likely to be found online, when young people are more likely than ever to move to cities and not partner up and have kids until later in life, and when the demand for rental housing in the United States is higher than it has been in the last few decades.[1] We also live in a time when achieving a perfectly decorated and aesthetical-ly pleasing home is highlighted as attainable by some and presented as laughably difficult to attain by others. If this weren't the case, we would not have Pinterest and Pinterest Fail, the yin and yang of domestic status-making. In both cases, the appreciation for at least attempting to have an aesthetically pleasing home is quite present in our world, even if we're not all good at it, and even if we may not stay in the apartment we're renting for the next six months.

Given how families have changed, it is also no wonder that how we think of our home spaces and objects may not carry the same meaning as they did for our grandparents. The idea of home seems increasingly transitory. We question the attachment of identity and status to things in a world of overconsumption and materialism. We have loads of cri-tiques in the ether that show how damaging inequalities that relate to our homes can be (from those who cannot afford a home, to those who are steered away from homes because of their race, to those who are tied to the home as a devalued work space). Necessarily, then, our meaning of home has changed. But what has not changed is the impor-tance we should place on understanding how this meaning is con-structed.

Home spaces and objects do not have the same meaning across time and geographic space. That we have a birch-colored particleboard Ikea table in our home rather than a cherished heirloom walnut coffee table that lasts a hundred years does not mean that the do-it-yourself Swedish table is somehow less meaningful than the heirloom table (or that the particleboard can't last a hundred years). Both are equally meaningful. But *why* and *how* they are meaningful may be different. One may tell us that pathways within our family lives are always in flux and our values are focused on ease and movement. The other may tell us that permanence and memory matter for our families. In both cases, we are told a family story about larger cultural values. For some of us, that may be exciting, and for others, unsettling.

As with individual families, values and roles change over time and life stages, and with this change comes a revised aesthetic representation of family life. Regardless of whether our home is a stopover on the way toward a different future place, or a "forever home," home spaces and objects tell the stories of families at a particular time and in a particular place—stories that could be kept behind a fence, or that could be shown to connect with other stories on a pathway toward greater understanding of families as they really are. Without this understanding, we may make decisions in our own families, or about all families, that are based on myths—decisions that can end up widening inequalities and increasing misunderstandings about the people we hold near and dear. These stories—the real ones, not the myths—are worth sharing. These stories are the stuff of family life.

NOTES

I. FAMILIES, HOME SPACES, AND OBJECTS

1. For a thorough interdisciplinary review of the definition and use of the terms *home*, *house*, and *family* that offers a solid foundation into the academic study of these concepts and that goes beyond this brief introduction of the terms here, see Shelley Mallett, "Understanding Home: A Critical Review of the Literature," *Sociological Review* 52, no. 1 (2004): 62–89. For a thorough discussion of the sociology of homes, from the meaning of home to larger societal-level influences in how we think about homes, see Rowland Atkinson and Keith Jacobs, *House, Home and Society* (London: Palgrave, 2016). For a vivid portrayal of the everyday lives of families, with excellent academic insights about the social meaning of homes, see Jeanne E. Arnold and Anthony P. Graesch, *Life at Home in the Twenty-First Century: 32 Families Open Their Doors* (Los Angeles: Cotsen Institute of Archaeology Press, 2012).

2. Christena Nippert-Eng, *Islands of Privacy* (Chicago: University of Chicago Press, 2010).

3. Tony Chapman and Jenny Hockey, eds., *Ideal Homes? Social Change and Domestic Life* (London: Routledge, 1999), xi.

4. For discussion of how things carry social meaning, see Aafke Komter, "Heirlooms, Nikes and Bribes: Towards a Sociology of Things," *Sociology* 35 (2001): 59–75; see also Arjun Appadurai, ed., *The Social Life of Things: Commodities in Cultural Perspective* (Cambridge: Cambridge University Press, 1986).

5. Conspicuous consumption is discussed in Thorstein Veblen, *The Theory of the Leisure Class* (New York: Vanguard Press, 1934 [1899]).

6. For discussions on home décor, objects, and spaces as they relate to identity and status, see Rachel Hurdley, "Dismantling Mantelpieces: Narrating Identities and Materializing Culture in the Home," *Sociology* 40, no. 4 (2006); Suzanne Reimer and Deborah Leslie, "Identity, Consumption and the Home," *Home Cultures* 1, no. 2 (2004); Daniel Miller, ed., *Home Possessions* (Oxford: Berg, 2002); Pierre Bourdieu, *Distinction: A Social Critique of the Judgment of Taste* (Cambridge, MA: Harvard University Press, 1984); and Mihaly Csikszentmihalyi and Eugene Rochberg-Halton, *The Meaning of Things: Domestic Symbols and the Self* (Cambridge: Cambridge University Press, 1981).

7. Josee Johnston, Kate Cairns, and Shyon Baumann, *Introducing Sociology Using the Stuff of Everyday Life* (New York: Routledge, 2017), 22.

8. Alison Blunt, "Cultural Geography: Cultural Geographies of Home," *Progress in Human Geography* 29, no. 4 (2005): 507.

9. Carl Knappett, "Photographs, Skeumorphs and Marionettes: Some Thoughts on Mind, Agency and Object," *Journal of Material Culture* 7, no. 2 (2002): 97–98. For a detailed discussion of the conceptual separation and dualism of people and objects, see Igor Kopytoff, "The Cultural Biography of Things: Commoditisation as Process," in *The Social Life of Things: Commodities in Cultural Perspective*, ed. Arjun Appadurai (Cambridge: Cambridge University Press, 1986). For a sociological theory of things, see Alex Preda, "The Turn to Things: Arguments for a Sociological Theory of Things," *Sociological Quarterly* 40, no. 2 (1999): 347–66.

10. Winifred Gallagher, *House Thinking: A Room-by-Room Look at How We Live* (New York: HarperCollins, 2006), 33.

11. Antonius Robben, "Habits of the Home: Spatial Hegemony and the Structuration of House and Society in Brazil," *American Anthropologist* 91, no. 3 (1989): 570–88.

12. Thomas Gieryn, "A Space for Place in Sociology," *Annual Review of Sociology* 26 (2000): 466.

13. See Michel de Certeau, *The Practice of Everyday Life*, 3rd ed., trans. Steven F. Rendall (Berkeley: University of California Press, 2011).

14. Wendy Griswold, Gemma Mangione, and Terence E. McDonnell, "Objects, Words, and Bodies in Space: Bringing Materiality into Cultural Analysis," *Qualitative Sociology* 36, no. 4 (2013): 343–64.

15. Daniel Miller, *Stuff* (Cambridge: Polity, 2009), 50.

16. Heather Whitmore, "Value That Marketing Cannot Manufacture: Cherished Possessions as Links to Identity and Wisdom," *Generations* 25, no. 3 (2001): 60–61.

17. LATs as a new family form as experienced in Norway and Sweden are discussed in Irene Levin, "Living Apart Together: A New Family Form," *Current Sociology* 52, no. 2 (2004): 223–40.

2. FROM CHILDHOOD TO ADULTHOOD

1. Richard Fry, "Millennials Overtake Baby Boomers as America's Largest Generation," Pew Research Center, Washington, DC, April 25, 2016, http://www.pewresearch.org/fact-tank/2016/04/25/millennials-overtake-baby-boomers.

2. Pell Institute, *Indicators of Higher Education Equity in the United States: 45 Year Trend Report* (Philadelphia: Pell Institute and PennAhead, 2015), accessed July 6, 2016, http://www.pellinstitute.org/downloads/publications-Indicators_of_Higher_Education_Equity_in_the_US_45_Year_Trend_Report.pdf.

3. Liz Kenyon, "A Home from Home: Students' Transitional Experience of Home," in *Ideal Homes? Social Change and Domestic Life*, ed. Tony Chapman (New York: Routledge, 1999), 87.

4. Jeff Sherwood, "Tweens, Teens, and Twentysomethings: A History of Words for Young People," *OxfordWords Blog*, January 13, 2015, http://blog.oxforddictionaries.com/2015/01/tweens-teens-twentysomethings-history-words-young-people .

5. Gill Valentine, "Boundary Crossings: Transitions from Childhood to Adulthood," *Children's Geographies* 1, no. 1 (2003): 38.

6. Siân Lincoln, *Youth Culture and Private Space* (Basingstoke, UK: Palgrave Macmillan, 2012), 133; David A. Karp, Lynda Lytle Holmstrom, and Paul S. Cray, "Leaving Home for College: Expectations for Selective Reconstruction of Self," *Symbolic Interaction* 21, no. 3 (1999): 254.

7. For a full description of the concept of emerging adulthood, see Jeffrey Arnett, *Emerging Adulthood: The Winding Road from the Late Teens through the Twenties*, 2nd ed. (Oxford: Oxford University Press, 2014). For interdisciplinary commentary on the myriad ways this life stage may be classified by contemporary scholars, see John Bynner, "Rethinking the Youth Phase of the Life-Course: The Case for Emerging Adulthood?" *Journal of Youth Studies* 8, no. 4 (2005): 367; and Fry, "Millennials Overtake Baby Boomers."

8. Karp, Holmstrom, and Cray, "Leaving Home for College," 255.

9. Frances K. Goldscheider and Calvin Goldscheider, *The Changing Transition to Adulthood: Leaving and Returning Home* (Thousand Oaks, CA: Sage, 1999).

10. To understand how the transition to adulthood has been elongated, see Betty G. Farrell, *Family: The Making of an Idea, an Institution, and a Controversy in American Culture* (Boulder, CO: Westview Press, 1999).

11. Fry, "Millennials Overtake Baby Boomers."

12. Pell Institute, *Indicators of Higher Education Equity*; Drew Desilver, "Increase in Living with Parents Driven by Those Ages 25–34, Non-College

Grads," Pew Research Center, Washington, DC, June 8, 2016, http://www.
pewresearch.org/fact-tank/2016/06/08/increase-in-living-with-parents-driven-
by-those-ages-25-34-non-college-grads.

13. Clara H. Mulder, "Family Dynamics and Housing: Conceptual Issues
and Empirical Findings," *Demographic Research* 29, no. 14 (2013): 355–78.

14. For a discussion of how a country's economic standing affects student
housing markets, see Janet Ford, Julie Rugg, and Roger Burrows, "Conceptu-
alising the Contemporary Role of Housing in the Transition to Adult Life in
England," *Urban Studies* 39, no. 13 (2002): 2455–67.

15. Tom Acitelli, "The Dormification of Manhattan," *Observer*, July 31,
2007, accessed June 8, 2016, http://observer.com/2007/07/the-dormification-
of-manhattan.

16. Lincoln, *Youth Culture and Private Space*, 147.

17. Julie Rasicot, "Dormify," *Bethesda Magazine*, accessed May 28, 2016,
http://www.bethesdamagazine.com/Bethesda-Magazine/May-June-2011/
Dormify.

18. Mulder, "Family Dynamics and Housing," 355–77.

19. Jane Kroger and Vivienne Adair, "Symbolic Meanings of Valued Personal Objects in Identity Transitions of Late Adulthood," *Identity* 8, no. 1 (2008):
5–24.

20. Ira Silver, "Role Transitions, Objects, and Identity," *Symbolic Interaction* 19, no. 1 (1996): 1–20.

21. Ellen Galinsky and Susan Ginsberg, "Taking Her Old Teddy Bear to
College," *Work and Family Life* (September 2013): 3.

22. Silver, "Role Transitions, Objects, and Identity," 7.

23. Lincoln, *Youth Culture and Private Space*, 147.

24. Elizabeth Aries and Maynard Seider, "The Interactive Relationship Between Class Identity and the College Experience: The Case of Lower Income
Students," *Qualitative Sociology* 28, no. 4 (2005): 419–43.

25. Michelle Janning and Maya Volk, "Where the Heart Is: Home Space
Transitions for Residential College Students," *Children's Geographies*, published online January 6, 2017, http://dx.doi.org/10.1080/14733285.2016.
1277183.

26. Judith Thomsen, "Home Experiences in Student Housing: About Institutional Character and Temporary Homes," *Journal of Youth Studies* 10, no. 5
(2007): 577–96.

27. Martin Heilweil, "The Influence of Dormitory Architecture on Resident
Behavior," *Environment and Behavior* 5, no. 4 (1973): 377–411.

28. Naz Kaya and Margaret J. Weber, "Territorial Behavior in Residence
Halls: A Cross-Cultural Study," *Environment and Behavior* 35, no. 3 (2003):
400–414.

29. Silver, "Role Transitions, Objects, and Identity," 12.
30. Ibid., 7.
31. Thomsen, "Home Experiences in Student Housing," 581.

3. COUPLEHOOD

1. In this chapter about couples I try to use language that can refer to any type of romantically involved couple, regardless of sexual orientation or marital status. So, while a lot of research is done on heterosexual married couples, the ideas presented here are not meant to be limited to that kind of relationship.

2. The information about the historical evolution of master bedrooms comes from Erika Riggs, "Evolution of the Master Bedroom," *Zillow Porchlight*, June 23, 2011, accessed May 1, 2016, http://www.zillow.com/blog/evolution-of-the-master-bedroom-48286.

3. "In Residential Real Estate, Bid Farewell to the 'Master Bedroom,'" *Washington Business Journal*, April 15, 2013, accessed March 28, 2016, http://www.bizjournals.com/washington/blog/2013/04/in-residential-real-estate-bid.html.

4. Margaret Gibson, "Death and the Transformation of Objects and Their Value," *Thesis Eleven* 103, no. 1 (2010): 59.

5. Marianne Gullestad, *The Art of Social Relations: Essays on Culture, Social Action and Everyday Life in Modern Norway* (Oslo: Scandinavian University Press, 1992), 63–64.

6. For a full discussion of group size and social forms in classical social theory, see Georg Simmel, *Sociology: Inquiries into the Construction of Social Forms*, volumes 1 and 2, trans. and ed. Anthony J. Blasi, Anton K. Jacobs, and Mathew Kanjiranthinkal (Boston: Brill, 2009).

7. For an updated discussion of polygamy (socially recognized mating with more than one partner), polyandry (one woman with two or more men), and polygyny (one man with two or more women), including reference to the classic 1967 work by anthropologist George Murdock, see Katherine E. Starkweather and Raymond Hames, "A Survey of Non-Classical Polyandry," *Human Nature* 23, no. 2 (2012): 149–72.

8. The U.S. Centers for Disease Control and Prevention, along with other governmental agencies, keep track of marriages and divorces each year. These data, under the "Marriage and Divorce" section presented by the National Center for Health Statistics, are available at https://www.cdc.gov/nchs/fastats/marriage-divorce.htm.

9. For a full discussion of the relationship between housing and marriage, see Samantha Nelson, Lucy Delgadillo, and Jeffrey P. Dew, "Housing Cost

Burden and Marital Satisfaction," *Marriage and Family Review* 49, no. 6 (2013): 546–61.

10. Susan L. Brown, Jennifer Roebuck Bulanda, and Gary R. Lee, "Transitions Into and Out of Cohabitation in Later Life," *Journal of Marriage and Family* 74, no. 4 (2012): 774–75; and Gary R. Lee and Krista K. Payne, "Changing Marriage Patterns Since 1970: What's Going On, and Why?" *Journal of Comparative Family Studies* 41, no. 4 (2010): 537.

11. Irene Levin, "Living Apart Together," *Current Sociology* 52, no. 2 (2004): 223.

12. Tyler B. Jamison and Lawrence Ganong, "'We're Not Living Together': Stayover Relationships Among College-Educated Emerging Adults," *Journal of Social and Personal Relationships* 28, no. 4 (2011): 536–57.

13. Aziz Ansari and Erik Klinenberg, *Modern Romance* (New York: Penguin, 2015).

14. Sharon Sassler and Amanda Miller, *Cohabitation Nation: Gender, Class, and the Remaking of Relationships* (Berkeley: University of California Press, 2017); and Stephanie Coontz, *Marriage, a History: How Love Conquered Marriage* (New York: Penguin, 2005).

15. Lauren Collins, "The Love App: Romance in the World's Most Wired City," *The New Yorker*, November 25, 2013, accessed July 31, 2015, http://www.newyorker.com/magazine/2013/11/25/the-love-app.

16. For a full discussion of heating and cooling objects and Belk's work, see Amber Epp and Linda Price, "The Storied Life of Singularized Objects: Forces of Agency and Network Transformation," *Journal of Consumer Research* 36, no. 5 (2010): 820–37.

17. For a full description of the love letters study, see Michelle Janning and Neal Christopherson, "Love Letters Lost? Gender and the Preservation of Digital and Paper Communication from Romantic Relationships," in *Family Communication in an Age of Digital and Social Media*, ed. Carol J. Bruess (New York: Peter Lang, 2015).

18. "Broadcast Firsts," accessed July 6, 2016, http://www.tvacres.com/broad_bed.htm.

19. "National Sleep Foundation Bedroom Poll Summary of Findings," National Sleep Foundation, Washington, DC, 2012, https://sleepfoundation.org/sites/default/files/bedroompoll/NSF_Bedroom_Poll_Report.pdf.

20. Paul Rosenblatt, *Two in a Bed: The Social System of Couple Bed Sharing* (Albany: State University of New York Press, 2006), 1.

21. The research findings in this section are from Simon Williams, Robert Meadows, and Sara Arber, "The Sociology of Sleep," in *Sleep, Health and Society: From Aetiology to Public Health*, ed. Francesco P. Cappuccio, Mi-

chelle A. Miller, and Steven W. Lockley (Oxford: Oxford University Press, 2010).

22. Rosenblatt, *Two in a Bed*, 25.

23. Ibid.

4. PARENTS AND CHILDREN

1. Caroline Bologna, "New LEGO Slippers Will Spare Parents the Unique Pain They Know All Too Well," *Huffington Post*, November 16, 2015, http://www.huffingtonpost.com/entry/new-LEGO-slippers-will-spare-parents-the-unique-pain-they-know-all-too-well_us_564a4cc5e4b06037734a6857.

2. Edwin Heathcote, *The Meaning of Home* (London: Frances Lincoln, 2012), 34.

3. Tammy Schotzko, personal phone interview, March 30, 2016.

4. Dennis Cauchon, "Childhood Pastimes Are Increasingly Moving Indoors," *USA Today*, July 12, 2005, accessed July 7, 2016, http://usatoday30.usatoday.com/news/nation/2005-07-11-pastimes-childhood_x.htm.

5. The Forum on Child and Family Statistics publishes population reports such as "America's Children in Brief: Key National Indicators of Well-Being, 2016," which are easy to access at https://www.childstats.gov/americaschildren/tables/pop2.asp.

6. For a thorough overview of psychological, sociological, and social constructionist understandings of childhood, see William Corsaro, *The Sociology of Childhood*, 4th ed. (Thousand Oaks, CA: Sage, 2014).

7. Jeffrey Arnett, *Emerging Adulthood: The Winding Road from the Late Teens through the Twenties*, 2nd ed. (Oxford: Oxford University Press, 2014).

8. Carie Green, "'Because We Like To': Young Children's Experiences Hiding in Their Home Environment," *Early Childhood Education Journal* 43, no. 4 (2015): 327–36.

9. See Corsaro, *The Sociology of Childhood*, for an overview of recent trends in research to include children's subjective voices.

10. Olivia Stevenson and Alan Prout, "Space for Play?," *Home Cultures: The Journal of Architecture, Design and Domestic Space* 10, no. 2 (2013): 135–58.

11. Tristan Bridges, "On the Social Construction of Childhood: Making Space for Babies," *Inequality by (Interior) Design*, January 21, 2013, https://inequalitybyinteriordesign.wordpress.com/2013/01/21/on-the-social-construction-of-childhood-making-space-for-babies.

12. Irene Cieraad, "The Family Living Room: A Child's Playpen? A Recent History of Material Colonization," *Home Cultures: The Journal of Architecture, Design and Domestic Space* 10, no. 3 (2013): 287–314.

13. For a thorough review of the debates and theories surrounding children, marketing, and consumer culture, see David Buckingham, *The Material Child* (Cambridge: Polity, 2011).

14. Allison Pugh, *Longing and Belonging: Parents, Children, and Consumer Culture* (Berkeley: University of California Press, 2009).

15. For an overview of past research on gender and family photography, see Michelle Janning and Helen Scalise, "Gender and Intensive Mothering in Home Curation of Family Photography," *Journal of Family Issues* 26, no. 12 (2015): 1702–25.

16. See Deborah Chambers, "Family as Place: Family Photograph Albums and the Domestication of Public and Private Space," in *Picturing Place: Photography and the Geographical Imagination*, ed. Joan M. Schwartz and James R. Ryan (London: I. B. Tauris, 2003), 96–114.

17. See Gillian Rose, "Family Photographs and Domestic Spacings: A Case Study," *Transactions of the Institute of British Geographers* 28, no. 1 (2003): 5–18.

18. Abigail Durrant, David Frohlich, Abigail Sellen, and Evanthia Lyons, "Home Curation versus Teenage Photograph: Photo Displays in the Family Home," *International Journal of Human-Computer Studies* 67, no. 12 (2009): 1005–23.

19. Sharon Hays, *The Cultural Contradictions of Motherhood* (New Haven, CT: Yale University Press, 1996).

20. For an example of memory work as a research methodology, see Claudia Mitchell, "Expanding the Memory Catalogue: Southern African Women's Contributions to Memory-Work Writing as a Feminist Research Methodology," *Agenda* 29, no. 1 (2014): 92–103.

21. "Girls' LEGOs Are a Hit, but Why Do Girls Need Special LEGOs?" NPR, June 29, 2013, http://www.npr.org/sections/monkeysee/2013/06/28/196605763/girls-LEGOs-are-a-hit-but-why-do-girls-need-special-LEGOs; "The LEGO Gender Gap: A Historical Perspective," *Thinking Brickly*, January 2, 2012, http://thinkingbrickly.blogspot.com/2012/01/LEGO-gender-gap.html; and "LEGO Friends," accessed July 7, 2016, http://www.LEGO.com/en-us/friends.

22. Annette Lareau, *Unequal Childhoods: Class, Race, and Family Life*, 2nd ed. (Berkeley: University of California Press, 2011).

23. Kathy Merlock Jackson, "From Control to Adaptation: America's Toy Story," *Journal of American and Comparative Cultures* 24, no. 1/2 (2001): 139–45.

5. GENDER AND HOUSEHOLD DIVISION
OF LABOR

1. Lauren Smith, "13 Lovely 'She Sheds' to Inspire Your Own Garden Escape," *House Beautiful*, March 10, 2016, accessed July 9, 2016, http://www.housebeautiful.com/room-decorating/outdoor-ideas/g2614/she-sheds-ideas.

2. This chapter focuses primarily on research findings that do not disrupt the categories of "man" and "woman" and that tend to be more applied to heterosexual living arrangements. This, of course, is a limitation and does not capture everyone's experience. One of the challenges of talking about homes and families is to simultaneously recognize the varied combinations of partnerships, gender identities, and sexual orientations along with the ever-present use of two categories of experience along both gender and sexuality lines—categories that are present in both research and popular culture. Joshua Gamson's *Modern Families: Stories of Extraordinary Journeys to Kinship* (New York: New York University Press, 2015) captures this variation much better than I do. For your reading of this chapter, please take the research findings with the recognition of their limitations but also recognize ways that expectations about what men and women are supposed to do can be present regardless of the sexual orientation or sexual identity of household partners.

3. Tristan Bridges, "Where Are Men and Women Happiest in Their Homes?" *Inequality by (Interior) Design*, January 31, 2012, accessed June 20, 2016, https://inequalitybyinteriordesign.wordpress.com/2012/01/31/where-are-men-and-women-happiest-in-their-homes.

4. Tristan Bridges, "A Brief History of the Masculinization of the Garage," *Inequality by (Interior) Design*, January 3, 2013, accessed June 20, 2016, https://inequalitybyinteriordesign.wordpress.com/2013/01/03/a-brief-history-of-the-masculinization-of-the-garage.

5. Elizabeth C. Cromley, *The Food Axis: Cooking, Eating, and the Architecture of American Homes* (Charlottesville: University of Virginia Press, 2011).

6. Winifred Gallagher, *House Thinking: A Room-by-Room Look at How We Live* (New York: HarperCollins, 2006), 73–91.

7. "Division of Labor in Households with Two Full-Time Working Parents," Pew Research Center, Washington, DC, November 2, 2015, accessed July 7, 2016, http://www.pewsocialtrends.org/2015/11/04/raising-kids-and-running-a-household-how-working-parents-share-the-load/st_2015-11-04_working-parents-02; and "Average Minutes per Day Men and Women Spent in Household Activities," Bureau of Labor Statistics American Time Use Survey, 2014, accessed June 18, 2016, http://www.bls.gov/tus/charts/household.htm.

8. Kelley Holland, "Division of Labor: Same-Sex Couples More Likely to Share Chores, Study Says," NBCnews.com, June 4, 2015, accessed January 17,

2017, http://www.nbcnews.com/business/consumer/division-labor-same-sex-couples-more-likely-share-chores-study-n369921.

9. Arlie Hochschild and Anne Machung, *The Second Shift: Working Families and the Revolution at Home*, rev. ed. (London: Penguin, 2012).

10. It is important to note that most of the research discussed in this section applies to heterosexual couples, but the norms associated with gender roles matter for any type of partnership. Same-sex couples negotiate gender role norms, too, though they are complicated by the alignment of idealized masculinity with attraction toward women and idealized femininity with attraction toward men. The significance of fairness versus equality is relevant for any kind of couple.

11. For classic and updated research on status-reversed couples, see Maxine P. Atkinson and Jacqueline Boles, "WASP Wives as Senior Partners," *Journal of Marriage and Family* 46, no. 4 (1984): 861–70; and Chiung-Yin Hu and Yoshinori Kamo, "The Division of Household Labor in Taiwan," *Journal of Comparative Family Studies* 38, no. 1 (2007): 105–24.

12. Tristan Bridges, "Gendering Your Household by Smell," *Inequality by (Interior) Design*, October 10, 2012, accessed June 20, 2016, https://inequalitybyinteriordesign.wordpress.com/2012/10/10/gendering-your-household-by-smell; and Tristan Bridges, "Color by . . . Gender?" *Inequality by (Interior) Design*, November 15, 2013, accessed June 20, 2016, https://inequalitybyinteriordesign.wordpress.com/2013/11/15/color-by-gender.

13. For a great discussion of occupational gender segregation and gender and home improvement, see Tristan Bridges, "On Masculinity and Home Improvement," *Inequality by (Interior) Design*, September 17, 2012, accessed June 20, 2016, https://inequalitybyinteriordesign.wordpress.com/2012/09/17/on-masculinity-and-home-improvement.

14. Susan Fornoff, "Home Improvement on the Tube: Craze or Just Plain Crazy?" *San Francisco Chronicle*, April 3, 2004, F1; and Carlise Peterson, "Designed for TV," *Chicago Sun-Times*, February 29, 2004, 1.

15. David Brooks, "Den of Dreams," *New York Times*, May 29, 2004, accessed June 3, 2004, http://www.nytimes.com/2004/05/29/opinion/den-of-dreams.html.

16. For examples of research on home décor and status groups, see David Halle, *Inside Culture: Art and Class in the American Home* (London: Routledge, 1993); Marianne Gullestad, "Home Decoration as Popular Culture: Constructing Homes, Genders and Classes in Norway," in *Gendered Anthropology*, ed. T. de Valle (London: Routledge, 1993); Orvar Löfgren, "The Sweetness of Home: Class, Culture and Family Life in Sweden," in *The Anthropology of Space and Place*, ed. Setha M. Low and Denise Lawrence-

Zuñiga (Malden, MA: Blackwell, 2003), 142–59; and Sarah Pink, *Home Truths: Gender, Domestic Objects and Everyday Life* (Oxford: Berg, 2004).

17. For an analysis of the politics of postwar housing design, gender inequality, and the future, see Dolores Hayden, *Redesigning the American Dream: The Future of Housing, Work and Family Life* (New York: Norton, 2002).

18. Daphne Spain, *Gendered Spaces* (Chapel Hill: University of North Carolina Press, 1992), 127.

19. Hayden, *Redesigning the American Dream*.

20. For a discussion of the observations I made while on the set of *Extreme Makeover: Home Edition*, see Michelle Janning, "Public Spectacles of Private Spheres: An Introduction to the Special Issue 'Spaces and Places of Family Life: Cultural and Popular Cultural Representations of Homes and Families,'" *Journal of Family Issues* 29, no. 4 (2008): 1–10.

21. Jessica Contrera, "The End of 'Shrink It and Pink It': A History of Advertisers Missing the Mark with Women," *Washington Post*, June 8, 2016, accessed June 9, 2016, https://www.washingtonpost.com/lifestyle/style/the-end-of-shrink-it-or-pink-it-a-history-of-advertisers-missing-the-mark-with-women/2016/06/08/3bcb1832-28e9-11e6-ae4a-3cdd5fe74204_story.html.

22. Ann Swidler, "Culture in Action: Symbols and Strategies," *American Sociological Review* 51, no. 2 (1986): 273–86. The empirical research findings referenced in this section stem from Michelle Janning and Lindsey Menard, "I Would Never Do That in My Own Home: Audience Reflexivity and the Decorating Television Viewing Culture," *Electronic Journal of Sociology* 10 (2006).

23. Jesse Rhodes, "Why Do Men Grill?" *Smithsonian*, June 14, 2012, accessed June 20, 2016, http://www.smithsonianmag.com/arts-culture/why-do-men-grill-121562921/?no-ist.

24. Roksana Badruddoja, *Eyes of the Storm: The Voices of South Asian-American Women*, 2nd ed. (San Diego: Cognella Academic Publishing, 2012).

25. Pink, *Home Truths*, 54.

6. HOME AND PAID WORK INTERSECTIONS

1. "One in Four American Households Have a Home Office; Most Are Used for Small Businesses Run from Home," *PR Newswire*, August 26, 1999, accessed May 15, 2016, http://www.prnewswire.com/news-releases/one-in-four-american-households-have-a-home-office-most-are-used-for-small-businesses-run-from-home-74138367.html.

2. Jean Andrey and Laura C. Johnson, "Being Home: Family Spatialities of Teleworking Households," in *Family Geographies: The Spatiality of Families*

and Family Life, ed. Bonnie C. Hallman (London: Oxford University Press, 2010), 68–87.

3. Frances Holliss, *Beyond Live/Work: The Architecture of Home-based Work* (London: Routledge, 2015).

4. Frances Holliss, "Space, Buildings and the Life Worlds of Home-Based Workers: Towards Better Design," *Sociological Research Online* 17, no. 2 (2012), accessed June 10, 2016, http://www.socresonline.org.uk/17/2/24.html.

5. Frances Holliss, "Home Is Where the Work Is: The Case for an Urban Design Revolution," *The Conversation*, July 24, 2012, accessed July 7, 2016, https://theconversation.com/home-is-where-the-work-is-the-case-for-an-urban-design-revolution-8147.

6. Thom File and Camille Ryan, "Computer and Internet Use in the United States: 2013," American Community Survey Reports, U.S. Census Bureau, November 2014, accessed April 20, 2016, https://www.census.gov/history/pdf/2013computeruse.pdf.

7. Penny Gurstein, *Wired to the World, Chained to the Home: Telework in Daily Life* (Vancouver: UBC Press, 2001).

8. Andrey and Johnson, "Being Home," 77.

9. Donell Holloway, "Gender, Telework and the Reconfiguration of the Australian Family Home," *Continuum: Journal of Media and Cultural Studies* 21, no. 1 (2007): 33–44.

10. Christena Nippert-Eng, *Home and Work: Negotiating Boundaries through Everyday Life* (Chicago: University of Chicago Press, 1996).

11. These data are taken from the "Women in the Labor Force" statistics produced by the U.S. Department of Labor, accessed at https://www.dol.gov/wb/stats/stats_data.htm.

12. Nikil Saval, "The Post-Cubicle Office and Its Discontents," *New York Times Magazine*, February 28, 2016, accessed February 28, 2016, http://www.nytimes.com/2016/02/28/magazine/the-post-cubicle-office-and-its-discontents.html.

13. "American Time Use Survey Summary," Bureau of Labor Statistics, June 24, 2016, accessed July 9, 2016, http://www.bls.gov/news.release/atus.nr0.htm.

14. Adia Harvey Wingfield, "How 'Service with a Smile' Takes a Toll on Women," *The Atlantic*, January 25, 2016, accessed February 15, 2016, http://www.theatlantic.com/business/archive/2016/01/gender-emotional-labor/427083.

15. Eileen Patten and Jens Manuel Krogstad, "Black Child Poverty Rate Holds Steady, Even as Other Groups See Declines," Pew Research Center, Washington, DC, July 14, 2015, accessed June 1, 2016, http://www.

pewresearch.org/fact-tank/2015/07/14/black-child-poverty-rate-holds-steady-even-as-other-groups-see-declines.

16. Jens Manuel Krogstad, "One-in-Four Native Americans and Alaska Natives Are Living in Poverty," Pew Research Center, Washington, DC, June 13, 2014, accessed May 1, 2016, http://www.pewresearch.org/fact-tank/2014/06/13/1-in-4-native-americans-and-alaska-natives-are-living-in-poverty.

17. Richard Fry and Rakesh Kochhar, "Are You in the American Middle Class? Find Out with Our Income Calculator," Pew Research Center, Washington, DC, May 11, 2016, accessed May 25, 2016, http://www.pewresearch.org/fact-tank/2016/05/11/are-you-in-the-american-middle-class.

18. Drew Desilver, "Tepid U.S. Jobs Data Conceal Modest Momentum for Blacks and Hispanics," Pew Research Center, Washington, DC, August 2, 2013, accessed June 1, 2016, http://www.pewresearch.org/fact-tank/2013/08/02/tepid-u-s-jobs-data-conceal-modest-momentum-for-blacks-and-hispanics.

19. Drew Desilver, "Job Shifts Under Obama: Fewer Government Workers, More Caregivers, Servers and Temps," Pew Research Center, Washington, DC, January 14, 2015, accessed June 1, 2016, http://www.pewresearch.org/fact-tank/2015/01/14/job-shifts-under-obama-fewer-government-workers-more-caregivers-servers-and-temps.

20. Kim Parker, "Women More Than Men Adjust Their Careers for Family Life," Pew Research Center, Washington, DC, October 1, 2015, accessed June 1, 2016, http://www.pewresearch.org/fact-tank/2015/10/01/women-more-than-men-adjust-their-careers-for-family-life.

21. "Raising Kids and Running a Household: How Working Parents Share the Load," Pew Research Center, Washington, DC, November 4, 2015, accessed May 1, 2016, http://www.pewsocialtrends.org/2015/11/04/raising-kids-and-running-a-household-how-working-parents-share-the-load.

22. Jennifer Glass, "CCF Brief: Parenting and Happiness in 22 Countries," Council on Contemporary Families, June 15, 2016, accessed June 15, 2016, https://contemporaryfamilies.org/brief-parenting-happiness.

23. Tammy Schotzko, personal telephone interview, March 30, 2016.

24. Michelle Janning, "The Efficacy of Symbolic Work-Family Integration for Married Professionals Who Share Paid Work: A Descriptive Study," *Journal of Humanities and Social Sciences* 3, no. 1 (2009): 8.

25. Anthony P. Graesch, "Material Indicators of Family Busyness," *Social Indicators Research* 93 (2009): 85.

26. Ibid., 86.

27. For the theoretical and methodological background of this research and an elaboration of the research I conducted on work-home boundaries for married coworkers, see Michelle Janning, "Put Yourself in My Work Shoes: Variations in Work-Related Spousal Support for Professional Married Co-Workers,"

Journal of Family Issues 27, no. 1 (2006): 85–109; and Michelle Janning, "A Conceptual Framework for Examining Work-Family Boundary Permeability for Professional Married Co-Workers," *Women and Work: A Journal of the Business and Professional Women's Foundation* 1 (1999): 41–57.

7. SEPARATED FAMILIES

1. For a discussion of the process of figuring out the "spoils" of divorce, see Jackie Goode, "Whose Collection Is It Anyway? An Autoethnographic Account of 'Dividing the Spoils' Upon Divorce," *Cultural Sociology* 1, no. 3 (2007): 379.

2. Isolina Ricci, *Mom's House, Dad's House for Kids: Feeling at Home in One Home or Two* (New York: Touchstone, 2006), 63.

3. Judith Wallerstein, "Growing Up in the Divorced Family," *Clinical Social Work Journal* 33, no. 4 (2005): 409.

4. Anat Hecht, "Home Sweet Home: Tangible Memories of an Uprooted Childhood," in *Home Possessions: Material Culture Behind Closed Doors*, ed. Daniel Miller (Oxford: Berg, 2001), 141.

5. Bella De Paulo, *How We Live Now: Redefining Home and Family in the 21st Century* (Hillsboro, OR: Atria Books/Beyond Words, 2015), 19.

6. Radhika Sanghani, "'Bird's Nest Custody': The Smart New Way to Divorce," *Telegraph*, February 7, 2016, accessed March 1, 2016, http://www.telegraph.co.uk/women/family/birds-nest-custody-the-smart-new-way-to-divorce.

7. For an overview of past research on divorce's effects on children, both positive and negative, see Caitlyn Collins and Michelle Janning, "The Stuff at Mom's House and the Stuff at Dad's House: The Material Consumption of Divorce for Adolescents," in *Childhood and Consumer Culture*, ed. David Buckingham and Vebjørg Tingstad (London: Palgrave, 2010), 163–77.

8. Constance Ahrons, *The Good Divorce* (New York: William Morrow, 1995).

9. For discussion of children's and teens' room culture, see Sarah Louise Baker, "Pop in(to) the Bedroom: Popular Music in Pre-Teen Girls' Bedroom Culture," *European Journal of Cultural Studies* 7, no. 1 (2004): 75–93; and Jeanne R. Steele and Jane D. Brown, "Adolescent Room Culture: Studying Media in the Context of Everyday Life," *Journal of Youth and Adolescence* 24, no. 5 (1995): 551–68.

10. See Herb Childress, "Teenagers, Territory, and the Appropriation of Space," *Childhood* 11, no. 2 (2004): 195–205.

11. Jill A. McCorkel, "Going to the Crackhouse: Critical Spaces as a Form of Resistance in Total Institutions and Everyday Life," *Symbolic Interaction*

21, no. 3 (1998): 227–52. See also Siân Lincoln, *Youth Culture and Private Space* (Basingstoke, UK: Palgrave Macmillan, 2012).

12. For a discussion of custody trends in the United States (including increasing shared custody but retention of mother as primary custody holder), see Joan B. Kelly, "Children's Living Arrangements Following Separation and Divorce: Insights from Empirical and Clinical Research," *Family Process* 46, no. 1 (2006): 35–52.

13. Goode, "Whose Collection Is It Anyway?," 367.

14. For a thorough discussion of the research on divorce and kids' bedrooms, see Michelle Janning, Caitlyn Collins, and Jacqueline Kamm, "Gender, Space and Material Culture in Divorced Families," *Michigan Family Review* 15, no. 1 (2011): 35–58; Michelle Janning, Jill Laney, and Caitlyn Collins, "Spatial and Temporal Arrangements, Parental Authority, and Young Adults' Post-Divorce Experiences," *Journal of Divorce and Remarriage* 51 (2010): 413–27; and Collins and Janning, "The Stuff at Mom's House and the Stuff at Dad's House," 163–77.

15. Gail Green, "The Art of Change: At Home and through Divorce," *Resource Furniture*, June 9, 2015, accessed June 20, 2016, http://resourcefurniture.com/the-art-of-change-at-home-and-through-divorce.

16. Diana Shepherd, "Smart Solutions for Small Spaces," DivorceMagazine.com, August 15, 2006, accessed July 2, 2016, http://www.divorcemag.com/articles/smart-solutions-for-small-spaces.

17. Monica Anderson, "Technology Device Ownership: 2015," Pew Research Center, Washington, DC, October 29, 2015, http://www.pewinternet.org/2015/10/29/technology-device-ownership-2015.

18. Lawrence Ganong, Marilyn Coleman, Richard Feistman, Tyler Jamison, and Melinda Markham, "Communication Technology and Postdivorce Co-parenting," *Family Relations* 61, no. 3 (2012): 397–409.

19. Caitlyn Collins and Michelle Janning, "My Room at Mom's House v. My Room at Dad's House: Material and Technological Representations of Divorce for Adolescents" (paper presented at the annual meeting of the Society for the Study of Social Problems, New York, New York, August 10–12, 2007).

20. For example, see Larry Bodine, "Using 'T&A' to Sell Divorce," *Law Marketing Blog*, May 8, 2007, http://blog.larrybodine.com/2007/05/articles/advertising/using-ta-to-sell-divorce.

21. Abigail Abrams, "Divorce Rate in U.S. Drops to Nearly 40-Year Low," *Time*, November 17, 2016, accessed January 17, 2017, http://time.com/4575495/divorce-rate-nearly-40-year-low.

8. BEYOND SINGLE (NUCLEAR) FAMILIES

1. Edwin Heathcote, *The Meaning of Home* (London: Frances Lincoln, 2012), 51.

2. Lisa Wade, "The Architecture of Gentrification; Or, the Dining Rooms Are Coming," *Sociological Images at the Society Pages*, May 30, 2016, accessed June 1, 2016, https://thesocietypages.org/socimages/2016/12/29/the-architecture-of-gentrification-or-the-dining-rooms-are-coming.

3. Tammy Schotzko, Certified Professional Organizer, telephone interview, March 30, 2016.

4. Stephanie Coontz, *The Way We Never Were: American Families and the Nostalgia Trap*, rev. and updated ed. (New York: Basic Books, 2016).

5. Therese Richardson, "Spousal Bereavement in Later Life: A Material Culture Perspective," *Mortality* 19, no. 1 (2014): 61–79.

6. Gabriella V. Smith and David J. Ekerdt, "Confronting the Material Convoy in Later Life," *Sociological Inquiry* 81, no. 3 (2011): 377–91.

7. Richard Fry, "Millennials Overtake Baby Boomers as America's Largest Generation," Pew Research Center, April 26, 2016, accessed January 5, 2017, http://www.pewresearch.org/fact-tank/2016/04/25/millennials-overtake-baby-boomers.

8. "Health, United States, 2015," National Center for Health Statistics, 4, http://www.cdc.gov/nchs/data/hus/hus15.pdf#015.

9. "Accessory Dwelling Units: What They Are and Why People Build Them," AccessoryDwellings.org, accessed June 15, 2016, https://accessorydwellings.org/what-adus-are-and-why-people-build-them.

10. "The Cohousing Directory," Cohousing Association of the United States, accessed June 1, 2016, http://www.cohousing.org/directory.

11. See Pepukayi Chitakunye and Tamandeep Takhar-Lail, "Materiality and Family Consumption: The Role of the Television in Changing Mealtime Rituals," *Consumption Markets and Culture* 17, no. 1 (2014): 50–70, for a discussion on changing norms and how smartphones and other technologies now are increasingly present at mealtimes, sometimes with teenagers chatting with friends and reporting back to family members about the conversation, and sometimes with more negative effects (expressed primarily by parents). This is the paradox of multitasking—technology at the table can distract from in-person communication, yet it can enhance communication overall.

12. Jane Kroger and Vivienne Adair, "Symbolic Meanings of Valued Personal Objects in Identity Transitions of Late Adulthood," *Identity: An International Journal of Theory and Research* 8, no. 1 (2008): 19.

13. Lindsey Menard and Michelle Janning, "Shared Spaces, Shared Responsibility? The Gendered Division of Labor in Cohousing Communities," Working Paper, 2013.

14. Heather Sullivan-Catlan, "Feeding the Communal Family: 'Family Time' and the Division of Household Labor in Cohousing," *Michigan Family Review* 18, no. 1 (2014): 39–56.

15. David J. Ekerdt and Julie F. Sergeant, "Family Things: Attending the Household Disbandment of Older Adults," *Journal of Aging Studies* 20 (2006): 202.

16. Kroger and Adair, "Symbolic Meanings of Valued Personal Objects," 16.

17. Rachel Hurdley, "Dismantling Mantelpieces: Narrating Identities and Materializing Culture in the Home," *Sociology* 40, no. 4 (2006): 717–33.

18. Jacqueline J. Goodnow and Jeanette A. Lawrence, "Inheritance Norms for Distributions of Money, Land, and Things in Families," *Family Science* 1, no. 2 (2010): 73–82.

19. Kroger and Adair, "Symbolic Meanings of Valued Personal Objects," 7–8. Kroger and Adair note that

> Erikson, Erikson, and Kivnick (1986) were among the early researchers to observe the importance of cherished possessions to late-life adults. They investigated varied psychosocial issues among older parents (aged 75 to 95) whose children had been participants in the Oakland and Berkeley Growth Studies and the Guidance Study during 1928 and 1929.

20. Ibid., 8–9. Kroger and Adair review gerontology and material culture theory and research that suggests that older adults, by virtue of their experience with many changes over the course of a lifetime, keep valued objects that remain unchanging as a symbol of a person's story. When older adults are relocated to long-term care facilities, they lose a part of their self, since many possessions must be left behind. For this reason, scholars and practitioners stress the importance of cherished possessions to preserve identity and prevent a loss of sense of self among these individuals.

21. Ibid., 17.

22. Mihaly Csikszentmihalyi and Eugene Rochberg-Halton, *The Meaning of Things* (Oxford: Cambridge University Press, 1981).

23. Smith and Ekerdt, "Confronting the Material Convoy in Later Life."

24. Richardson, "Spousal Bereavement in Later Life," 65.

9. FAMILIES, HOMES, AND SOCIAL CHANGE

1. E. Holte, "Tidsånd på badet (Zeitgeist in the bathroom)," *Bonytt* 10, no. 7 (2003). Translated from Norwegian by Thomas Berker (2013).

2. Allen Chun, "Flushing in the Future: The Supermodern Japanese Toilet in a Changing Domestic Culture," *Postcolonial Studies* 5, no. 2 (2002): 169.

3. Drue Lawlor and Michael A. Thomas, *Residential Design for Aging in Place* (Hoboken, NJ: Wiley, 2008).

4. Alexander Kira, *The Bathroom* (New York: Viking, 1976).

5. Julie Beck, "The Private Lives of Public Bathrooms," *The Atlantic*, April 15, 2014, accessed April 20, 2016, http://www.theatlantic.com/health/archive/2014/04/the-private-lives-of-public-bathrooms/360497. See also Sheila Cavanagh, *Queering Bathrooms* (Toronto: University of Toronto Press, 2010).

6. Marc Linder and Ingrid Nygaard, *Void Where Prohibited: Rest Breaks and the Right to Urinate on Company Time* (Ithaca, NY: Cornell University Press, 1998).

7. Beck, "The Private Lives of Public Bathrooms."

8. Erving Goffman, *The Presentation of Self in Everyday Life* (Garden City, NY: Doubleday, 1959).

9. Spencer E. Cahill et al., "Meanwhile Backstage: Public Bathrooms and the Interaction Order," *Journal of Contemporary Ethnography* 14, no. 1 (1985): 33–58.

10. Harvey Molotch and Laura Noren, eds., *Toilet: Public Restrooms and the Politics of Sharing* (New York: New York University Press, 2010).

11. Edgar Alan Burns, "Bathroom Politics: Introducing Students to Sociological Thinking from the Bottom Up," *Teaching Sociology* 31, no. 1 (2003): 110–18.

12. Ibid.

13. For a helpful historical overview of changes in bathrooms, see Katherine Ashenburg, "A Short History of the Newest and Sometimes Smallest Room," in *The Domestic Space Reader*, ed. Chiara Briganti and Kathy Mezei (Toronto: University of Toronto Press, 2012), 221–24. See also Witold Rybczynski, *Home: A Short History of an Idea* (New York: Penguin, 1986); and Winifred Gallagher, *House Thinking: A Room-by-Room Look at How We Live* (New York: HarperPerennial, 2007).

14. Edwin Heathcote, *The Meaning of Home* (London: Frances Lincoln, 2012), 11.

15. Maria Kaika, "Interrogating the Geographies of the Familiar: Domesticating Nature and Constructing the Autonomy of the Modern Home," *International Journal of Urban and Regional Research* 29, no. 2 (2004): 265–86.

16. Lawlor and Thomas, *Residential Design for Aging in Place*.

17. For a discussion on poverty and precarious housing, see Matthew Desmond, *Evicted: Poverty and Profit in the American City* (New York: Crown, 2016).

18. Merrit Kennedy, "Lead-Laced Water in Flint: A Step-by-Step Look at the Makings of a Crisis," NPR, April 20, 2016, accessed June 10, 2016, http://www.npr.org/sections/thetwo-way/2016/04/20/465545378/lead-laced-water-in-flint-a-step-by-step-look-at-the-makings-of-a-crisis.

19. Marianne Gullestad, *The Art of Social Relations: Essays on Culture, Social Action and Everyday Life in Modern Norway* (Cambridge: Oxford University Press), 67.

20. For a discussion on household toxins and environmental health, see Alissa Cordner, *Toxic Safety: Flame Retardants, Chemical Controversies, and Environmental Health* (New York: Columbia University Press, 2016).

21. World Health Organization, "Housing and Health: 'Healthy Housing'—Experts Call for International Guidelines," accessed June 1, 2016, http://www.who.int/hia/housing/en.

22. Andrew Rice, "The Elusive Small-House Utopia," *New York Times Magazine*, October 15, 2010, accessed June 1, 2016, http://www.nytimes.com/2010/10/17/magazine/17KeySmallHouse-t.html.

23. Vladas Griskevicius, Joshua M. Tybur, and Bram Van den Bergh, "Going Green to Be Seen: Status, Reputation, and Conspicuous Conservation," *Journal of Personality and Social Psychology* 98, no. 3 (2010): 392–404.

24. Kaika,"Interrogating the Geographies of the Familiar."

25. See Chun, "Flushing in the Future," for an overview. For discussion of cultural practices associated with fecal events and how emotions play out in bodies in bathrooms, see Martin S. Weinberg and Colin J. Williams, "Fecal Matters: Habitus, Embodiments, and Deviance," *Social Problems* 52, no. 3 (2005).

26. Chun, "Flushing in the Future," 168.

27. Kaika, "Interrogating the Geographies of the Familiar."

28. Martin Hand, Elizabeth Shove, and Dale Southerton, "Explaining Showering: A Discussion of the Material, Conventional, and Temporal Dimensions of Practice," *Sociological Research Online* 10, no. 2 (2005), accessed June 1, 2016, http://www.socresonline.org.uk/10/2/hand.html.

29. Thomas Berker, "'In the Morning I Just Need a Long, Hot Shower:' A Sociological Exploration of Energy Sensibilities in Norwegian Bathrooms," *Sustainability: Science Practice and Policy* 9, no. 1 (2013): 57–63.

30. Kaika, "Interrogating the Geographies of the Familiar," 273.

EPILOGUE: SPATIAL, MATERIAL, AND SOCIAL BOUNDARIES FOR FAMILIES

1. For a discussion on changes in temporariness of people's conceptions of home, see Sarah Amandolare, "The Real Reason You Still Shop at Ikea—and Probably Always Will," *Guardian*, June 26, 2016, accessed July 8, 2016, https://www.theguardian.com/lifeandstyle/2016/jun/26/why-shop-ikea-home-decor-convenience. Besides social change in terms of rental housing demand, it is also important to revisit how the precariousness of renting tells us about definitions of home that are not be attainable to all. This is poignantly discussed in Matthew Desmond's epilogue to *Evicted*, where he reminds us that "at home, we can 'be ourselves' [and that] the home is the wellspring of personhood" (293). When a stable home is not within our reach, we lose out on the protection and personal reflection that such a home may provide.

INDEX

ABOUT THE AUTHOR

Michelle Janning is professor of sociology at Whitman College in Walla Walla, Washington. Her research and writing focus on the intersections between family relationships and spatial design. She teaches sociology courses and conducts research on family, childhood, education, social class, and gender, and has received numerous teaching awards. She has also received a Fulbright Specialist Grant and served as a visiting professor at the Danish Institute for Study Abroad.

Michelle lives in Walla Walla with her husband, son, and dog, all of whom are occasionally dismayed when she rearranges the stuff in their home. She has a blog at http://www.michellejanning.com, where she explores the "between-ness" of social life. Her goal is to tell humorous stories and share sociological ideas in an accessible way so that people can relate the ideas to their own lives and relationships. Ideas and stories inspired by *The Stuff of Family Life: How Our Homes Reflect Our Lives* can be explored at https://www.facebook.com/thestuffof familylife.